Turn a
BOWL

with Ernie Conover

Turn a BOWL

Getting great results
the first
time around

with Ernie Conover

The Taunton Press

Cover photographer: **RANDY O'ROURKE**

Publisher: **JIM CHILDS**
Associate Publisher: **HELEN ALBERT**
Associate Editor: **STROTHER PURDY**
Editor: **PETER CHAPMAN**
Copy Editor: **CANDACE B. LEVY**
Indexer: **PETER CHAPMAN**
Layout Artist: **ROSALIE VACCARO**
Photographer: **ERNIE CONOVER**
Illustrator: **MARIO FERRO**

Taunton
BOOKS & VIDEOS

for fellow enthusiasts

Text © 2000 by Ernie Conover
Photographs © 2000 by The Taunton Press, Inc.
Illustrations © 2000 by The Taunton Press, Inc.

Printed in the United States of America
10 9 8 7 6 5 4 3 2 1

The Taunton Press, Inc., 63 South Main Street, PO Box 5506, Newtown,
CT 06470-5506
e-mail: tp@taunton.com

Distributed by Publishers Group West

Library of Congress Cataloging-in-Publication Data
Conover, Ernie.
      Turn a bowl : getting great results the first time around / with Ernie Conover.
        p. cm.
      Includes index.
      ISBN 1-56158-293-X
      1. Turning. 2. Woodwork. 3. Bowls (Tableware). I. Title.
TT201.C664   2000   99-047134

684'.083—dc21   CIP

ABOUT YOUR SAFETY
Working wood is inherently dangerous. Using hand or power tools improperly or ignoring standard safety practices can lead to permanent injury or even death. Don't try to perform operations you learn about here (or elsewhere) unless you're certain they are safe for you. If something about an operation doesn't feel right, don't do it. Look for another way. We want you to enjoy the craft, so please keep safety foremost in your mind whenever you're working with wood.

To Rude Osolnik, my friend and mentor
and the patriarch of woodturning today

Foreword

I was delighted when Ernie Conover asked me to write a foreword for his new book on bowl turning. I can well remember first meeting Ernie (and his wife, Susan) at a conference at Arrowmont School of Arts and Crafts in Gatlinburg, Tennessee, in 1985. Turners had gathered with the purpose of forming an American woodturning society, and it was here that we formed the American Association of Woodturners. Ernie and I served on the charter board of directors and co-chaired the first AAW symposium in Lexington, Kentucky, the following year.

Soon after the conference, Ernie stopped at my shop for a visit on his way to Atlanta. We cemented a friendship that endures to this day. Ernie has been a frequent visitor to my shop, and I've also spent a good deal of time with him and Susan teaching many workshops at their school, Conover Workshops. Ernie has always been very interested in learning all that a person could do with a lathe. He is an apt student, willing to learn new techniques, but he has also developed a good many of his own. Ernie is fascinated by all aspects of woodturning and has explored the use of a broad range of tools, materials, and techniques for the wood lathe. He is a versatile turner equally at home with spindle work, faceplate work, and metal spinning.

Ernie's real gift is that he can express in words what most woodturners cannot. His book will guide you past all the pitfalls that can trap a turner with clear, concise prose, photos, and illustrations. I highly recommend this book for novice and advanced turners alike. It has something for everyone.

Rude Osolnik
Berea, Kentucky
June 1999

Acknowledgments

My wife, Susan, and I first met Rude Osolnik at Arrowmont School of Arts and Crafts during the Woodturning Visions and Concepts Symposium in 1985. He invited me to stop and visit when I passed through Berea, Kentucky, which I did about a month later. When I called him from a service station by the freeway, he directed me up to "Poverty Ridge," his tongue-in-cheek name for his beautiful home on a mountain overlooking Berea. I called about three in the afternoon, figuring on spending a couple of hours before driving a further five or six hours south to Atlanta. What transpired was one of the most interesting and engaging conversations of my life. Oh, we talked about turning, sure; but we also talked about our children, politics, the economy, and the relative merits of Scotch whiskey as opposed to Kentucky bourbon. (Of the latter, we felt sampling was necessary to make a definitive opinion.) I also met his wife, Daphne, a lovely and engaging lady, known to be a friend to children.

They fed me supper and talked me into staying the night on Poverty Ridge. In the morning, we started talking where we had left off and proceeded to Rude's workshop to actually do some turning. I left sometime far after lunch at the last possible minute to still get to Atlanta that day.

So started a friendship that has lasted to this day. He and Daphne stayed at our house frequently during numerous classes he did here at Conover Workshops. He became a mentor to me, and I owe much of my woodturning to him. The thing that has always most impressed me about Rude, however, is his willingness to share any and all of his knowledge with anyone. In many ways, the openness and free exchange of information that American woodturning enjoys today can be credited directly to Rude. The current generation of woodturners owes much to him. I hope this book continues woodturning's cornerstone of sharing laid down by Rude's example.

I would also like to thank the following people for their help and advice on technical issues: Darel Nish of Craft Supplies, Brad Packard of Packard Woodworks, Jerry Glaser of Glaser Engineering, Peter Gill of Sorby, and Tim Clay of Oneway on tools and equipment; Jonny Doucette of Jonsered and Jim Peck of Origon on chainsaw use; David Puett of Klingspor and Chris Minick of 3M on sanding; Charlie Van-Zandt of Oster, Brooks Titcomb of Woodbury Pewterers, and David Jones on pewter spinning.

Finally, I would like to thank my editors at The Taunton Press: Helen Albert, Peter Chapman, and Candace Levy.

Contents

Introduction

Turning a bowl is the most popular project in the turning seminars that I run. My five-day workshops start with spindle turning; and after two days of spindle exercises, there is a buoyant mood when students chuck up bowl blanks and take bowl gouges in hand. It is much like watching traditional Olympic ice-skating. After the compulsory figures program, the free skating is a joy. People get excited and really start having fun. There is something magical about turning a bowl, because it is both creative and useful. In this age of mass-produced, plastic look-alike housewares, the knowledge that you have produced something real, artistic, and unique is a splendid touchstone.

Most beginners are daunted by the prospect of turning a bowl and don't know where to begin. The act of turning a bowl is easy, but the tools and procedures to do the job are not generally understood. Without guidance, the beginner starts with a scrap of 8/4 dry wood, a 6-in. faceplate, and a gouge that is not properly sharpened. He or she may even try to use a spindle gouge rather than a bowl gouge; and either tool, as delivered from the factory, will not be sharpened correctly.

The experienced turner starts with a better-prepared blank, mounted on a 3-in. faceplate (or a variety of other chucks), and uses a properly sharpened bowl gouge. The 3-in. faceplate allows you to form a base that is proportionally correct, whereas the larger faceplate makes for a clunky, oversized base. Properly prepared wood is much easier to work with, and a properly sharpened bowl gouge is a joy to use. This is all to say that having a teacher to guide you through the initial steps and set you on the right path saves time and frustration. After all, the idea is to have fun.

This book is an action manual for anyone who wants to turn a bowl. I have taught hundreds of people to turn bowls, and I can teach you. We will accomplish that end with a "roll up your sleeves and let's get to work" approach. This book is short on text and long on photos and illustrations. It is really a series of photo essays, which explain all aspects of bowl turning from the simplest to the most advanced. What's more, you don't have to read the entire book to get started. You may skip the chapters on tools and equipment and get right to the first bowl-turning essay, which will then direct you to the sanding, finishing, and reverse-turning sections. Once you have mastered this basic technique, you can move on to more advanced techniques, which in turn cross-reference appropriate basic information.

I've even covered pewter spinning, which, to my knowledge, hasn't been covered in any other book written in recent times. Although this was an active hobby use of the wood lathe up through the early 1950s, it seems to have since been largely forgotten. When I was a boy, I watched my father spin a set of pewter plates after we returned from a trip to Colonial Williamsburg. The price in the gift shop stopped him from buying, so he spun his own, which were indistinguishable from those at Williamsburg. Spinning pewter does not require sophisticated tools. My dad made his from old broomsticks, and you can do the same.

Bowl turning is many faceted. It runs the gamut from simple, functional bowls that the baby-sitter can run through the dishwasher with impunity to ultrathin art forms that demand to be held but that are not functional beyond holding peanuts. I offer many options in this book, and it is up to you to find the style that is right for you. So take off your watch and ring, roll up your sleeves, and let's get turning.

1 Lathes and Chucks

The primary tool for turning is a lathe. A lathe allows wood to spin in two ways, between two points (called centers) or by itself, attached only to the headstock on a chuck called a faceplate. Bowl turning is pure faceplate turning. Turning on the headstock alone, without aid of the tailstock, places much greater demands on a lathe than does spindle work. For that reason, you'll need a more substantial lathe for bowl turning than you will for spindle work. If you're thinking of buying a lathe, you'll want to consider the requirements for bowl turning discussed in this chapter. If you already own a lathe, you'll find advice on how to improve its performance.

This classic cast-iron Welles lathe, made in Massachusetts, was originally designed for metal spinning; but it makes an excellent woodturning lathe.

The Ideal Bowl-Turning Lathe

Faceplate turning requires more from a lathe than does spindle turning. In the initial stages of turning, most bowls are out of balance; and a light lathe can literally walk across the floor. So a bowl-turning lathe needs to be of sturdy construction, both in the bed and stand and in the headstock and tailstock. Beyond this, there are other features to consider when choosing a lathe, including the amount of swing and speed control.

Bed and stand construction

Cast-iron construction has always been held in high esteem by turners, and many fine lathes are made from this time-honored material. Recently, a number of fabricated lathes have become available. Instead of cast iron, the lathe is welded together from pieces of structural steel. Most commonly, such lathes are hybrids: The bed is welded structural steel, and the headstock and tailstock are cast iron. Others are built entirely of fabricated parts. In theory, a cast-iron lathe should have a lower frequency of vibration. In practice, fabricated lathes seem to work just as well.

The Oneway 2436 is a hybrid lathe with fabricated bed and cast-iron components.

Spindle Turning vs. Faceplate Turning

SPINDLE TURNING

Grain runs parallel to rotational axis of lathe.

Grain

FACEPLATE TURNING

Grain runs at right angles to rotational axis.

Grain

What to Look For in a Bowl-Turning Lathe

- Sturdy construction (cast iron or hybrid with structural-steel bed and cast-iron components); heavy bearings.
- At least 10 in. of actual swing over the tool base (13 in. of advertised swing).
- 1¼-in. or larger spindle nose.
- Morse tapers in the headstock and tailstock.

- A tool base and tool rest that are easy to adjust and position in any orientation and at any height.
- A solid stand (this can be improved or replaced, if necessary).
- Provision for outboard turning.
- 1 hp or bigger motor.
- Distance between centers is unimportant for bowl turning.

The stand is just as important to a solid lathe as is the lathe itself. Unfortunately, manufacturers often skimp on stand design, and the lathe can jump around as a result. Test that the stand is solid by giving it a good shake—the stand shouldn't move at all. Fortunately, it is easy to reinforce a weak stand or build a replacement (see "Improving Your Lathe," p. 11).

The tool rest is of particular concern to the bowl turner, because frequent fine adjustment of the rest angle and height is necessary. The tool rest is composed of two parts: the base and the rest itself. The base can be positioned anywhere on the bed and in any alignment. Look for a sturdy base that adjusts easily but stays put once locked in place. A tool base that needs Herculean strength to lock and/or creeps all the time under heavy loads is annoying at best and dangerous at worst. Similarly, the tool rest should lock quickly and easily at any height or angle with only moderate strength on your part.

Headstock and tailstock

Much more is demanded from a headstock in faceplate turning than in spindle turning. Look for sturdy construction, a heavy spindle, and robust bearings. The most popular spindle-nose size is 1 in. by 8 threads per inch, which was originally adopted by the Milwaukee Delta Company (now Delta International) in the early part of the 20th century. Although this is a great size for spindle turning and light faceplate work, it's undersized for heavy faceplate work. A 1-in. spindle will flex under the high loads placed on it by heavy faceplate turning; a 1¼-in. or larger spindle is preferable.

The sturdiness of the tailstock generally mimics the heftiness of the headstock, so it's not a feature you have to worry about. And as long as you buy a sturdy lathe, it will have heavy bearings as a matter of course. Morse tapers in both the headstock and the tailstock are a must. As you'll learn in the course of this book, there is no end to the accessories that use Morse-taper mounting. But beyond that, it's a quality issue. Morse tapers

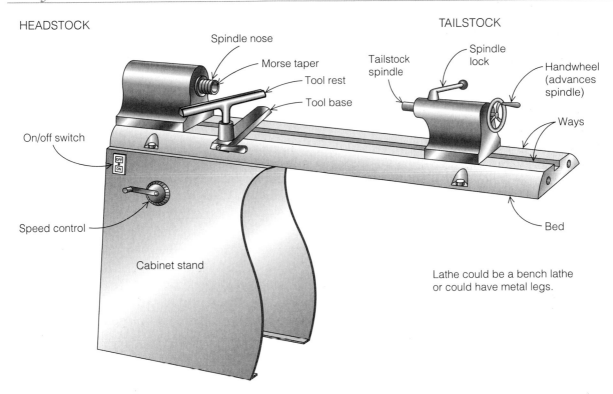

HEADSTOCK

Spindle nose

Morse taper

Tool rest

Tool base

On/off switch

Speed control

Cabinet stand

TAILSTOCK

Tailstock spindle

Spindle lock

Handwheel (advances spindle)

Ways

Bed

Lathe could be a bench lathe or could have metal legs.

are a watershed feature that separates well-constructed and well-designed lathes from inferior ones.

Swing

Lots of swing is an advantage in a bowl-turning lathe. Although an 8-in. swing is sufficient for most of the spindle turning carried out in a typical woodworking shop, 10 in. to as much as 18 in. is better for bowl turning. What is "swing" exactly? Manufacturers list this specification as the diameter of the work that can be swung over the bed. In fact, the *actual* swing is the diameter of the work that can be swung over the tool base. Often a lathe with an advertised swing of 13 in. has an actual swing in the neighborhood of 10 in. To find the actual swing, subtract twice the height of the tool base from the manufacturer's stated swing.

A useful option that allows a good deal of extra faceplate swing on a small lathe is a swing-head design (see the top photo on p. 8). The headstock can be slid toward the center of the bed and rotated 90° so that the work is turned in front of the bed. The tool base is then mounted on the left side of the headstock. Usually there is an extension piece that fits into the tool base to get the tool rest where it should be.

One final way to get greater bowl-turning capacity is to turn off the "wrong" end of the headstock—what is usually referred to as outboard turning. The usual scheme is to put a left-hand thread, equivalent to that of the nose, on the back end of the spindle. Although Delta threads their

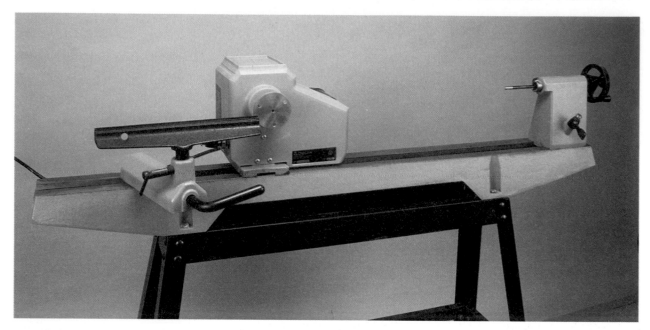

A lathe with a swing-head design allows you to pivot the headstock at a right angle to the bed so that you can turn in front of the lathe.

A floor-stand tool rest is one way of managing outboard turning. Because it does not have the rigidity of a normal tool base, it should be used only with light cuts.

faceplates in both directions, other manufacturers supply separate left- and right-hand threaded faceplates. Another scheme is to turn the existing headstock around or to place it on the tailstock end of the bed, which means only right-hand faceplates are needed.

When outboard turning, you can support the tool rest in one of two ways. One is to use a floor-stand tool rest, as shown in the photo at left. You need a sturdy floor stand with a large stable base (mine has a heavy tripod base). Floor-stand rests do not have the rigidity of fixed tool rests, so they should be used with a good deal of caution to avoid the risk of tipping them over. A second way to provide support is with an outboard tool base that attaches to the base of the lathe, as shown in the photo on the facing page. This is a nice arrangement, because it gives you both a conventional spindle lathe and an outboard bowl lathe.

Speed control

For bowl turning you rarely need speeds higher than about 1,500 rpm; but the more control over the speed you have, the better. A traditional configuration is a four-step pulley that gives a low speed of about 700 rpm, a second speed around 1,100 rpm (the main faceplate speed), a third speed around 1,700 rpm (the main spindle-turning speed), and a high speed somewhere between 2,800 rpm and 3,600 rpm (for sanding spindle work and for miniature turning). Many modern lathes have five to as many as eight speeds, with the low end down in the 200-rpm to 300-rpm range.

The Delta Top Turn 16 has an outboard rest, designed specifically for bowl turning, built into the base of the lathe.

This is good news for the bowl turner, because there are times when you need to go quite slowly and to have minute control over the speed.

Variable speed is a great advantage in a bowl-turning lathe, because it allows you to choose the exact speed needed for the job. Often a few revolutions per minute faster or slower can make the difference between annoying vibration and smooth running. Variable speed can be achieved in two ways: with variable-width sheaves or with a variable-speed motor.

The normal setup for variable-width sheaves includes a mechanical control that adjusts the width of the drive pulley, as shown in the drawing on p. 10. Moving the two halves of the pulley apart decreases the diameter, and squeezing the two halves back together increases the diameter. The mating pulley (usually on the headstock) is similarly split, but spring loaded, so it automatically adjusts to the state of the drive pulley. This easily gives a wide range of infinitely variable speeds. The only drawback is the fairly high wear and tear on the belt, so belts need to be changed relatively frequently.

A variable-speed motor is a better way to control speed, but it is also the more expensive option. I use a DC motor, but variable-speed AC controls are now available for about the same price as the DC. With either system, it is best to keep a step-pulley arrangement for several reasons. Most important is that if the speed control goes berserk (don't laugh, it can happen), your lathe cannot go faster than the pulley combination you are

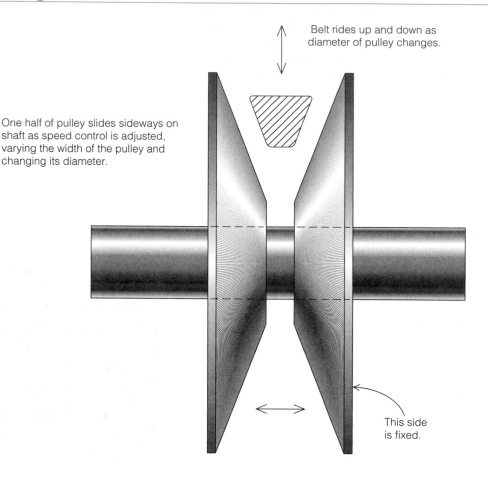

Belt rides up and down as diameter of pulley changes.

One half of pulley slides sideways on shaft as speed control is adjusted, varying the width of the pulley and changing its diameter.

This side is fixed.

using. In short, you limit your liability. The second reason is that by going to a lower speed range, you increase the torque at the spindle, which is a great help when working with large diameters. (The larger the diameter you are turning, the more leverage the tool has against the motor.) A good way to think of this arrangement is that the step pulleys are the gearbox in your car and the speed-control knob is the accelerator.

The not-so-ideal lathe

With all of the above in mind, however, don't lose sight of the goal—to turn bowls and have some fun. A bowl always looks bigger off the lathe than when mounted. Most beginners seem to want to chuck up a truly huge piece of wood and turn a gargantuan bowl. It is like eating at a smorgasbord, our eyes are bigger than our bellies, and we take more food than we can eat. In truth, a bowl bigger than about 14 in. in diameter is not particularly useful. It takes too much fruit to fill it up, and the bowl takes up too much cupboard space. Whether utilitarian or of a more artistic flair, the most useful bowls are 6 in. to 12 in.

Note that most wood lathes have at least an 8-in. actual swing and a 1-in. spindle, which are adequate to make lots of useful bowls. If you have a ¾-in. spindle and a 6-in. swing, fear not, you can still have lots of fun. Turn some bowls, get some experience, and next December tell Santa you need a bigger lathe. With all the experience you are going to get, starting right now, you will be ready to enjoy the full potential of your dream lathe come Christmas morning.

■ Improving Your Lathe

If you are a woodworker, you may already own a lathe. Now that you've read about the requirements for a bowl lathe, you may be wondering if your machine is equal to the job. Even if your lathe doesn't have all the features described in the previous section, there are some simple things you can do to help your lathe perform adequately for bowl turning.

Stands

One of the first things you can do is to beef up the stand. The stand is just as important as the lathe itself; and all too often, stands on modern lathes are bolted together from light structural steel and sheet metal. On economy lathes, the stands often appear to be an afterthought; and you're better off building a new one from wood.

A sturdy stand can be made from 2×4 building material (or poplar milled to a true 2×2, if you want a cabinetmaker's look to your stand) and plywood. As shown in the drawing on p. 12, you can build a box section into the stand and fill it with sand. The sand will add weight to your lathe and help adsorb vibration; it's well worth the effort. Many lathes have enclosed sheet-metal stands that are sturdy but resonate badly. A good tactic here is to put bags of sand inside the stand. A few bags of sand can make a tin drum seem like a cast-iron monolith.

The stand should not be made much larger than the lathe, because flat surfaces collect chips. Shelves and tool holders built into the stand tend to do the same thing—especially with the volume of shavings made in bowl turning. If you want to include a shelf at the back or under your stand, build it with dowels so the chips fall through but your tools and accessories do not. I use shelves like these under my lathes and workbenches (see the photo at right).

Tool rests

Tool rests are subject to a great deal of wear and tear; and over time you may notice a definite low spot in the center of your rest, to say nothing of a multitude of nicks and dents. Both conditions will hinder your turning ability. The best tool for removing these defects is a large single-cut mill file in either bastard or first cut. Draw-file the tool rest by turning the file sideways and alternately pulling and pushing it over the rest, almost as if it

Shelves under the lathe stand should be built with dowels so that chips and shavings don't collect there.

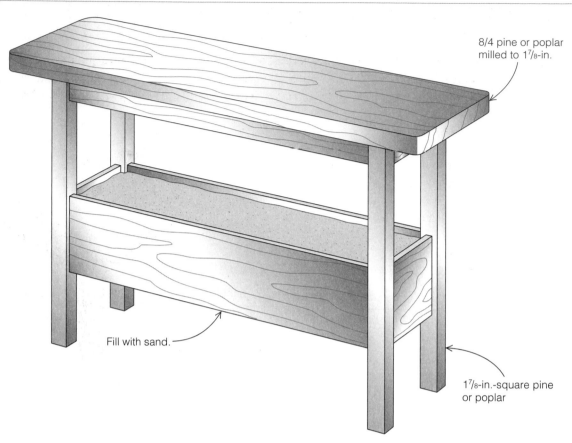

8/4 pine or poplar milled to 1⁷/₈-in.

Fill with sand.

1⁷/₈-in.-square pine or poplar

were a spokeshave. (Only a single-cut file will work for this process; a double-cut file will not.) Once you get the hang of it, you'll be rewarded with long ribbons of steel or iron and a tool rest that allows you to slide your tools smoothly along its length.

Bearings

Most lathes built in the last 100 years have "sealed-for-life" ball bearings in the headstock, but the term is a little misleading. In this case, *life* refers to the grease packed in before sealing. The trouble is that the lubricant may have long ago expired under the seal. If your bearings are more than five years old, they could probably do with changing. It's a simple matter to press the spindle and bearings out of the headstock and replace them. Most bearings have a shield number engraved on the sides. Armed with this number you can go to any bearing supplier (found under "Bearings" in the Yellow Pages) and obtain replacements—usually at a much cheaper price than you can get them from the manufacturer of your lathe. If you don't want to tackle the job yourself, most automotive repair shops will replace the bearings for you.

Making Your Own Tool Rest

It's easy to make your own tool rest. Find a short length of cold-rolled steel of the proper diameter for the neck and have a piece of flat stock brazed or welded to it at the proper angle (45° to 60°). If you do not have welding equipment, any weld shop can do the job for a nominal price.

Once the rest is welded, draw-file the top to the desired shape. Two handy shapes are shown at right. The S-curve is particularly useful for bowl turning (and it is easy to make because the flat stock doesn't have to be welded at an angle). One end does the inside of a bowl and the opposite end does the outside. Another handy shape for faceplate work is the right angle, which allows you to work on the side and the base of a bowl (or the inside) without having to move the tool rest.

Some Useful Tool-Rest Shapes

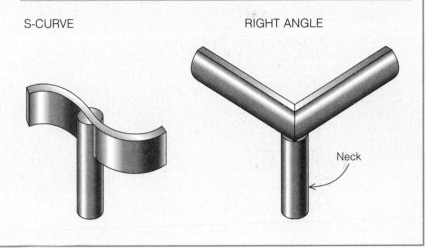

S-CURVE

RIGHT ANGLE

Neck

Belts and pulleys

Replacing the belt will often breathe new life into a tired lathe, especially if it has a variable-width pulley speed control. (For more on speed control, see pp. 8–10.) V-belts drive off their flanks, and the inside surface of the belt should never touch the bottom of the pulley groove. A worn belt will touch the bottom of the groove, leading to loss of power transmission and strange thumps.

Belts, much like tires, range greatly in price, quality, and performance. The difference between the average hardware or discount-store belt and a good-quality belt is like the difference between bias-ply and radial tires. A cheap belt will be stiff and have an uneven cross section, which can cause noise and vibration. For less than $20 you can obtain a high-quality replacement belt. Again, bearing stores are the best source. Gates Green Belts are always a good bet; the belts are of constant cross section and supple. It's good shop practice to replace the belt every time you replace the bearings.

Most modern lathes use V-belts for power transmission. The belts should be replaced every time you replace the bearings.

Pulleys are often a cause of problems, especially strange, vibration-causing thumps and bumps. Sometimes dirt and rubber from the belt will build up in the pulley grooves and cause a clunk (the belt suddenly rides up in the pulley at this point). The buildup can usually be removed with solvent, but sometimes you may have to use sandpaper or a file. The moral here? When replacing belts, always scrupulously clean the pulleys.

Motors

Bowl turning requires more power than does spindle turning, because of the greater diameter of the work. Often an older motor is a bit anemic. The motor may simply be old, or it may be experiencing the rigors of large faceplate work for the first time. If you decide to replace the motor, it's a good idea to buy a more powerful motor (providing it will fit the space and mounts). If you have a ½-hp motor, you might go to a ¾-hp, for instance. This is also an opportunity to upgrade to variable speed.

Vibration

Most lathes have some vibration, usually at a specific speed. Often such problems are speed related, which is one reason why I prefer variable speed. Sometimes the work itself will be the culprit, and tweaking the speed up or down a bit is an instant cure.

Pulleys and belts are the most common sources of vibration, and they should be the first place to look. Cheap pulleys are often out of balance. The dynamic balance of the pulleys and the spindle is the next most likely cause. Many automotive machine shops have dynamic balancing machines and can remedy the problem for you. When adjusting the headstock pulley, both the spindle and the pulley should be balanced as a unit. This will give you a super-running lathe. Don't overlook the possibility that the motor is out of balance; although not that common, it can happen.

For detailed information on lathe maintenance and reconditioning, see *The Lathe Book* (The Taunton Press, 1993).

Holding the Work

Now that you know what you need in a lathe for bowl turning, let's take a look at how to hold the work. A "chuck" is any device that holds work in the lathe—a spur or drive center, a faceplate, a screw chuck, a metal-spinning form, or a live center for the tailstock. The traditional chucks for spindle turning are a set of centers; and for faceplate work, the chuck of that name. Today, however, there's a mind-boggling array of chucks beyond faceplates. Let's look at the many ways to hold bowls.

Centers
Most lathes come with a set of centers—traditionally, a two- or four-prong drive center for the headstock and a dead center for the tailstock. More often today, a live center is provided instead of a dead center, which is a welcome improvement, because the former allows more tailstock pressure and requires no lubrication. If you don't have a live center, you'll want to buy one. I prefer a simple 60° center, because it has a small footprint and holds well. You can save a lot of money by going to a metalworking supply house and buying a center for a metalworking lathe.

Although we usually think of centers as spindle-turning chucks, they can be handy for bowls as well. Often the best way to grab a really odd-shaped piece of wood is to hold it between centers, turn a flat spot for a faceplate or a glue block, and then transfer it to a faceplate. Turners of rough-top bowls do this all the time. Centers can also be used to retrue a dried blank (which was turned wet and has dried oval), so that an expanding scroll chuck may be employed to hold the work.

A live center in the tailstock is a real help for securing work mounted on faceplates. After first mounting a bowl blank, you should make it a habit (like fastening your seat belt) to bring the tailstock up and secure the work against the faceplate with a live center. This takes all the axial load off the screws that secure the work on the faceplate; they now have to hold only the radial load. Using the tailstock in this way is one of the easiest ways to ensure your safety. Later, once things are in balance and true, the tailstock can be redrawn and the real work of shaping your bowl can begin.

A word of advice (which I learned the hard way): Remove the center from the tailstock after it is redrawn. Once while using a big dome scraper on the inside of a bowl, I backed my elbow into the point of the center. I

A lathe is a safe tool; but, as with any tool, knowing about the potential dangers will ensure a good safety record. The main areas of concern are flyers, work flying out of or coming apart in the lathe; speed, which is closely related to the former; clothing, jewelry, and hair, which can become entangled in the spinning work; and dust, which can get into your eyes, nose, and mouth. In addition, your lathe must be properly grounded to prevent the risk of electric shock; if in doubt, have it checked by a licensed electrician.

FLYERS AND SPEED

Work flying out of the lathe or work (especially glued-up pieces) flying apart in the lathe constitutes the biggest danger in turning. Accidents can almost always be traced back to starting the lathe at too high a speed for the turning situation.

You need to work out a drill that will prevent flyers. Get into the habit of turning your lathe back to its lowest speed at the end of every turning session. Unplugging the machine and draping the cord across the bed when you're done is a great reminder. You have to think about the speed before you plug the cord in. Make speed concerns the foremost thought in your mind as you approach the lathe, and make setting the appropriate speed the first order of business when chucking up work. Finally, if you are the least unsure, step to the left of the lathe and turn it on. If the work is going to fly, you'll be out of the way and won't get hurt.

Appropriate speed is a difficult thing to specify. As when driving a car, you can negotiate higher speeds with experience. Except for miniature work, you should never turn bowls at a speed higher than 1,400 rpm. Similarly, sanding is best done at the final turning speed and does not need higher speeds.

Bowl turning is pure faceplate work and is more prone to flyers than is other work because of the greater diameter of the piece and the greater difficulty in centering. For work up to 10 in. in diameter, 600 rpm to 800 rpm is a good roughing speed, with 1,100 rpm being an appropriate finishing speed. Faceplate work need never be done at a speed greater than 1,400 rpm, and a speed from 1,100 rpm to 1,200 rpm is optimum. For large-diameter faceplate work, speeds as low as 200 rpm may be necessary.

Chucking work correctly in the lathe is an important part of the flyer equation. The biggest danger is at the very beginning, because the work is out of balance and out of round. If it flies at this time, the uneven weight will make it sail off with great force (and if a protruding edge catches the tool rest, the force is multiplied). Once a bowl is round and faced true, a piece that comes out of the chuck is much less dangerous, because the work is in balance (and tends to spin in

Although more commonly used for spindle turning, centers can also be used to hold bowls. This bowl was turned wet and will be re-turned between centers.

the air in its own axis) and has no protruding edges.

Of prime importance when starting a turning session is to mount a live center in the tailstock and secure it against the freshly mounted blank. This pins the work to the faceplate (or chuck), taking the axial load off of the screws (or jaws). Bringing the tailstock into play with a live center is one of the cheapest insurance policies you can write yourself. It is something even seasoned veterans should do. Once the work is round, the tailstock may be withdrawn and the center removed; then the work can progress normally.

CLOTHING, JEWELRY, AND HAIR

Good shop practice is to roll up your sleeves, remove jewelry, and restrain long hair. Turning is not for the suit-and-tie crowd. You want your clothing to be devoid of dangling ends that can become entangled in the lathe.

When finishing your work, never use sandpaper or a rag bigger than about 4 in. square. A small rag will be pulled from your fingers, whereas a larger one can drag them with it. Paper-backed sandpaper is safer than cloth-backed paper, because it will tear if it wraps in the work.

DUST

Some sort of eye protection is a must when turning. A minimum is a pair of shatterproof glasses, preferably with side shields. For some types of work, such as turning wood that still has bark on it or exceptionally splintery material, a full-face shield should be worn.

Equally important is protection from inhaling dust. Wood dust can be quite toxic and may be carcinogenic. As a rule of thumb, the more tropical the wood, the more harmful it probably is. A paper dust mask, like those worn in automotive body shops, is a minimum requirement. Better

protection is afforded by a respirator, which looks like a military gas mask and has replaceable cartridge-type filters. On the downside, respirators are hot and tiring to wear, because they are powered by your own lungs. They are also a problem for turners with beards, because the respirator won't seal properly.

My preferred form of protection is an air helmet. Air helmets offer the safety of a full-face shield and hard hat with excellent dust protection that does not tax your respiratory system. They have a motor that pumps air into the helmet, which provides positive air pressure inside the shield, excluding dust and preventing fogging. Although some air helmets will filter only dust, others will also filter organic vapors from finishing products. Air helmets are quite expensive; but if you do much woodworking, they are well worth the price.

jerked forward, and the scraper was flipped around by the spinning bowl and slammed down on my thumb, which was on the rest. The result was a very unhappy month for my left thumb. Always remove the live center when not in use!

Faceplates

Faceplates are the most useful holding device for turning bowls. A faceplate is simply a metal disk with a threaded hub that screws onto the lathe's spindle (see the drawing on p. 18). It has three or more holes to accept screws that hold the work on the disk; standard sizes are 3 in., 4 in., 6 in., and 9 in. Lathes are usually sold with a faceplate.

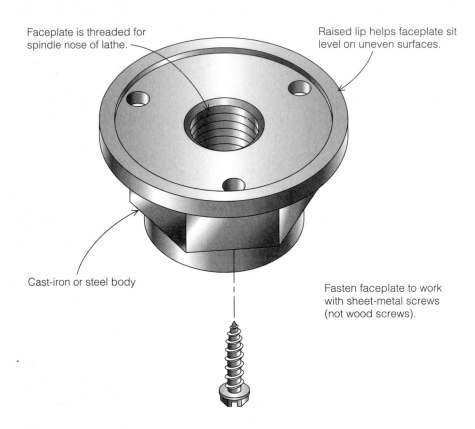

Faceplate is threaded for spindle nose of lathe.

Raised lip helps faceplate sit level on uneven surfaces.

Cast-iron or steel body

Fasten faceplate to work with sheet-metal screws (not wood screws).

A cast-iron or turned-steel faceplate is best for bowl turning. Faceplates with a raised rim tend to seat better on uneven surfaces, such as roughsawn blanks.

One of the first mistakes an aspiring bowl turner can make is to pick a faceplate that's far too large. There's a popular misconception that a 6-in. faceplate is the best all-around size. The best diameter size for bowl turning (and faceplate turning in general) is about 3 in. In fact, a 3-in. faceplate is often called a bowl chuck. Any larger and it's difficult to make a small enough base on your bowl. Many manufacturers cast their small faceplates from aluminum. Although aluminum is fine for small bowls, it's not strong enough for heavy faceplate turning. If you get into larger green-wood turning, you'll want to have some steel or cast-iron models. Aftermarket steel faceplates for most makes of lathes are available from Craft Supplies USA, Packard Woodworks, and Woodcraft (see p. 34).

A second important consideration for faceplates is the type and size screw you use to hold them to the work. A standard tapered wood screw is the conventional choice, but it's not the best one. A sheet-metal screw, sometimes called a self-tapping screw, is much better; it has a straight (rather than a tapered) body and 45° (rather than 60°) threads, which bite into the wood better. It is best to use #10 or bigger screws; I find that #10 by 1-in.-long screws do for the lion's share of my work; I use #10 by 1¼-in.-long screws when extra holding power is necessary.

I like to use hex-head screws because I can drive them with a socket wrench and a cranklike automotive tool called a "speeder" (see the photo at right). Using a speeder, I never have to worry about overtorquing the screws (which is a real problem in green wood); and I never have to hunt for a charged battery or an extension cord. Best of all, in most situations I don't have to drill a starting hole—I can crank the self-tapping sheet-metal screws right in. Armed with sheet-metal screws and a speeder, it's possible to mount and change faceplates quickly and easily.

Glue blocks

Instead of screwing the work directly to the faceplate, there are times when it's desirable to put a secondary piece of wood between the bowl and the faceplate. This piece of wood is screwed to the faceplate and then glued to the center of the work—hence the name "glue block." Why use a glue block? One reason is to get a deeper bowl from a given piece of wood, which is possible because the holding screws are in the glue block and not in the actual turning blank (see the drawing on p. 20). Another reason is that the glue block can be made into a chuck for reverse chucking a bowl, as we will see in later chapters. Reverse chucking is the main reason I like to have plenty of faceplates. Then I don't have to remove the primary faceplate from a bowl in progress to set up a glue block for a reverse-chucking job.

It's best to use 1-in. to 1½-in. material for the glue blocks. This thickness gives you plenty of room to cut off above the screws when you separate the finished bowl from the glue block. Avoid 2-in. material, because the work gets too far from the faceplate for good stability, especially on a lathe that has a light spindle. Roughsawn lumber works fine for a glue block. I like to use 5/4 material and to bandsaw a dozen or so rounds about ¼ in.

A fast and reliable way to secure a faceplate to a bowl blank is to use hex-head screws and a speeder.

Face a glue block flat with a large round-nose scraper.

Glue Block

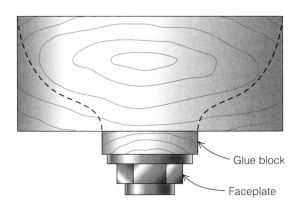

Using a glue block allows you to turn a much deeper bowl for any given blank.

Glue block

Faceplate

bigger in diameter than my faceplates so they're ready at hand as the need arises. Mount the glue block to the faceplate with 1-in. sheet-metal screws (in dry wood, it's a good idea to drill pilot holes to prevent splitting). Mount the faceplate in the lathe, and then scrape the glue block flat with a large round-nose scraper. The result is a glue block that is square and true with your lathe.

If you're gluing a glue block to green wood, standard wood glues (such as Elmer's or Titebond) will not work. You must use a medium-viscosity

cyanoacrylate glue (Super Glue). If you're gluing to dry wood, be sure you have an exact surface-to-surface joinery-level fit between the glue block and the bowl blank, and follow the glue manufacturer's directions for clamping and curing times.

Screw chucks

A screw chuck is a handy, cost-effective chuck for the bowl turner. As the name implies, this chuck is nothing more than a screw projecting from a flat plate, which mounts on the headstock spindle. An appropriately sized hole is drilled in the work, which is then threaded over the screw. For bowl turning, you need a heavy screw chuck that screws over the spindle nose, not one that is built on a Morse taper. Look for a heavy screw ¼ in. to ⅜ in. in diameter.

As you will see in later chapters, a screw chuck is a handy way to hold the bowl blank for the initial turning of the outside of the bowl. A hole is drilled into the area that will be the interior of the bowl, and the blank is mounted on the screw chuck. After the outside of the bowl is turned, a glue block (which has to be thicker than the length of the screw) can be screwed onto the chuck, and the partially completed bowl can be reverse chucked so the inside can be turned. Finally, when it is time to turn the foot, a large disk of wood can be mounted on the screw chuck to make a jam chuck (see p. 78). A screw chuck gives good chucking value indeed.

Commercial chucks

Many novice bowl turners buy commercial chucks in the mistaken belief that they will solve all their turning problems. Although such chucks can make life easier once you have learned to turn reasonably well, they don't do anything the glue block, faceplate, or jam chucks can't do. Initially, it's much better to put your money into good tools and sharpening jigs than into commercial chucks. In short, learn to use the shop-built chucks before moving onto commercial chucks.

Once you're ready to try commercial chucks, I recommend that you opt for a four-jaw self-centering scroll chuck (see the photo at right). There are three readily available, moderately priced scroll chucks designed specifi-

The Nova chuck (shown here disassembled) grips the workpiece with four jaws, which can be adjusted with a scroll. The scroll engages the rack on the bottom of the base jaw, moving it in or out, depending on which direction the scroll is turned.

To open and close a lever chuck, place the two steel bars in the holes in the body of the chuck and scroll plate and turn them in opposite directions.

cally for woodturning: the Nova chuck, which was the first on the market and is made in New Zealand; the Vickmark (Australia); and the Oneway (Canada). They are all lever chucks, which means the scroll is actuated by two metal levers that are inserted into holes in the body of the chuck and the scroll itself. All three chucks come with a heavy screw that can be gripped in the medium-size jaws that come with the chucks. This turns the scroll chuck into a large screw chuck.

Although we tend to think of scroll chucks gripping by compressing around the outside of the work (compression hold), their real value in bowl turning is expanding inside a recess in the base of the bowl (expansion hold). The Nova, Vickmark, and Oneway chucks all have jaws that are angled on the outside (see the top drawing on p. 68). By scraping a dovetailed (undercut) recess in the base of the bowl the chuck can be expanded to hold securely.

There are a couple of safety issues when working with scroll chucks. First, never extend the jaws more than halfway out of the chuck body. If you inadvertently extend one or more jaws beyond the grip of the scroll, the jaws will fly out of the body when you start the lathe, leading to potentially fatal consequences. Second, take great care not to touch (or brush up against) the jaws or chuck body. At best, the spinning jaws are real knuckle busters; at worst, they can maim. If the job demands working close to the chuck, wrap the chuck and jaws with duct tape. The tape covers sharp edges and helps brush fingers and body parts away rather than catching them on the spinning jaws. Shop-built chucks seldom present these dangers.

2 Turning Tools

The lathe is only one part of the bowl-turning equation. You'll also need tools to turn your bowls (the subject of this chapter) and material to turn the bowls from (discussed in chapter 3). Fortunately, you don't need a large number of tools to turn attractive bowls. If you already have tools for spindle turning, the only new tool you'll really need for bowl turning is a bowl gouge. In the long run, you'll also want to add some big round-nose scrapers to your turning arsenal, but these can be shopmade or improvised. You may also want to consider buying a combination gouge.

A few spindle-turning tools can be used for bowl turning (such as parting tools and scrapers), but it is dangerous to use a roughing-out gouge or a skew chisel for faceplate work. You can use a spindle gouge for bowl turning, but it's not something I recommend (the tool catches too easily).

Traditionally, turning tools were made out of high-carbon steel. Today, standard tools are still made from carbon steel. However, high-speed steel (HSS) is used in most, if not all, premium turning tools. The main difference between the two metals is that HSS stands up under heat and still maintains a sharp edge. Although HSS tools cost more than carbon-steel tools, they will last much longer; and you don't have to worry about overheating during grinding, because HSS can be turned red hot on the grinder without affecting the temper. Although I don't recommend getting your tools that hot, by removing the worry of ruining your tool by overheating you can concentrate on grinding even bevels of the correct angle. (For more about sharpening, see pp. 31–41.)

◾ The Bowl Gouge

The most important tool for any bowl turner is the bowl gouge, which differs significantly from a spindle gouge in that it has a deeper flute and an asymmetric grind. The nose is ground to a short bevel, whereas the sides are ground to a medium bevel. Most beginners make the mistake of grabbing a spindle gouge when they first try to turn a bowl. The result is invariably a lot of frustration—if not a nasty catch. That's because bowl turning is faceplate turning, and the grain of the wood runs across the axis of the lathe, as shown in the top drawing on the facing page, not parallel to the axis as in spindle turning.

As woodworkers, we are taught always to try to cut with the grain; but in the case of faceplate turning, we have to cut against the grain in two areas on every revolution of the lathe. A spindle gouge is ground to a long bevel, because a low angle of attack works best for cutting with or across the grain (as in spindle turning). However, it works against you in bowl turning, since it tends to dig into the reverse grain—sometimes seriously.

A twofold solution to the reverse-grain problem was worked out long ago in the form of the bowl gouge. At first glance, a bowl gouge may look just like a big spindle gouge; but in fact, it is quite different. A bowl gouge has a much deeper parabolic-shaped flute and is ground to a medium bevel. The traditional grind is 45° all the way round, as shown in the top drawing on p. 26. The resulting higher angle of attack renders the tool

The Wrong Tool for the Job

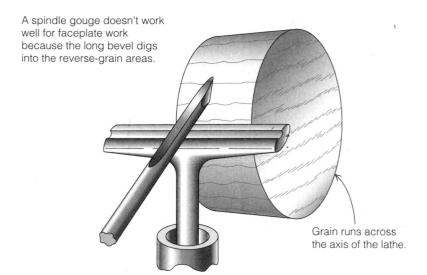

A spindle gouge doesn't work well for faceplate work because the long bevel digs into the reverse-grain areas.

Grain runs across the axis of the lathe.

Turning-Tool Grinds

Throughout this book we will be speaking of tools being ground to a short, medium, or long bevel.

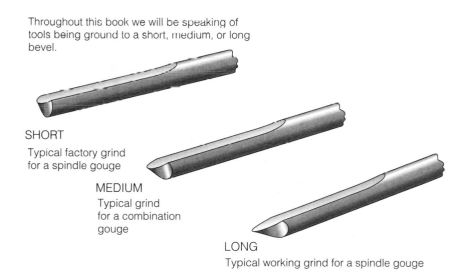

SHORT
Typical factory grind for a spindle gouge

MEDIUM
Typical grind for a combination gouge

LONG
Typical working grind for a spindle gouge

much less likely to dig into reverse-grain areas. Second, a bowl gouge does not cut at right angles to the axes of rotation, as the spindle gouge does, but rather parallel to it. The third drawing in the bowl-gouge evolution series on p. 26 shows a modified version of the traditional gouge, with the same 45° bevel angle but with the face raked back a bit to get the top corners out of the way for a typical cut, which renders the tool better for inside bowl work. Regardless of the grind, the bottom half of the flute does all of the work, and the nose bevel rides on the surface generated by the

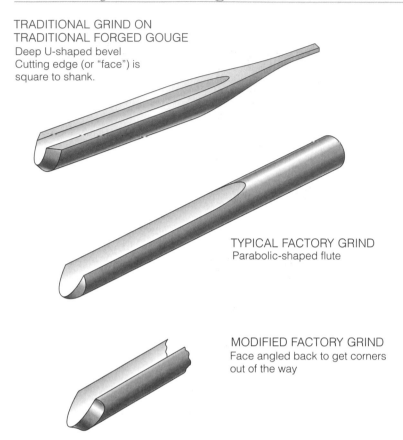

**TRADITIONAL GRIND ON
TRADITIONAL FORGED GOUGE**
Deep U-shaped bevel
Cutting edge (or "face") is
square to shank.

TYPICAL FACTORY GRIND
Parabolic-shaped flute

MODIFIED FACTORY GRIND
Face angled back to get corners
out of the way

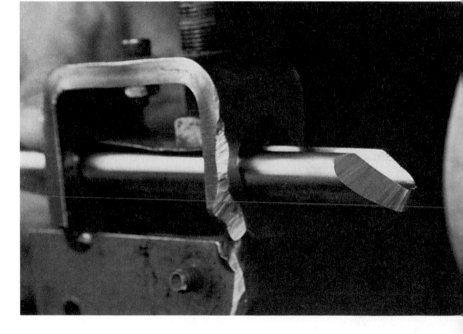

*The bowl gouge has a short nose
bevel and medium side bevels. This
modified version has the top corners
of the face raked well back, which
makes them less likely to catch when
cutting inside a bowl.*

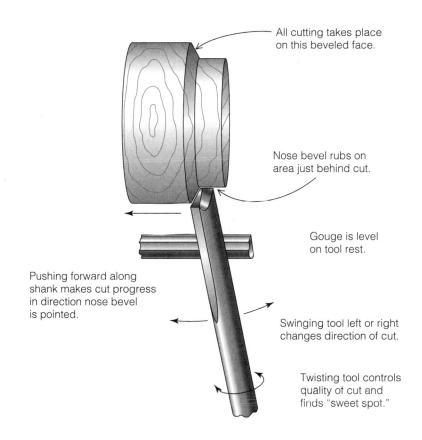

All cutting takes place on this beveled face.

Nose bevel rubs on area just behind cut.

Gouge is level on tool rest.

Pushing forward along shank makes cut progress in direction nose bevel is pointed.

Swinging tool left or right changes direction of cut.

Twisting tool controls quality of cut and finds "sweet spot."

cut. This prevents the gouge from following the reverse grain, resulting in a nice cut.

Bowl gouges are commonly sold in ¼-in., ⅜-in., and ½-in. sizes (see the sidebar on p. 28). If you're just learning to turn bowls, I'd recommend starting with a ½-in. gouge. Add a ¼-in. gouge and possibly a ⅜-in. tool as budget allows. There's an extra-large bowl gouge offered these days (often under the name "Texas Turning Tool") that's milled from ¾-in. bar stock, but it's much too big to be useful. Stick with ½ in. and smaller.

The Combination Gouge

A combination gouge is a compromise between a true spindle gouge and a bowl gouge. It has a deeper flute than the average spindle gouge, but the flute is a radius rather than a parabola. A combination gouge is ground to a medium bevel of about 45°, which allows it to be used in spindle and faceplate work. (In fact, most combination gouges cannot be ground to a

Bowl-Gouge Size

Traditionally, deep-fluted bowl gouges are sized by the approximate distance across the top of the flute. Because HSS bowl gouges are milled from round bar stock, a ½-in. bowl gouge is made from a ⅝-in.-diameter bar. The word "approximate" is key here, because I have seen flute widths that varied as much as ⅛ in. from the stated size and noted great differences in flute widths among tools from the same company.

As a result, some companies have started to size bowl gouges by the diameter of the bar they are made from. This is probably a truer measure. You need to read advertising copy carefully to find out which system the company (or reseller) is using. The chart below lists the three sizes of bowl gouges in both systems. All bowl-gouge sizing used in this book is in the traditional measure.

TRADITIONAL MEASURE (distance across flute)	NEW MEASURE (diameter of bar)
¼ in.	⅜ in.
⅜ in.	½ in.
½ in.	⅝ in.

How a Combination Gouge Differs from a Spindle Gouge

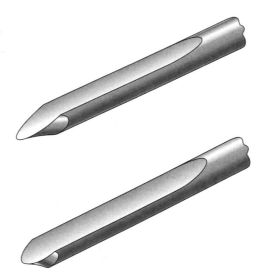

SPINDLE GOUGE
Long grind makes the spindle gouge awkward to use in faceplate work.

COMBINATION GOUGE
Deeper flute and 45° grind make the combination gouge excellent for final cleanup of faceplate work (but just adequate for spindle work).

Cross section

long bevel because the deep flute precludes it.) Although it is just adequate for spindle work, a combination gouge is excellent for the final shaping and cleanup of faceplate work. It is easier for most workers to control the direction of a combination gouge than of a bowl gouge, so a smoother cut is usually the result. (For information on using a combination gouge, see p. 87.)

Combination gouges are sized the same as bowl gouges—by the distance across the flute. I like to use a fairly large combination gouge (½ in. or bigger). Although I find small bowl gouges very useful, I do fine with just the one ½-in. gouge. If you don't own a combination gouge, don't rush out and buy one. Perfect your bowl gouge and scraper techniques and pick this tool up later when you have more confidence.

Scrapers

While the bowl gouge is the preeminent tool of the bowl turner, scrapers are the workaday implements that get the job done. A gouge is the best way to cut wood, because it leaves the smoothest finish; but it requires a fair amount of skill to master and cannot reach blind areas, such as reverse forms, undercut areas, and the bottom of a bowl. A scraper cuts wood handily in all situations and requires only a modicum of skill. Scrapers can be ground to complicated shapes, which makes duplication of details easy. Most bowl turners use scrapers as tools of necessity.

Using a scraper is quite different from using other turning tools, and at first it can seem a little unnerving. Most books on turning encourage turners to sheer cut, which requires keeping the bevel of the tool rubbing on the work surface. To use a scraper, you have to point the tool downhill and drag the burred edge for it to cut properly (see p. 88). In fact, pointing a scraper uphill can result in a nasty catch. As can be seen in the drawing on p. 30, a turning scraper works exactly like a cabinet scraper and is

A combination gouge is an excellent tool for the final shaping and cleanup of faceplate work, because it leaves a really smooth surface.

A scraper is a good tool to use in areas that would be hard to turn with a bowl gouge. Here, a large square-corner scraper starts the cut to get beyond the natural edge of a rough-top bowl.

Making Scrapers

You can buy turning scrapers from woodworking stores and tool catalogs, but they're also easy to make yourself. Driving a cement nail into a piece of wood makes a quick-and-easy miniature scraper, as shown at far left in the photo. Some of my best scrapers are discarded tools. A screwdriver makes a great detail scraper; worn files are always handy to turn into small form scrapers; and chisels for pavement breakers (air hammers) make dandy bowl scrapers.

I purchased my pavement chisels at a scrap yard for 50¢ a pound, but even new they are only

$15 to $20. The round or faceted shank allows the tool to be rolled on the tool rest, which makes it great for inside bowl work. Its weight makes it rock steady and easy to control.

Left to right: a scraper made from a cement nail in a wooden block, a screwdriver scraper, two scrapers formed from old files, a pavement-chisel scraper, and two commercial scrapers.

How a Scraper Cuts

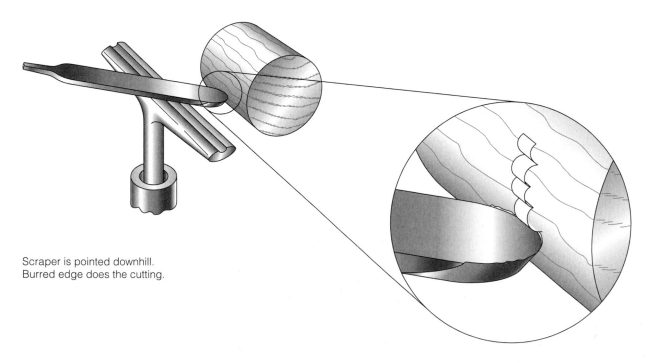

Scraper is pointed downhill.
Burred edge does the cutting.

sharpened to a burr. It's the burr that does the work, a micro cutting edge that, because of its short length, removes only a set amount with each revolution of the lathe.

■ Sharpening

You can't turn without sharp tools, so sharpening is as important a skill as turning itself. As delivered from the factory, most turning tools are not even ground to the correct shape, let alone made sharp, which is why turning can be so frustrating for beginners. Sharpening is the most difficult part of the learning-to-turn equation; the good news is that it's not difficult for anyone to become proficient at turning once they've mastered the art of sharpening.

Sharpening lathe tools can be divided into three distinct operations: establishing the correct shape and bevel angle, light grinding, and honing. Establishing the correct shape and bevel angle is really a heavy grinding operation; after the correct shape is obtained, only light grinding is necessary to maintain the tool. Honing makes the ground edge really sharp but is generally unnecessary for faceplate tools. Relatively large cross sections combined with two encounters with the end grain per revolution render burrs meaningless. Therefore, bowl gouges can be used directly from the grinder; and the burr is purposely left on scrapers, because the burr is what does the cutting. If you elect to purchase a combination gouge, you will find that the tool benefits from honing before the final pass over your nearly finished bowl. With all of this in mind, I always hone spindle tools but almost never hone faceplate tools.

An 8-in. bench grinder is a good size for sharpening turning tools.

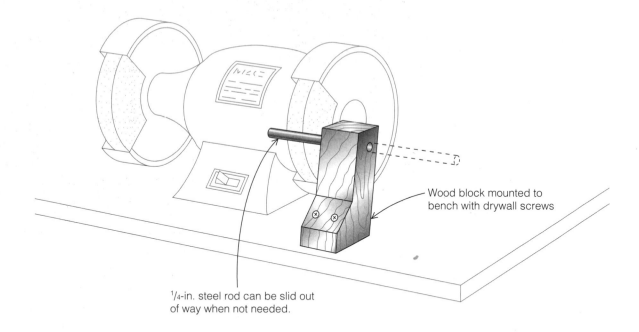

Wood block mounted to
bench with drywall screws

¹/₄-in. steel rod can be slid out
of way when not needed.

Grinding

You'll have to shape new turning tools that you buy, because they rarely
come from the factory ground to the correct angle. You'll also have to
regrind your tools as they wear down from use. In these endeavors, the
bench grinder will be your constant companion.

Grinders Bench grinders for home use up through those for light-
industrial use come in 6-in., 7-in., 8-in., and 10-in. sizes. The three smaller
sizes are generally built on a 3,450-rpm motor frame, whereas the 10-in.
model is constructed on a 1,725-rpm frame. Many people think the larger
machine grinds cooler because of the slower speed, but there's really
not much difference (5,416 ft. per minute for the 6-in. grinding wheel vs.
4,516 ft. per minute for the 10-in. wheel). Several companies offer 6-in.
grinders built on a 1,725 rpm motor, which gives a surface speed of
2,710 ft. per minute.

   Although the virtue of low-speed grinding has been touted, there is
actually a loss of efficiency at speeds much below 4,000 ft. per minute.
There is, however, a gain in control, because things happen more slowly,
which is why beginners are more comfortable with these machines.
If, as I recommend, you are going to use a jig to sharpen your tools (see
"Sharpening Jigs"), a normal-speed 8-in. grinder will work best; a low-
speed grinder wastes time, because sharpening takes longer.

Sharpening jigs allow novice turners to grind gouges correctly and consistently to any bevel angle. Shown here are the Sorby jig (left; grinding a combination gouge) and the Oneway jig (right; grinding a bowl gouge).

Most beginners make the mistake of using too fine a grinding wheel. I normally mount a 46-grit wheel on the left-hand side of my grinder and an 80-grit on the right. I do the initial shaping of a new tool and sharpen bowl gouges on the coarse wheel. I use the fine wheel for grinding spindle-turning tools, combination gouges, parting tools, and scrapers.

All grinders come with some sort of rest, which is useful for sharpening scrapers, but it must be removed if you are going to use a jig. If you elect to sharpen freehand (without a jig), it's better to make your own rest. For gouges, a rest that emulates the tool rest on your lathe works best (see the drawing on the facing page). Such a rest will allow you to roll the tool easily to create the complex shape required of a bowl or combination gouge.

Sharpening jigs For a long time, I was a firm believer in sharpening freehand; but over the years, I've come to appreciate the value of using sharpening jigs, especially for novice turners. A jig allows a beginner to grind gouges correctly and consistently to any grind angle. The advantage of starting your bowl-turning career with correctly shaped tools and being able to consistently repeat the initial results is so overwhelming as to make the cost of the jig insignificant.

There are two jigs widely available to turners: the Sorby and the Oneway. Although they look quite different, they both work essentially the same. The tool is mounted in an articulated holder, which can swing on its axis at any angle to the grinding wheel. You can obtain any ratio of nose-to-side-bevel grind by varying the angle of articulation and the angle at which the axis of the jig contacts the wheel.

At $75, the Sorby is the less expensive of the two jigs. It exhibits beautiful workmanship and finish but comes with rather poor directions. It works with any size grinder and is simple to operate. The one disadvantage is that the Sorby jig is designed to work with only one of the two wheels on your grinder, because it is made to be permanently mounted.

A fingernail sharpening jig is available for the Tormek SuperGrind Sharpening System, a low-speed wet grinder. The jig comes with an angle adjustment for easy setup (shown with a bowl gouge).

However, it's easy to work out some sort of rapid clamping fixture to locate the jig at either wheel or get it out of the way when not grinding gouges.

At $175 for all the necessary pieces, the Oneway jig is more expensive; but it can also be used to grind other woodworking tools, such as plane irons and bench chisels, in addition to lathe tools. For this reason, it's a good value. The Oneway works best with an 8-in. grinder, though 6-in. and 7-in. grinders work acceptably, if they're blocked up. The basic Oneway Wolverine System gives you a mounting device that goes under each wheel to hold either the Variable Angle Platform Rest or the V-arm that comes with the system. The Variable Angle Platform Rest is good for general woodworking tools and bowl-turning scrapers. To sharpen gouges with the Oneway, you also need the fingernail Vari-grind, which is used in combination with the V-arm.

For both the Sorby and the Oneway I recommend mounting your grinder on a piece of ¾-in. plywood and then attaching the jig to this sub-base. This keeps the relationship of the jig and the grinder constant but allows the grinder to be portable. I like to attach four rubber feet to the bottom of the sub-base; the feet adsorb the vibration and help the grinder stay put.

There is also a fingernail jig for the Tormek SuperGrind Sharpening System (see the photo on the facing page). The Tormek is a low-speed wet grinder for general woodworking tools, such as plane irons and bench chisels. With the addition of the fingernail jig, it works well for bowl and combination gouges; but it is much slower than the Sorby and Oneway. If you already own a Tormek grinder, it makes sense to buy the fingernail jig (for about $60); otherwise, I'd stick with the Sorby or the Oneway.

Sharpening a bowl gouge

The secret to sharpening a bowl gouge is to grind the gouge in halves. Start at one corner of the bevel and roll the tool toward the center. Then go to the other corner and execute a mirror image of the procedure. The photo essay on pp. 36–37 shows techniques both for freehand grinding and for using a sharpening jig (the Oneway). Grinding by eye takes a fair amount of skill and a good deal of practice to get it right; try to work with a fluid, steady motion. The photos demonstrate an asymmetric grind suitable for general bowl work, with a medium bevel on the sides of the tool and a short nose bevel.

Bowl-gouge grinds The factory grind of the bowl gouge varies greatly among manufacturers, and most turners find the tool can be made more useful by modifying the grind. The simplest modification is to rake the face of the tool back at least 15° while retaining the 45° bevel, as shown at top left in the drawing on p. 38. By getting the top corners of the bevels raked back out of the way, they are much less likely to catch in tight quarters, such as the transitional area where the side wall meets the bottom on the inside of bowls. Further modification entails going to an asymmetric grind

Sharpening a Bowl Gouge

Freehand

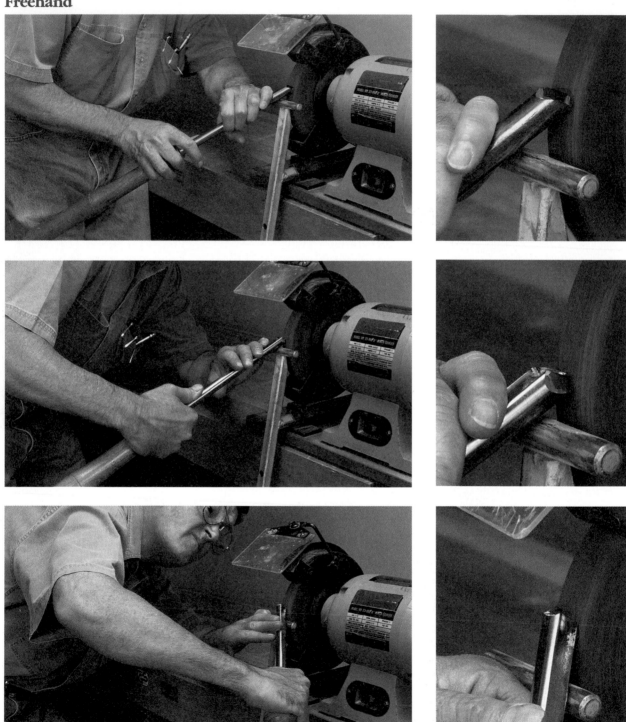

With Jig

1. *Whether sharpening freehand (far left) or with the aid of a jig (left), start with the left-hand bevel so you can stand well to the left of the grinding wheel and step toward the wheel as the grind progresses. Slant the tool up to the desired bevel angle. From your side vantage point, you can compare the existing bevel angle to the wheel as the two kiss.*

2. *Once sparks break over the edge (which signals that the entire bevel has been ground), roll the tool toward the nose and simultaneously raise the handle. Stop at the tip of the nose or just slightly past it. Grind quicker and lighter on the nose to avoid grinding it back behind the side bevels.*

3. *If sharpening freehand, now do the mirror image on the other bevel, starting on the side, rolling the tool while raising the handle, and stopping at the tip of the nose. If you are using a jig, simply continue to grind the right bevel. Increase the pressure slightly once past the nose. The entire grind should be one continuous, slow, and fluid motion.*

MODIFIED FACTORY GRIND

ASYMMETRIC GRIND

Nose bevel
flattened

ADVANCED GRIND

INCORRECT GRIND

Tool starts to cut here
before nose bevel
can engage.

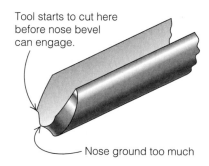

Nose ground too much

in which the nose bevel is flattened (to 75° to 80°) in relationship to the side bevels, which remain at 45°, as shown at top right above.

The asymmetric grind is much better for turning the inside of deep bowls, because the nose bevel doesn't lose contact when it goes around the transitional area between the side wall and the bottom. In a deep bowl, a 45° nose bevel loses contact at this area, resulting in a rough cut. Many bowl turners grind the side bevels back farther still and increase the length of the bevel, as shown at bottom left above. In skilled hands, this grind is able to cut through reverse grain in green wood, but it negates much of the forgiving nature of a bowl gouge. Instead of rolling out of trouble, it tends to dig in deeper. Furthermore, I believe that this grind actually tears out worse in dry wood. I strongly recommend that you become technically proficient with one of the milder grinds before progressing to this one.

A common grinding mistake, which makes the bowl gouge difficult to use, is demonstrated at bottom right above. It's easy to grind more on the nose than on the side bevels, resulting in the shape shown. This will make the tool very hard to start, because the lower side bevel will begin cutting before the nose has a chance to engage itself on the ledge created by the cut. Because the nose is small in relation to the side bevels, it will be ground away more quickly if you don't take care to grind fairly lightly in this area. With a properly ground bevel, the nose engages simultaneously with the start of the lower bevel cutting.

After grinding the combination gouge, hone it to a fine edge on a buffing wheel. Hold the bevel at a tangent to the wheel.

Sharpening a combination gouge

A combination gouge is ground in exactly the same way as the bowl gouge. The only difference is that after grinding the bevel, I hone the combination tool on a buffer (it's the only faceplate tool I hone). The honing results in a noticeable reduction in tearout in the reverse-grain areas—and a great reduction in the amount of sanding you have to do.

Sharpening a scraper

Although sharpening a gouge by eye can be difficult for the novice turner, sharpening scrapers is simplicity itself. All you need is a grinder and a platform rest. It doesn't even matter much whether you use a coarse or a fine grinding wheel. The object is just to create a burr.

Grinding a Burr on a Scraper

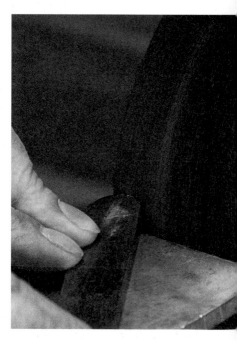

1. *To grind the burr on a round-nose scraper, set the platform rest slightly uphill, and swing the tool across the wheel.*

2, 3, 4. *Using moderate pressure against the wheel, start on the left-hand end of the curve, and swing the bevel from side to side until a burr is formed.*

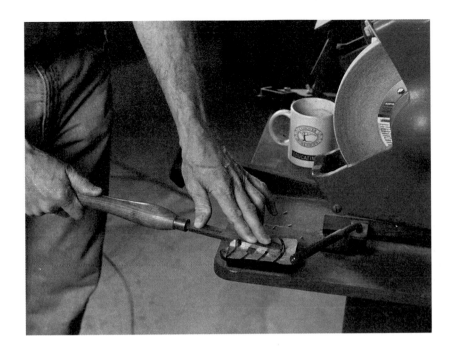

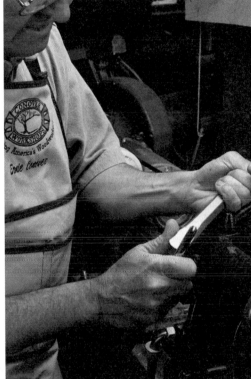

High-speed steel scrapers can be burnished using the Veritas burnishing fixture. Place the tool in the fixture, with the cutting edge down, and lever the cutting edge against the fulcrum pin and the carbide cone to roll the burr.

Use a cabinetmaker's burnish to roll the burr on a carbon-steel scraper.

You can create the burr in two ways: by grinding or by burnishing. Grinding a scraper is easy: Simply grind the desired shape on any reasonably hard piece of steel. I set my grinding rest very slightly uphill so that about an 80° bevel (10° of relief) is created. Contrary to popular wisdom, the tool does not have to be turned upside down during grinding—no better burr is created if you do. Grinding right side up is much better, because you can concentrate on shaping the tool correctly.

The main thing is to swing the tool with smooth, fluid motions for curved shapes (see the photo essay on the facing page) and slide it laterally across the rest in a straight line for straight edges. Use moderate pressure against the wheel until sparks break over the edge. If you're grinding a HSS tool, you don't have to worry about burning, but with carbon steel you should frequently quench the scraper in water.

The second way to create the burr is by burnishing, in the same way a cabinet scraper is sharpened. The only problem is that HSS scrapers are too hard to burnish unless you use the Veritas burnishing tool shown in the photo above. Traditionally, a scraper was drawn back to a milder temper (about Rc50 to Rc55 on Rockwell C scale, which is spring temper) than other turning tools (in the Rc58 to Rc62 range). If you have a spring-steel scraper and a cabinetmaker's burnish, you can roll a burr in the same way as you would sharpen a cabinet scraper. Start by grinding the shape you desire, even if you are just resharpening the same shape. Then use an oilstone or a waterstone to remove all trace of the burr and grind marks from the bevel. Now burnish, and you are ready to go.

3 Wood for Turning

Inside that log, there's a bowl just waiting to come out.

Wood is the raw material we start with in the process of turning bowls. In this plastic age, wood is the substance that gives our bowls their unique characteristics, which never fail to delight anyone who holds or uses them. Like it or not, to be a bowl turner you are going to have to learn a lot about wood: how to gather it, how to select the best grain for your purposes, and how to cut it into usable chunks that fit in your lathe.

There are three ways to go about obtaining wood for a bowl blank: buy air- or kiln-dried wood; gather and cut green wood yourself; or glue up bowl blanks from small blocks of wood (a process known as tiling).

Buying Wood

The first way to obtain wood for turning is straightforward: Simply buy a heavy air- or kiln-dried plank and bandsaw round bowl blanks from the plank. There are two drawbacks to this option. The first is that it is difficult to buy wood thicker than 8/4, which is actually about 2⅛ in. thick. The second is that dried wood is expensive; the thicker it is, the more expensive it becomes. Above 8/4, the price rises dramatically for each additional ¼ in. Still, you can turn a good many nice bowls from an 8/4 or 10/4 plank, as long as you use a glue block so that you get the full depth from the plank (see pp. 19–20).

Gathering Wood

A much cheaper way to obtain quality wood for bowl turning is to gather it yourself. And when you consider that you can have a blank for a bowl of any size and depth, and you can find wood of unbelievable grain pattern and beauty, gathering your own becomes the only game in town.

Where to look
If you look around, you'll soon find that great bowl turning wood is being thrown away every day. Sources to pursue include power companies, tree services and tree surgeons, town maintenance departments, construction companies, and sawmills.

Using a glue block allows you to get full depth out of a dry-wood bowl.

You can get some wonderful burl wood suitable for turning bowls just by asking around at power companies, tree services, and other local sources.

Seldom does a week go by that I don't drive by a power-company crew working on clearing a roadway. Simply stopping and asking will usually put a log or two of any length in the back of your car. Wood is just a nuisance that has to be hauled away, so your doing some hauling for them is greatly appreciated. You can sweeten the deal with $5 or $10, but a much better sweetener is the offer of a finished bowl. Once the bowl is delivered, the recipient often becomes a scout for you and will save burls or logs of interesting grain and species.

Tree services and tree surgeons can be found listed in the Yellow Pages. As with the power companies, wood is just a nuisance that has to be disposed of. I've gotten some marvelous burl just by asking. Also consider contacting your local town maintenance department. Every town has to remove trees now and then, and maintenance crews will invariably be willing to drop off the offending trees at your house rather than hauling them to the town dump. Housing developments are great places to find green wood. As with the other sources, merely asking an on-site construction crew will usually put any amount of wood in your vehicle.

Most sawmills will gladly sell you a log. In fact, they often have logs they cannot use because they suspect they contain metal—from nails to railroad spikes and fence wire—that will ruin their saws. Often these logs are partially milled to the point at which the sawyer spotted discoloration in the wood, a telltale sign of metal deeper down. Rather than risk the saw, he rolled the questionable piece off the carriage and moved on to safer logs. As bowl turners, we can easily work with this wood. Simply cut around the areas where the suspected metal is; at worse, you'll end up with a badly dulled or ruined chain. Because I buy chain at less than $15 per loop this is a small price to pay.

I have on a number of occasions persuaded a sawyer to mill a log or two for me. I simply have him mill 3-in.- to 6-in.-thick planks to either side of the heart, which, as you will see, is exactly what I do with a chainsaw (see the photo essay on pp. 46–47). This saves a lot of chainsaw work. Wax these planks with Anchorseal, Sealtite, or a similar preservative, and the planks will keep for some time. (How long depends on where you live and the time of year. Cut wood will last longer in cold, wet weather than in hot, dry weather. Storing it in a cool place out of the sun always helps. At worst, your wood will last at least a month.) Now all you have to do is crosscut the plank to the diameter of the bowl desired.

Be aware that a log suitable for bowl turning can be almost any log in almost any condition short of rotten. Logs that a sawmill would not look at twice often prove a bonanza to the bowl turner. Although grade lumber comes from the branchless trunk section (called the bole) of the tree, intersecting branches, crotches, and grown-over wounds usually add interesting figure to wood and present little problem to the turner. It's definitely a case of the ugly duckling becoming a swan. Some of my best bowls have come from trees that you might even pass over for firewood.

Cutting your own wood

Unless you elect to have a mill slab off some thick boards for you, you'll need a chainsaw for harvesting wood for bowl turning. Chainsaws are inherently dangerous and should always be treated with caution (see "Chainsaw Safety" on p. 46 for some important tips). There are two types of chainsaw chain: safety and professional. Nonprofessionals, if not all users, should use safety chain. Fortunately, most homeowner saws on the market today come equipped with safety chain, but check to make sure.

Safety chain digs in less during a kickback, which can occur because the operator inadvertently brings the upper quadrant of the chainsaw's bar nose in contact with something, usually wood (see the drawing on p. 47). The possibility of a kickback is why you should never stand directly behind a saw, always keep both hands on the grips, and wear a hard hat with a face shield and other safety clothing. Always pay close attention to where the nose is and what it can touch—and use full throttle. It's easy to be concentrating on a cut and inadvertently touch the upper quadrant of the bar nose to an adjacent piece of wood. A few simple precautions will all but eliminate kickbacks.

Anchorseal is a product used by the wood industry to seal end grain. It is good for sealing the ends of logs (as shown here), coating rough-turned bowls, or sealing freshly cut blanks.

Chainsaw Safety

- Always wear proper safety equipment: hard hat, ear protection, face shield, safety glasses, safety gloves, chaps, and safety shoes.

- Always wear gloves when installing and maintaining chain.

- Always watch the nose of the bar carefully and make sure that you never cut with the upper quadrant of the nose.

- Never use a chainsaw with a left-hand grip (chainsaws are built for right-handed people).

- Always use full throttle during a cut.

- Never make a cut higher than your shoulders.

- Never stand directly behind a saw but rather just to the left so that any kickback goes by your head.

- Always make sure the chain is properly tensioned. A loose chain is more prone to kickbacks and can be thrown by the saw.

- Always have a first-aid kit close at hand.

- Make sure your saw has a mechanical and inertial chain brake, as well as safety chain.

Cutting Planks from a Log

1. *If the log has been sitting for some time, slice 6 in. to 12 in. off the end to get into fresh green wood. Then measure a length of log just shorter than the usable bar length of your chain saw.*

2. *Crosscut the log.*

3. *Use a lumber crayon to lay out planks on the end of the log. On small logs I generally cut through the exact center. On larger logs, I cut an inch or so to either side of center to be entirely clear of a complete annular ring.*

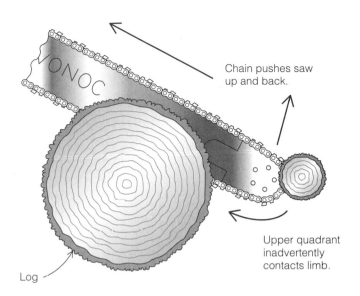

Chain pushes saw up and back.

Upper quadrant inadvertently contacts limb.

Log

4. *Support the log on a suitable surface, such as two other logs or a heavy plank. If necessary, insert wedges at either side of the log to keep it from rolling while you are cutting. The main thing is to get the log off the ground so that you cannot hit a stone when you come though the bottom and to ensure that the nose of the saw will not touch anything unexpectedly—causing a kickback.*

5. *Rip flatsawn planks to your layout lines. Keep the bucking spikes against the end of the log and the bar pointed slightly uphill throughout the cut.*

6. *The finished planks, ready for cutting into bowl blanks.*

Cutting Bowl Blanks from Chainsawn Planks

1. *Lay out the bowl blanks with dividers or trammels. Go over the circles with a pencil to make it easier to follow the layout.*

2. *Cut just outside the lines. Work slowly and carefully, watching that you are allowing the blade to cut rather than twisting it. Make sure the cut is supported at all times and that the work is not going to tip.*

3. *Cut out from the circle to allow the waste to fall away once or twice during the cut. Avoid backing up. (It's better to cut a flat spot in the circle than to back up.)*

Understanding wood movement

The photo essay on pp. 46–47 and "Cutting Bowl Blanks from Chainsawn Planks" (above) show you how to obtain a usable bowl blank directly from a tree. Before attacking a log with a chainsaw, however, you need to understand a bit about wood technology. Turning bowls from green wood is an age-old process. In fact, when all lathes were human powered, using green wood was the only way the job could be done, because green wood turns much more easily than does dry wood and can be reduced to lathe-

Once you've cut the flatsawn planks with a chainsaw, they need to be further processed into bowl blanks using a bandsaw. This must be done soon after chainsawing, otherwise water loss will cause checking problems. I can get between one and four blanks from one of my flatsawn planks. A word of safety: It's very important that the wood sits level and even on the bandsaw table, because a piece that rocks on the table can cause the blade to catch, possibly leading to injury. If necessary, level the plank with an adze, ax, or handplane.

I like to use a coarse, skip-tooth blade, because it cuts green wood fast and efficiently. I find that a skip pattern of 0.025 in. thick, ⅜ in. wide, and 4 teeth per inch works best. The ⅜-in. width turns any radius in bowl turning and yet resists snapping if you get into trouble.

The finished blanks need to be turned immediately (you have a window of only a few hours) or stored in a tightly sealed plastic bag to keep them wet until turning. I use plastic trash bags. After wrapping the blanks well and expelling all the air from the bags, I tape them.

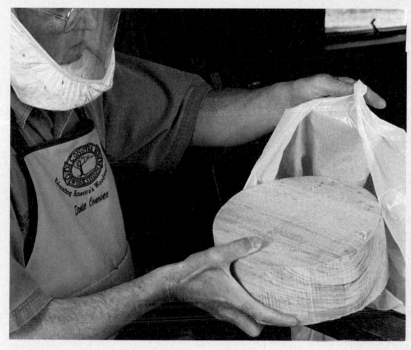

4. *If you're not going to turn the finished blank immediately, store it in a tightly sealed plastic bag to keep it wet until its used.*

Depending on the climate and the type and condition of the wood, the blank will keep between three weeks and three months. If you have room in your freezer, the bagged blank can be kept indefinitely (but it needs to be thawed before turning). All this is to say, the sooner you can turn your blank the better.

size chunks with pioneering tools. It is important to understand that the wood for a bowl must be green, and the greener the better. The trick is to turn the bowl from a piece of green wood and to do the drying after the turning process. As woodworkers, we all understand the importance of properly dried wood and that wood shrinks as it dries. But let's be a bit more specific.

As shown in the drawing on p. 50, wood does not shrink significantly along the grain. In the case of bowls, we can consider the shrinkage to be

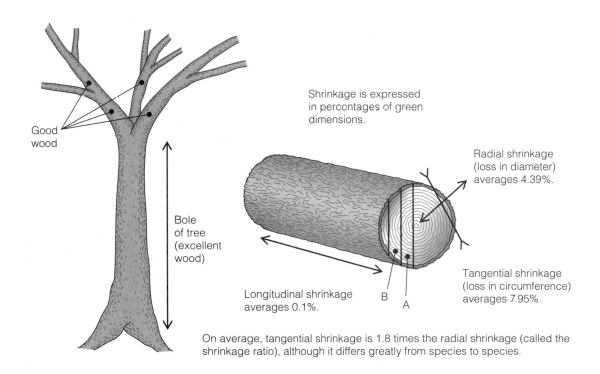

Good
wood

Bole
of tree
(excellent
wood)

Shrinkage is expressed
in percentages of green
dimensions.

Radial shrinkage
(loss in diameter)
averages 4.39%.

Longitudinal shrinkage
averages 0.1%.

B   A

Tangential shrinkage
(loss in circumference)
averages 7.95%.

On average, tangential shrinkage is 1.8 times the radial shrinkage (called the
shrinkage ratio), although it differs greatly from species to species.

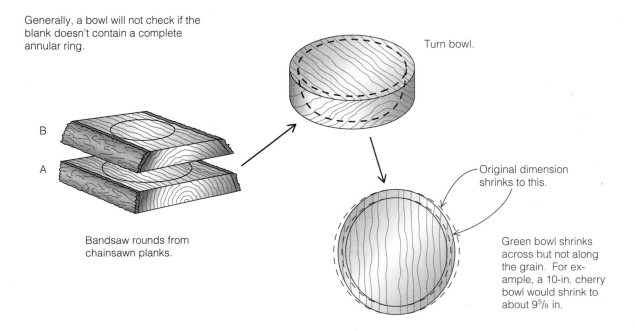

Generally, a bowl will not check if the
blank doesn't contain a complete
annular ring.

B

A

Turn bowl.

Original dimension
shrinks to this.

Bandsaw rounds from
chainsawn planks.

Green bowl shrinks
across but not along
the grain. For ex-
ample, a 10-in. cherry
bowl would shrink to
about $9\frac{5}{8}$ in.

*A bowl that's turned from green
wood will dry oval rather than
round.*

zero. Across the grain, there is significant shrinkage, ranging from an average of 4.39% in the radial plane to 7.95% in the tangential plane. These are average figures, however; and American beech is going to shrink a lot more than black walnut will. This means that a freshly turned green-wood bowl ends up oval. How oval depends on the species of wood and the orientation of the tangential and radial planes in relation to the turning blank. The best orientation of the grain for the strength and longevity of your bowl is with the base toward the outside of the tree, but there are no hard-and-fast rules. Other orientations often give more interesting grain, so don't be afraid to experiment.

As an example, a 10-in.-diameter cherry bowl would end up measuring about 9⅝ in. across the grain but would remain 10 in. along the grain. As long as there is not a complete annular ring in the turning blank, there is little likelihood of the wood cracking as a result of stress, which is called checking. If you don't object to an oval bowl, you can simply turn a bowl from green wood and let it dry to oval. Any type of oil finish will seal the end grain sufficiently to result in equal water losses from all surfaces of the bowl, preventing checking. It takes three to six weeks for the average green-turned bowl to come to its final shape.

If you don't want to end up with an oval bowl, there is another option: Rough-turn your bowl green, but leave the wall a bit heavy to facilitate future turning once drying and warping has taken place. You want to turn to a nice constant wall thickness; a good rule of thumb is to leave the wall about one-tenth the diameter. This means that our 10-in.-diameter bowl would be rough-turned to a 1-in.-thick wall. The rough turning is then allowed to air dry—generally, for about three months (the amount of time varies greatly, depending on the species, your climate, the time of the year, and the size of the bowl). Obviously, a large bowl with thick walls is going to take longer to dry than will a small bowl with lighter walls. Cherry takes

The author keeps a supply of rough-turned bowls on hand. Once the bowls are dry, they can be turned to their final shape.

less time than American beech, and so on. Once the bowl is dry, you can chuck it in the lathe again and turn it to the final shape. (For more on re-turning an air-dried, rough-turned bowl, see chapter 4.)

Although some turners get quite scientific about all this, employing weighing rituals and moisture meters, I like to keep things simple. I always keep a good supply of roughed-out bowls on hand, and if I see the supply getting low, I simply turn more. Whenever I complete a bowl from my rough-turned stock, I rough out one or more to replace it. I date my rough turnings so my inventory can be used sensibly.

As the rough-turned bowl dries, the greatest loss of water occurs in the first two to three weeks. Because wood loses water much faster from the exposed end-grain areas than from the face-grain areas, anything that can be done to retard evaporation from the end grain a bit is helpful. Each turner tends to have his or her own "secret" method, but all the techniques accomplish the same thing: slowing down the initial rapid water loss from the end grain.

One method is to coat the rough turning with wax; I have heard of turn-ers using everything from floor wax and paste wax to one of the commer-cial lumber water-soluble waxes such as Sealtite or Anchorseal. I don't like this option because it is time-consuming and messy (although I do use it for difficult-to-dry woods like American beech). A second method is to put the blank in a plastic bag and not seal the bag well. Some people even punch holes in the bag and reverse it daily until there is no condensation on the inside. I find this almost as time-consuming as the wax routine. A

third option is to bury the blank in a pile of the wet chips left from the rough turning. This works well and is simple, but I don't like the mess or the fire hazard of a pile of chips in my shop.

The simplest method I've come across is simply to wrap the freshly roughed bowl in several sheets of newspaper—much as you would wrap a gift. Newspaper breathes enough for the bowl to dry but keeps enough of a vapor barrier around the bowl to maintain an equilibrium between the end- and face-grain areas. I date the rough-turned bowl (using a ballpoint pen) on both the inside and the outside and again on the paper wrapping. After three weeks, the paper can be removed and discarded.

Tiling

The third way to obtain bowl blanks is to glue them up out of small blocks of wood—a process referred to as tiling or segmented turning. Tiling has several advantages. The grain of each tile can be oriented to an advantageous direction for turning, making the finished bowl easier to sand and finish. Usually this entails cutting the segment so that face grain is oriented to the outside of the bowl. Because end grain is not encountered anywhere in the bowl, there is little fear of tearout. This orientation of the wood also tends to show the grain pattern more equally on all surfaces of the bowl. When tiled from contrasting woods, interesting patterns can be

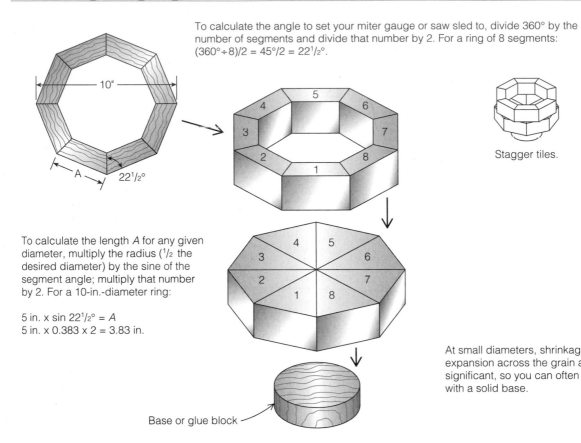

To calculate the angle to set your miter gauge or saw sled to, divide 360° by the number of segments and divide that number by 2. For a ring of 8 segments: $(360° \div 8)/2 = 45°/2 = 22\frac{1}{2}°$.

Stagger tiles.

To calculate the length *A* for any given diameter, multiply the radius ($\frac{1}{2}$ the desired diameter) by the sine of the segment angle; multiply that number by 2. For a 10-in.-diameter ring:

5 in. $\times \sin 22\frac{1}{2}° = A$
5 in. $\times 0.383 \times 2 = 3.83$ in.

At small diameters, shrinkage and expansion across the grain are not significant, so you can often get away with a solid base.

Base or glue block

Tiling with contrasting woods creates a finished bowl with an interesting pattern.

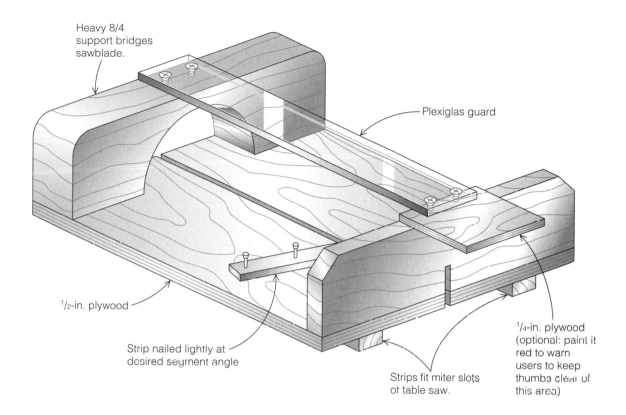

Heavy 8/4 support bridges sawblade.

Plexiglas guard

1/2-in. plywood

Strip nailed lightly at desired segment angle

Strips fit miter slots ot table saw.

1/4-in. plywood (optional: paint it red to warn users to keep thumbs clear of this area)

formed in the bowl. The turning community often refers to this effect, rather grandly, as polychromatic turning.

The downside of tiling is that it is time-consuming and requires exacting work. If done well, tiling results in bowls of exquisite beauty. But if the glue joints are not joinery-level fits, the result is not only ugly but also dangerous because the blank can come apart in the lathe. Even with the best of joinery and glue, speeds should always be kept moderate for segmented work.

As in green-bowl work, a knowledge of wood technology is important. One of the most important things to remember is that you cannot glue end grain and expect it to have much holding power. By staggering the joints in successive layers of tiles, much in the same way building bricks are laid, sufficient strength for turning can be attained. The blank is actually held together by the horizontal face-grain-to-face-grain glue joints between the layers of tiles. Glue between the vertical end-grain tiles is more of a filler than a structural element.

The most accurate way to cut the tiles is to use a shop-built sled on a table saw equipped with a high-quality carbide blade. The drawing on the facing page shows how to calculate the correct cutting angles for the tiles (if you don't want to do the math, refer to Appendix 1 on p. 148). A simple

2. *Dry-fit the blocks for each layer of tiles. If you have a really bad fit, you'll have to correct the angle on your cutting sled. If there is only a tiny bit of error, however, there is an easy solution: Simply disk-sand the last block for a perfect fit. No one but you will ever know.*

1. *After figuring out the cutting angles and length for each tile, nail two strips on the saw sled at the correct angle and cut the tiles. Use a push stick to hold the tile in place. (Note that the Plexiglas shield was removed from the sled for these photos.)*

3. *Lay out the tiles for each layer on a strip of duct tape, and apply glue to the mating surfaces.*

sled for your table saw is shown in the drawing on p. 55. I use an accurate dividing head, which came with my combination square, to lay out the correct angle on my cutting sled; then I lightly nail a strip of wood at this angle to use as a fence. The system can be changed to any angle quickly and is quite accurate. For small pieces, I use a push stick to hold the work so my fingers are kept at a safe distance from the blade.

It's important to choose the right glue for gluing up tiled bowls. For absolutely waterproof joints, epoxy glue is best; it also has the best gap-filling characteristics. It is, however, very messy. Be sure to use a 60-minute or longer epoxy to ensure sufficient open time to get everything placed

4. *Wrap up the tiles into a ring and secure with the ends of the duct tape.*

6. *Secure each ring with an automotive hose clamp and then clamp the tile assembly in a simple jig. Use waxed paper between the jig and the work to prevent sticking.*

5. *Stagger the joints in the layers of tiles and use plenty of glue between layers.*

correctly. I wear disposable rubber gloves, because epoxy is tough to get off your hands. I have also had very good success with Titebond Type II, which is weatherproof but not waterproof. This means it will stand everything but prolonged soaking in water. With a coat of finish on the completed bowl, there is ample protection from water and I have had no problems.

Another trick worth mentioning is to put strips of veneer of contrasting color between the joints—vertical, horizontal, or both. No calculations have to be made for the veneer, because it increases the size of the bowl only slightly. It is simple to do, and the effect can be very pleasing. For directions on turning a tiled bowl, see pp. 104–105.

4

Basic Turning Techniques

Now that you know all about lathes, turning tools, and preparing and holding the wood, it's time to turn a bowl. As you'll see from the photo essays in this chapter, there are many ways to go about the task. We'll start with the simplest method and work to the most complicated. You'll notice I didn't say the "hardest" or "most difficult" method. The later techniques are no more difficult than the first; in fact, they offer some advantages, because they make it easier for the novice to turn a pleasing shape. These methods are just a bit more complicated. Before we begin, let's first take a look at how to use a bowl gouge, the most basic of bowl-turning tools.

■ How to Use a Bowl Gouge

The bowl gouge may at first seem like a tricky tool to master, but it's not that difficult once you get the hang of it. The secret lies in riding the bevel.

The bowl gouge cuts parallel to the axes of rotation (see the drawing on p. 27). The tool is placed level to very slightly uphill on the rest; and the rest should be slightly below center so that the tip of the nose bevel touches the center of the work when the gouge is level on the rest. Approximately 90% of the control of the bowl gouge is done by the right hand. The left hand mostly acts as a sandbag to hold the tool down on the rest and keep it from bouncing. Twisting the tool with the right hand controls the quality of the cut; swinging the tool to the left or right controls the direction of cut. Pushing forward on the handle along its axis controls the speed of the cut (actually, the heaviness of the chip removed).

Starting the bowl gouge can be tricky; you must aim the nose bevel in the direction you want to cut. Depending on the angle of the nose bevel

1. *Start the bowl gouge by aiming the bevel in the direction you want to cut.*

2. *Twist the gouge a little to the left or right until you find the "sweet spot"; you'll know you're there when the gouge cuts a perfect shaving.*

3. *Direct the gouge by swinging the handle to the left or right.*

(which depends on the grind), the handle will at first be at what seems an odd angle. Hold the tool down firmly on the tool rest with your left hand and lightly touch the work with the bottom half of the tool. Once the gouge starts to cut, it's time to look for the "sweet spot."

The sweet spot is the position in which the tool cuts the best. It can be found by twisting the tool ever so slightly to the left or right. What you are looking for is the point at which the bottom bevel rides on the ledge that has been created ahead of the cut. This leaves the nose bevel riding on the area just behind the cut, which serves to guide the tool. With a little practice finding the sweet spot becomes a natural, almost involuntary action.

The bowl gouge is directed by swinging the handle to the left or right. Again, the nose bevel rides on the area just behind the ledge created by the cut, whereas the bottom half of the bevel is cutting away on the face of this ledge. The point at which the nose bevel makes contact acts as a fulcrum when you swing the handle left or right, making for a smooth transition in direction. Keep the entire tool fairly level on the rest during the whole operation. Do not use your left hand to pull or push the tool; as stated previously, that hand is there just to steady the tool. To make the tool go forward, push forward with your right hand along the axis of the tool. Once the tool is started, if everything is cutting correctly, you should be able to do the entire operation with just your right hand.

One-time chucking is the simplest way to turn a bowl, but the bowl's depth is dictated by the screws that hold the blank to the faceplate.

The Simplest Way to Turn a Bowl: One-Time Chucking

In the photo essay on pp. 62–67, I show you how to turn a finished bowl from freshly cut green wood. The one-time chucking method has been used by turners for centuries, and it produces a usable bowl with little or no fanfare. Furthermore, it is often the only method you can employ for re-turning an air-dried bowl (p. 83). The bowl blank is secured to a faceplate with #10 (or larger) × 1-in.-long hex-head sheet-metal screws and then mounted on the headstock spindle.

Although this method is the quickest way to turn a bowl and offers the most secure chucking, it does have a couple of disadvantages. First, the depth of the finished bowl is limited by the length of the screws used to attach the bowl blank to the faceplate. Second, it's difficult to use a bowl gouge in the area around the base of the bowl: The nose bevel of the gouge cannot be kept rubbing in the transition area between the base of the bowl and the bottom because the headstock is in the way, as shown in the drawing below. You must either drag the bowl gouge in this area or resort to a large round-nose scraper. If you happen to own a gap bed lathe (which has a notch in the bed just under the spindle to accommodate larger-diameter facework), you may not be able to get the tool rest positioned to turn the base of your bowl. You will have to use one of the methods discussed later in this chapter.

One-Time Chucking Problem

It is difficult to use a bowl gouge in the area around the base of the bowl because the headstock is in the way.

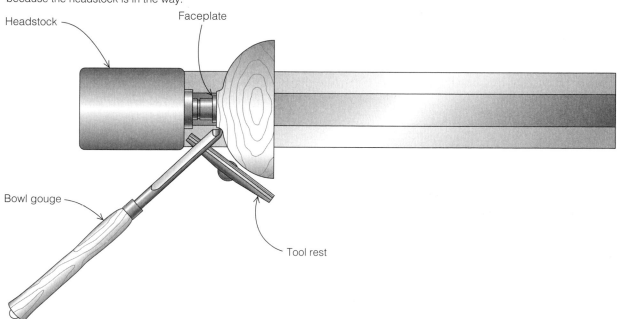

Headstock

Faceplate

Bowl gouge

Tool rest

One-Time Chucking

1. *Mount the bowl blank on a faceplate in the headstock spindle, and snug the tailstock with a live center up against the center of the blank. Set the lathe to a low speed (600 rpm or less); and using light cuts with a ¹/₂-in. bowl gouge, true up the blank and start to shape the outside of the bowl.*

2. *Work from the base of the bowl out toward the top.*

3. *Wood must be removed to a point above the screws that hold the work on the faceplate. This makes for an extra-long foot that will be shortened when the bowl is cut off.*

4. *It's impossible to stay on the nose bevel in the area adjacent to the foot, so you'll either have to drag the gouge in this area or resort to a big round-nose scraper (as shown).*

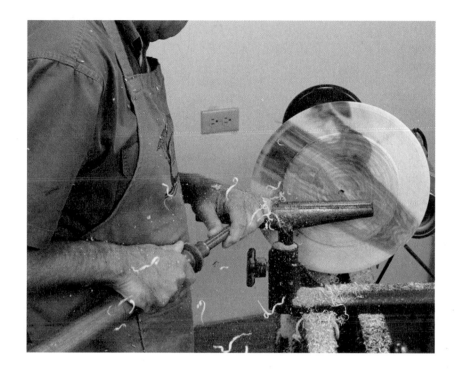

5. *Once the outside of the bowl is turned, withdraw the tailstock, remove the live center, and face the bowl level.*

6. *Work from the perimeter of the bowl toward the center.*

7. *Once the face is completely level, it's time to turn your attention to the inside of the bowl. Starting in the center, make a miniature version of your bowl that mimics the shape of the outside.*

8. *Remove wood in a series of overlapping cuts. The trick is to make passes with the bowl gouge, starting at the rim and working to the bottom center, that parallel the shape of the outside of the bowl.*

9, 10. *Keep hollowing out the interior of the bowl, making it incrementally wider and working from the rim down to the bottom until the wall is the desired thickness.*

11. *Whether you are working green wood or seasoned wood, it is important to work the inside wall to its final thickness progressively during the final passes. The wall should be of constant thickness after each pass.*

12. *Work in ½-in. steps and get everything perfect before moving down to the next step.*

Thinning the Wall of a Bowl

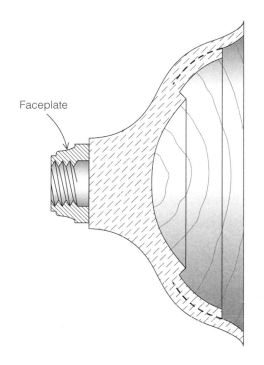

Faceplate

Thin by increments to keep strength in the wall.

13. *Once the bowl is turned, it's time to sand and finish the inside and outside. For sanding and finishing instructions, see chapter 6.*

14. *To prepare for the cutoff, check the depth of the bowl by touching a pencil to the bottom center and sighting across the rim. The trick is to cut the bowl off above the faceplate screws but below the bottom.*

15. *Hold the pencil on the outside of the bowl to judge where the bottom is.*

16. *Position the tool rest as close to the bowl as possible, and start in with the parting tool.*

17. *Once the parting tool starts cutting, place your left elbow on the headstock and wrap your fingers around the rim of the spinning bowl without actually touching it. (It's advisable to slow the lathe down.)*

■ A Better Way to Turn a Bowl: Work-and-Turn Chucking

The "work-and-turn" chucking method of turning a bowl is a bit more complicated from a chucking standpoint, but it gives you much more freedom to achieve a pleasing shape. It is my preferred method of turning a bowl, and the one I use most often.

As the name implies, work-and-turn chucking is a two-step operation. The first step is to mount a faceplate or screw chuck on the part of the blank that will be the mouth of the bowl (the exact opposite of the way we mounted the blank in one-time chucking) and then turn the outside of the bowl. Because there is no headstock in the way, it is easy to get a fluid, smooth cut from the base of the bowl to the rim using a bowl gouge. The second step is to flip the bowl around, attach it to a chuck, and turn the inside.

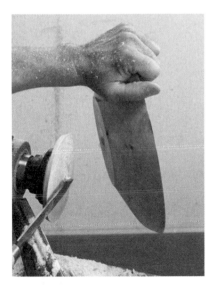

18. *As the bowl drops away, catch it! Trust me, it's easy; it only looks scary. (But if you prefer, don't cut the bowl all the way off. Leave a bit at the center, stop the lathe, and cut the final portion with a backsaw. Japanese saws work great for this.)*

19. *The almost completed bowl. All that is left to do is to turn away the chucking marks, leaving a decorative foot. For directions on "reverse chucking," see pp. 78–82.*

Two branches of work-and-turn chucking are shown on the following pages. The photo essay on pp. 69–75 demonstrates how to use a homemade glue-block chuck, and the photos on pp. 76–77 illustrate the use of a four-jaw commercial chuck. Most people who turn bowls eventually invest in a commercial chuck, but there's no need to rush out and buy one. Learn to use homemade chucks first. Although it seems as though it would be quicker to use a metal chuck, they are actually not that much faster. Also, you are limited to a foot that is slightly larger than the size of your chuck's jaws, which results in an oversize base on a small bowl. A glue-block chuck accommodates any size foot, so design is never compromised.

Using a metal chuck is much the same process as using a glue-block chuck, except for shaping the mortise in the base of the bowl. Instead of a straight-walled mortise, you need to scrape a wall that has a reverse taper, forming a dovetail-shaped mortise in the base of the bowl, as shown in the bottom drawing on p. 68. The dovetail mortise also needs to be a bit deeper (by ¹⁄₁₆ in. to ³⁄₁₆ in.) than the straight-walled mortise used with a glue block. For optimum holding power, the mortise must be the same diameter as that of the chuck's jaws when they form a perfect circle.

Glue-Block Chuck

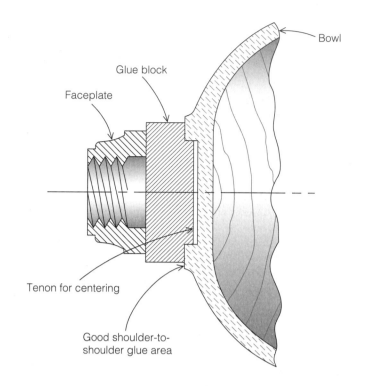

Faceplate

Glue block

Bowl

Tenon for centering

Good shoulder-to-shoulder glue area

Mounting a Bowl on a Four-Jaw Metal Chuck

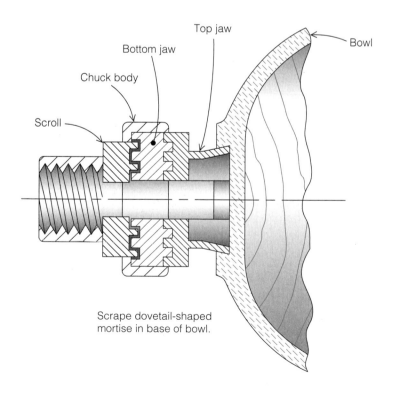

Top jaw

Bottom jaw

Bowl

Chuck body

Scroll

Scrape dovetail-shaped mortise in base of bowl.

Work-and-Turn Chucking: Using a Glue-Block Chuck

1. *Mount the blank on a faceplate, thread onto the headstock spindle, and then bring up the tailstock to support the blank for the initial shaping.*

2, 3. *Taking light cuts with a ½-in. bowl gouge, shape the outside of the bowl.*

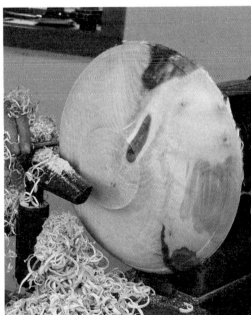

4. *Once the bowl has been rough turned, you can back off the tailstock and finish shaping the outside of the bowl and turn the foot.*

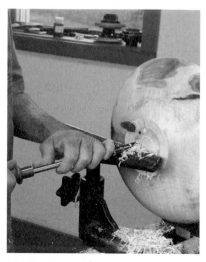

6. *Cut a mortise into the foot of the bowl to receive the glue block. Use a bowl gouge to remove the bulk of the wood.*

5. *Sand and finish the outside of the bowl (see chapter 6). Sanding the outside at this point pays some dividends. First, there's nothing in the way of the sander; and second, if you're turning to a thin wall, it's possible to sand through the wood if you leave the sanding of the inside and outside to the last.*

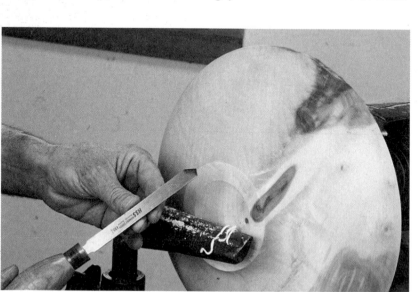

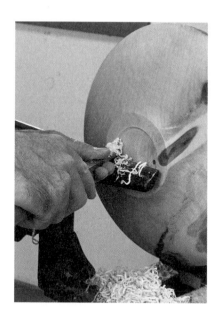

8. *Line up the left edge of the scraper with the axis of the lathe (which will put the leading edge parallel to the base of the bowl) and plunge straight forward with a light touch.*

7. *Switch to a small square-end scraper to finish off the mortise. The mortise doesn't have to be very deep—no deeper than ⅛ in. The important thing is to make sure that the mortise has perfectly straight walls and the shoulder around it is flat (parallel to the chuck).*

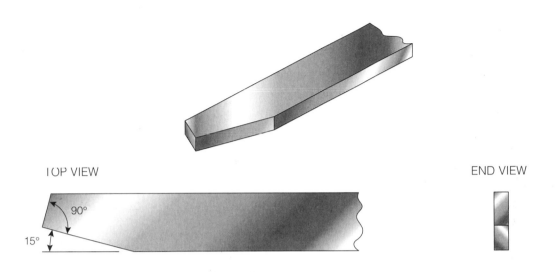

TOP VIEW

90°

15°

END VIEW

9. *Remove the bowl from the lathe and mount a fairly thick glue block on a faceplate (I like to start with 5/4 material), and face it flat with a round-nose scraper.*

10. *Set a pair of dividers to the diameter of the mortise in the base of the bowl.*

11. *Use the dividers to transfer the diameter of the mortise to the glue block. The trick is to center the dividers as best you can by eye then touch only the left leg lightly to the spinning work and see if the right leg lines up with the other side of the scribed circle. Adjust for any inaccuracies and then press the left leg a bit harder.*

12. *Use the square-end scraper to cut a short tenon almost to the scribed circle. Then chamfer the end of the tenon.*

13. *Test-fit the mortise in the bowl to the tenon on the glue block. If the mortise fits over the chamfer, you know you are close. If it doesn't, you can cut the tenon down to the chamfer and re-chamfer for another test-fit. Once the bowl drops over the tenon, shorten or lengthen the tenon so that it is just a bit shorter than the depth of the mortise. The idea is for the tenon not to bottom out.*

14. *Apply medium-viscosity cyanoacrylate glue to the shoulder around the tenon.*

15. *Spray the catalyst for the glue into the mortise.*

16. *Mate the bowl and the glue chuck, and position the tailstock so that it provides pressure to hold the two parts together. Wait about 10 minutes, and then test by grabbing and pulling. Now you're ready to turn the inside of the bowl.*

17. *Using a ½-in. bowl gouge, turn the inside of the bowl.*

18, 19. *As with one-time chucking, turn incrementally wider bowl shapes, working from the center of the bowl out toward the rim.*

20. Switch to a ¼-in. bowl gouge to do the final shaping of the interior.

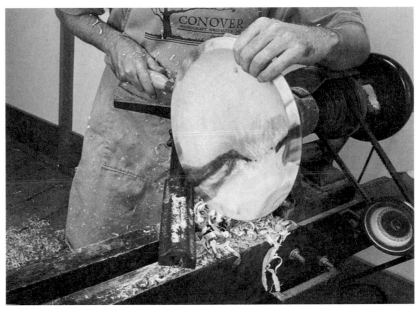

21. Sand the inside, and apply finish inside and outside the bowl (see chapter 6). Then cut off the bowl on the glue-block side of the glue line. The idea is for the right-hand edge of the parting tool to go through the glue line.

22. The completed bowl. All that remains is to turn and finish the base (see pp. 78–82).

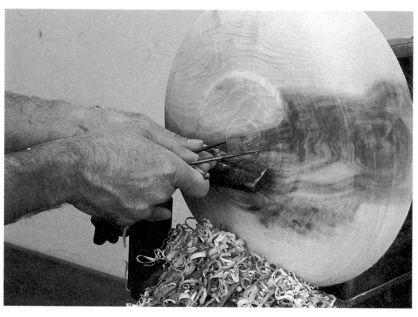

1. *Set a pair of dividers to the diameter of the jaws of the chuck.*

2. *Use the dividers to transfer the diameter to the base of the bowl.*

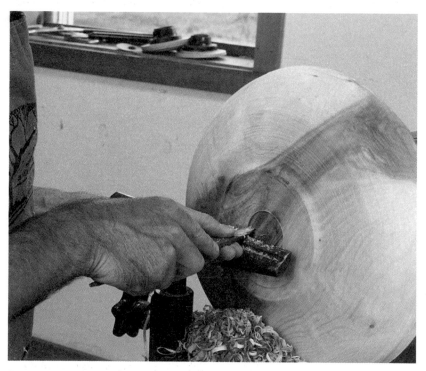

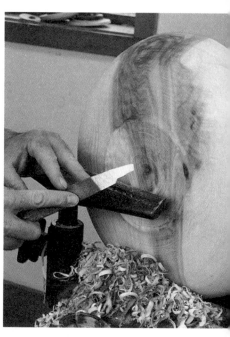

3. *Use a bowl gouge to remove most of the waste in the recess and then switch to a scraper to cut the taper.*

4. *This scraper (made from an old file) has a 75° to 80° tip that provides the necessary taper on the walls of the mortise.*

5. *Press the chuck into the dovetail-shaped mortise and expand the jaws.*

6. *Check the trueness of the chuck before removing the bowl from the faceplate or screw chuck. This can be done by extending a pencil from the tool rest and using it as a reference point to judge if the chuck runs true. Often loosening the chuck and turning it slightly, as well as pressing it firmly to the bottom of the dovetail-shaped recess, help bring things true.*

7. *Take the bowl off the lathe and mount the metal chuck on the headstock spindle. (You can see where the bowl was attached to the screw chuck.) Turn the inside of the bowl.*

Reverse Chucking

One of the hallmarks of a well-turned bowl is that there's no sign of any chucking. No plugged screw holes covered with felt, no dovetail recess, only a nicely undercut foot so that the bowl sits level on almost any surface. The signs of chucking are there in the first place simply because you can't get in to turn the base of the bowl when it's mounted to the chuck. To achieve the desired level of quality, you must take the bowl off the lathe and turn it around (hence "reverse chucking") to turn and sand the base. Fear not, it's a lot easier than it sounds.

For bowls that have a consistent rim (that is, the rim's the same height all round), jam chucking is a great way to reverse turn the base. It's called jam chucking, because you jam the bowl into the chuck to hold it. I save old squares of ¾-in. plywood and cutoff board ends that are 10 in. wide or wider to make my chucks from. The diameter of the chuck needs to be at least 1 in. bigger than your bowl's diameter, to leave a ½-in. wall all the way round. Don't be afraid to make the chuck much bigger than the bowl—it will always come in handy to chuck other bowls. Once you've bandsawn a round of suitable size, the chuck can be mounted on a faceplate or a screw chuck. I prefer to use a screw chuck, because the round can be mounted and dismounted quickly and repeatedly without tying up faceplates.

If the bowl you're turning has a rim diameter smaller than its interior diameter, the jam chuck just described won't work for reverse chucking. Instead of scraping a tapered recess in the chuck, you need to turn a raised cone (see the photos below). Slip the bowl over the cone and, if necessary, hold it in place with the tailstock.

Similarly, a jam chuck will not work for a bowl that has an uneven rim—what's known as a rough-top bowl. The method shown in the photos on p. 82 (which I call "nubbin chucking") will work fine, however.

To reverse turn a bowl that has a rim smaller than its interior, mount the bowl on a tapered cone.

Reverse Chucking a Bowl

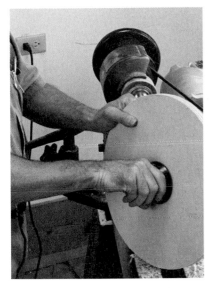

1. *Mount the plywood round on a screw chuck (or faceplate).*

2. *Mount the plywood round on the lathe and scrape a series of concentric circles on the face of the chuck.*

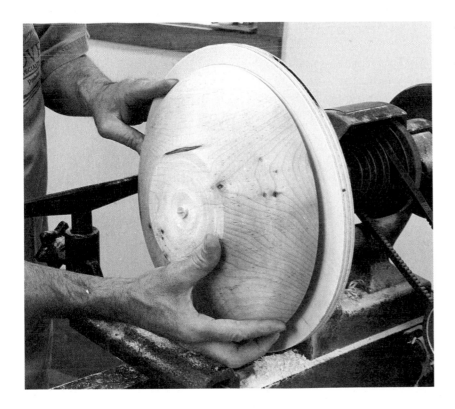

3. *Find the circle that most closely matches the rim diameter of your bowl.*

Reverse Chucking a Bowl *(continued)*

4. *Scrape a tapered recess in the chuck for the rim of your bowl. The idea is to cut a recess that has an outside diameter exactly the same as the outside diameter of the rim of your bowl. The wall of the recess, however, needs to have a 1° to 2° taper (it must taper in).*

5. *Tap the bowl into the recess with the heel of your hand. If you do not have enough taper, the bowl won't stay in the chuck (if you have too much taper, you won't get the bowl to go into the chuck in the first place). Turn the work manually in the lathe and inspect for trueness.*

6. *If you have trouble with the bowl staying in the chuck, apply some blackboard chalk to the tapered wall of the recess. It's like chalking a pool cue—the bowl won't slip. You can also put a few strips of masking tape or duct tape over the rim to hold the bowl in place.*

7. *Turn the base to its final shape, taking light cuts with a ¼-in. bowl gouge. You can also use a small round-nose scraper for this final shaping.*

8. *Check that the base is concave by holding the bowl gouge across the base.*

9. *Sand and finish the bottom part of the bowl, and then give it a gentle tap to remove it from the chuck.*

Reverse Chucking a Rough-Top Bowl

1. *Mount a scrap block of wood (it can be green) on a screw chuck or faceplate, and turn it to a rough approximation of the inside shape of the bowl.*

2. *Slip the bowl over the chuck. (Putting a piece of thin foam rubber between the chuck and the bowl will help prevent slippage of the chuck.)*

3. *Secure the bowl with a live center in the tailstock, and turn the base of the bowl to the desired shape.*

4. *Back off the tailstock, and remove the bowl from the lathe. Pare off the nubbin left under the live center with a fishtail carving gouge.*

Re-Turning a Bowl

If you like to turn green wood (as I do), you have to accept that your bowl is going to warp as it dries. For this reason, I rough turn the bowl, leaving the wall a little bit thicker than the final thickness, and then allow the bowl to air dry for about three months (see chapter 3). When I re-turn the bowl, I know that it will now maintain its shape.

So far, so good. But how are you going to chuck the air-dried bowl in the lathe for final turning? If you used a glue-block chuck (work-and-turn chucking) to rough turn the blank, it may or may not have separated as the blank dried and warped. A lot depends on size, because there is more wood movement in a larger bowl, so it is less likely that the glue block will hold.

If the glue block did hold, you only need to reattach the faceplate to the glue block. I usually reposition the faceplate slightly from the original alignment so as not to use the original holes, which no longer form a perfect circle. It's also a good idea to drill some shallow pilot holes into the glue block at the new location to prevent splitting. In the event that the glue block does not hold, you must attach a new one; for this you will have to scrape a new recess on the foot, as shown in the photo essay on pp. 84–85.

If you used a four-jaw commercial chuck to hold the work, the problems are about the same as with the glue block. The dovetail recess is probably oval as a result of warping and will need to be rescraped.

Scrapers for Re-Truing the Recess in an Air-Dried Bowl Blank

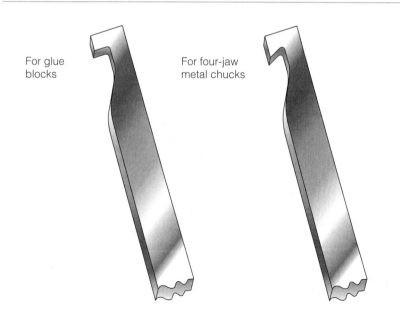

For glue blocks

For four-jaw metal chucks

Re-Turning a Rough-Turned, Air-Dried Bowl

1. *The easiest way to catch the bowl is between centers. By looking at the tool marks left from the rough turning, it is easy to find the original outside and inside center points. Turn the bowl over by hand so you can sight over the rim and see how true it is. Adjust the center points to get the rim running as true as possible.*

2. *Use a homemade scraper to re-true the recess in the foot. Also scrape the bottom flat. (If you are going to use a four-jaw metal chuck, you need to use a slightly different scraper, as shown in the drawing on p. 83.)*

3. *Turn a new glue block and glue the two together (as shown on p. 73).*

4. *Turn the outside, starting as near the foot as you can get with a bowl gouge and still stay on the nose bevel and ending at the rim.*

5. *Turn the inside to match, and then sand and finish the areas that you have re-turned.*

6. *Cut off the bowl at the glue block, and reverse chuck the bowl (for more on this, see pp. 78–82). Sand and finish the base and you are done.*

Tools and techniques for final turning of air-dried blanks

I am often asked whether dry, seasoned wood turns differently from wet, green wood. The answer is yes and no. The techniques are the same in regard to riding the bevel and the basic way the tools operate. Wet wood, however, cuts much more easily than does dry wood, because it is softer and the water lubricates the cut. You can take heavier cuts and take risks with wet wood that you cannot with seasoned material. Dry wood takes more precise bevel control, sharper tools, and lighter cuts. Medium-bevel angles tend to work better in dry wood. Cutting theory predicts this, and I find it to hold true, so I reserve my advanced-ground tools for green work.

One tool I find very handy for final passes on a dry-wood bowl is a ¼-in. bowl gouge (see the photo below). I keep it ground to a medium bevel and even hone it on a buffer for a final pass. Taking a final light (½₂ in. or less) pass with this tool will usually save lots of sanding. A ½-in. combination gouge ground to a medium bevel and buffed will do the same thing.

Finally, there are scrapers. If there were ever a 911 in turning that you could call when you were in trouble, it would be the scraper. Scrapers are ephemeral, workaday tools that can be made from any piece of steel, modified to the dictates of the job, and modified again when a new situation arises. Don't be afraid to grind a scraper to any shape that gets the job done. They are perishable tools that are meant to be used up.

Scrapers never improve a finish; but if used lightly, they will remove ridges and uneven spots (see the sidebar on p. 88). If pushed, they tear,

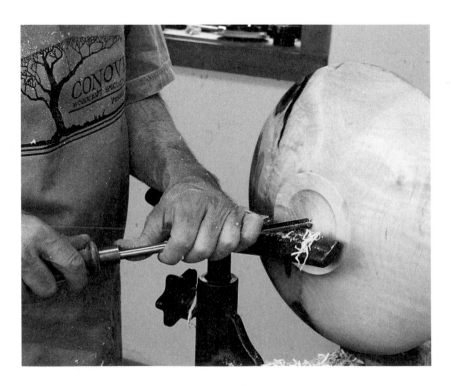

Use a ¼-in. bowl gouge for final turning of a dry, seasoned bowl.

How to Use a Combination Gouge

A combination gouge can be used for the shaping of a bowl, but its real value is in taking light final cuts, because it leaves a really smooth surface. Resist the urge to use the tool like a spindle gouge at right angles to the axis of rotation—the tool will catch. Use the combination gouge just like the bowl gouge, cutting to the left or right with the tool fairly level on the rest. (Often it is started a bit more uphill than a bowl gouge.)

Point the nose bevel in the direction you wish to cut and lightly touch the work. (The handle may seem to be at an odd angle to the work surface.) Once the gouge is cutting, twist it a little to the left or right with your right hand until you find the "sweet spot." Swing the handle to change the direction the gouge is cutting.

Use a combination gouge as you would use a bowl gouge for the final shaping of the surface.

and it is back to the gouge or a lot of sanding, depending on the situation and your enthusiasm for risk. For bowls with an interior bigger than the opening, scrapers are the only tool that can get the job done. As your gouge skill improves, your use of scrapers will decrease; but they will always be stalwart friends in the never-ending battle to achieve level surfaces and even wall thickness.

One final thought: It's all too easy to get caught up in technique and lose sight of design. An ugly bowl is ugly no matter how good the techniques used to make it. On the other hand, a beautiful form turns heads no matter how it was made. Never lose sight of form and function. If you make form number one, technique will take care of itself. Yes, you will have to sand your first bowls quite a bit; but they will be worth the effort, if they have good form. And you will be inspired to make more, allowing your technique to grow exponentially.

How to Use a Scraper

The trick to using a scraper effectively is to point it slightly downhill and touch it lightly to the work. On the inside of bowls it is necessary to raise the rest a bit for the tool to cut on center at the center. You will have to play around with how far downhill you slant your scrapers, depending on how you created the burr (see pp. 40–41). Burnished burrs need more slant than do ground burrs, and no two people burnish exactly the same way.

Simply pointing the tool slightly downhill isn't always enough, especially if you're using a dome scraper on the inside of a bowl. If you start a scraping cut at the inside center, your concentration is naturally on the tip of the tool. As you approach the side wall of the bowl, the side of the scraper starts to cut too. If you don't pay attention, you may find the side of the tool cutting uphill instead of downhill, resulting in a catch.

The trick is either to swing the handle to the right, to roll the tool on the rest, or to do both. This is why I like my big dome scraper made from a pavement-breaking

Use a scraper with a light touch to remove ridges and uneven spots; point the tool slightly downhill.

chisel (see p. 30). The round handle allows me to roll the tool easily on the rest as I approach the side wall.

The importance of using scrapers with a light touch cannot be overemphasized. Scrapers should be held loosely in the fingers and placed ever so lightly against the work. If a scraper is pushed, it goes from a positive angle cut by the burr to a negative-angle plow cut, resulting in tearout aplenty. Again, this is why I like my pavement-breaker scraper. Its sheer weight makes it easy to use with a light touch, because it doesn't jump around on the rest.

5 Advanced Turning Techniques

Turning a natural-edge bowl is one of many advanced techniques you'll be able to try your hand at once you've mastered the basics. This beautiful bowl, made from poplar by Rude Osolnik, is cockleshell thin and measures 10¼ in. in diameter by 9 in. high.

Once you've mastered the basics and can make the tools do what you want them to do (instead of what they want to do), there are a lot of interesting bowl-turning techniques that are worth exploring. Although the cone-separation technique, described first, simply allows you to get more bowls out of one piece of wood with less work, other techniques take bowl turning further toward an art form. Let's take a look at some of the interesting things that will take your bowl turning beyond the ordinary.

Cone Separations

Cone separation offers a way to turn two or more bowls from a single wood blank. In this technique, a Paul Bunyan–sized parting tool is used to remove the inside of a bowl as a cone, which can then be made into another bowl, and so on. With precious woods and burls, this can result in significant cost savings. Adding more joy to the process, cone separation is usually a bit quicker than hollowing out the bowl from scratch: Once the bowl is separated, the remaining cone is mounted on the lathe and running true; so it is a simple matter to shape it into the next bowl.

For cone separations, you need a giant parting tool to give you the leverage and control to do the job safely. A commercial cone-separation tool designed by Dennis Stewart (and also manufactured by Sorby) is available from Craft Supplies USA, Packard Woodworks, and Woodcraft (see p. 34). It is really a system of tools that centers on what Stewart calls an "Armbrace Handle." As you can see in the photo below, the handle

Sharpening a Cone-Separation Tool

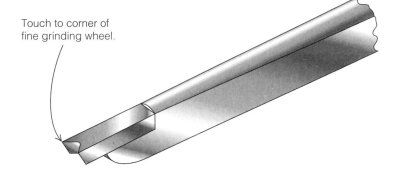

Touch to corner of fine grinding wheel.

The Armbrace Handle and slicer tool are perfect for cone separations. The other tool is an offset scraper for hollow-form work (see p. 103 for a photo of the scraper in action).

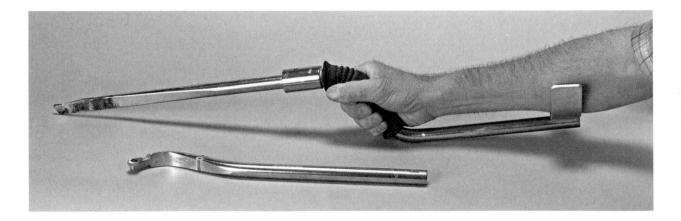

Cone Separation

This layout yields
three bowls.

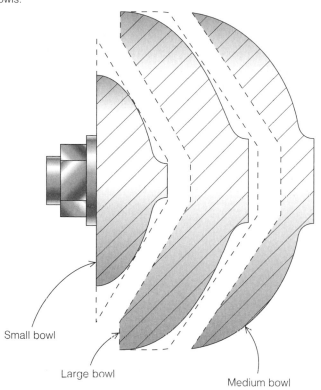

Small bowl

Large bowl

Medium bowl

becomes an extension of your forearm, affording great leverage as well as good radial control over the tool, which you affix in the handle via a setscrew.

If you have minimal metalworking skills, you can make a cone-separation tool yourself. You'll need a 3-ft. section of a ⅝-in. round structural steel bar and a ¼-in.-square M2 HSS metalworking lathe tool bit, eutectic silver braze, flux, torch, and wood billet to turn the handle from. The same solder and torch can also be used to replace the carbide bit that comes with the Armbrace tool with an HSS metalworking lathe tool bit. Replacing the bit is a good idea because you can grind the HSS bit to shape at your bench grinder in seconds (see the photo at right).

Making a cone separation is easy, but there are some safety issues to be aware of. First, the work needs to be securely mounted on a faceplate or screw chuck (one designed for bowl turning, such as the Glaser, which has a heavy threaded post). Second, speeds should be kept moderate, no more than 600 rpm or 800 rpm. Third, the lathe belt-drive system should not be too tight. You want the drive system to slip if the tool becomes stuck in the work. Cone separations should not be attempted with powerful gear-drive lathes, for which slippage is impossible.

To sharpen the slicer tool, adjust the platform rest to put a bit of relief in the ground edge, and then touch the tip of the tool to the corner of the wheel.

Making a Cone Separation

1. *After turning (and if necessary, sanding) the outside of the bowl, position the tool rest as shown. Make sure both the tool rest and the tool base are securely locked and will not move during the cone-separation process.*

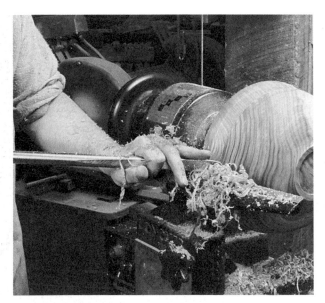

2. *With the lathe set to a low speed and the belt adjusted to slip if the tool catches, aim for the center of the bowl at a point about 1 in. above the bottom. Take overlapping cuts to give the slicer tool plenty of clearance. Because the shank of the tool is tapered, the entry point has to be made wider; the kerf will narrow to the center.*

3. *You don't need to sever the bowl from the cone. Depending on the diameter of the bowl, the species of the wood, and whether it is green or seasoned, you can leave a 1-in.- to 3-in.-diameter tenon. Hit the bowl (or pry in the kerf with a wood lever) on the face-grain side, and the bowl will break away.*

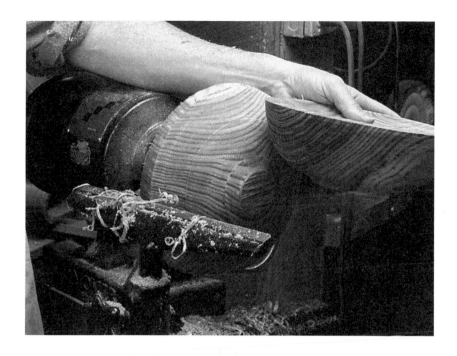

4. *The first bowl is separated. It has a recess in the base so that you can later chuck it to turn the inside.*

5. *Repeat the process to create the second and third bowls.*

■ Natural-Edge Bowls

Burl and crotch areas make interesting edges. The grain orientation of natural-edge bowls is different from that in traditional bowls, because the base is generally toward the center of the tree and the rim is at the outside edge.

As you start to hollow out the inside of a bowl, you are often presented with an original surface on the wood that would make an interesting rim—much more interesting than if you turned the rim to an even height. Every turner has been presented with this opportunity, and if you come to the conclusion that nature is a better sculptor than you are and decide to leave the rim as you found it, a natural-edge bowl is the result. Also called rough tops, natural-edge designs take turned wood bowls away from the purely utilitarian into the realm of the art gallery. Rough tops are fun to turn, and the result can be pleasing and whimsical.

The natural edge can be the chainsawn face of your blank or the original outside surface of the tree (or burl). If the tree is harvested during the winter months (when the sap is down), the edge can even include the bark; unfortunately, the bark usually falls off trees harvested at other times of the year. But even for a tree harvested in the dead of winter, it's good insurance, just before hollowing, to apply a bit of water-thin cyanoacrylate glue (Super Glue) where the bark meets the wood. Burls in particular offer a cornucopia of textured surfaces and are excellent for rough-top treatment. Root burls (such as rhododendron and manzanita) make stunning natural edges, although you may have to deal with the occasional stone trapped in the root system.

Going Natural

Starting in the 1950s, Rude Osolnik and Bob Stocksdale (working independently) found that, at craft shows, they could sell natural-edge bowls much easier than traditionally designed bowls. The public was ready for something new, and the natural edge spoke to art and nature. Rough tops could be turned directly from green wood, and the resulting warpage only added to the whimsy. In fact, the natural edge robbed most buyers of a reference to judge roundness by.

Today the market is flooded with rough tops, and I think the public may be moving back toward the traditional shapes; but don't let that deter you from giving natural edges a try. They can really be fun.

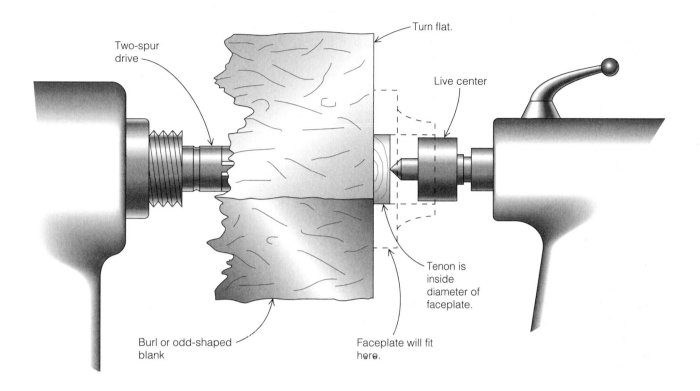

Two-spur drive

Turn flat.

Live center

Tenon is inside diameter of faceplate.

Burl or odd-shaped blank

Faceplate will fit here.

You do need to be careful when turning natural-edge bowls, especially when hollowing the inside. At speed, the uneven edge becomes a blur and woe to the careless turner who places his or her hands in the path of a protruding edge. A nasty cut can be the result. It's also best to always stop the lathe when positioning the tool rest.

I learned to turn natural-edge bowls from Rude Osolnik of Berea, Kentucky, who was one of the early developers of the art form (see "Going Natural" on the facing page). It is often easiest to start a natural edge between centers. This allows you to shape the outside and flatten a place for a chuck while giving you a chance to play around with the positioning between centers to get the most pleasing yield out of the billet. A large two-spur drive center and a 60° live center point are best for the job.

Turning a Natural-Edge Bowl

1. *Position the blank between centers, and turn the outside shape of the bowl.*

2. *Don't be afraid to play around with the center placement to achieve the most pleasing balance between the natural edge and the volume of the bowl.*

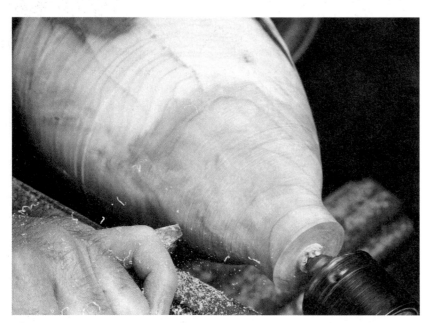

3. *Turn a base for chucking. This can be a dovetail recess (expansion hold) or a tenon (compression hold) to grab in a four-jaw commercial chuck or jam chuck. If you're using a faceplate, you simply need a flat spot with a tenon the diameter of the hole through your faceplate (see the drawing on p. 95).*

4. *Once the turned blank is chucked, position the tool rest and turn the work over by hand to ensure the work clears the rest. Now use a ½-in. bowl gouge to hollow out the inside.*

5. Once you get down to a thin wall, starting the bowl gouge is often a challenge, because of the interrupted nature of the cut. A good solution is to use a large square-corner scraper to start the cut and get beyond the natural edge.

6. The scraper leaves a ledge below the lowest point on the rim where you can place the bowl gouge and complete the cut. Get the nose of the gouge rubbing on the wall left by the scraper, and continue cutting on the face of the ledge.

7. Wrap sandpaper around the handle of the gouge to sand the interior. Reverse turn the base of the bowl as shown in "Reverse Chucking" on pp. 78–82.

8. The finished bowl.

Bird's-Mouth Bowls

Bob Stocksdale of Berkeley, California, is credited with developing the bird's-mouth bowl design. The name derives from the fact that the finished bowl looks like a baby bird in a nest waiting for food. The shape is achieved by turning the bowl directly from a small-diameter log. Bird's-mouth bowls ignore some basic principles of wood technology, but because of the small diameter involved and because a bulge or a crack only adds to the effect, the rules of physics bend nicely.

To turn a bird's-mouth bowl you need a small green log, 6 in. or smaller in diameter. If you want the bark to stay on the rim (a nice touch in a bird's mouth), the tree must be harvested in the winter months (January or February in the Northern Hemisphere). As mentioned earlier, don't be afraid to use a little water-thin cyanoacrylate glue on the bark before hollowing out the inside. Cut a section of log the same length as the diameter (i.e., a 6-in.-long section for a 6-in.-diameter log). Handplane or bandsaw a flat spot on one side of the log, and attach a glue block. Medium-viscosity cyanoacrylate glue is best for attaching the glue block to the wet wood. Attach a faceplate or screw center to the glue block, and you are in business. Or, if you have a commercial chuck, turn a tenon that can be grabbed with a compression hold.

After positioning the rest as close to the work as possible, turn the lathe over by hand to make sure everything clears. Start turning at 600 rpm to 800 rpm. Use a ½-in. bowl gouge, and reposition the tool rest as necessary to keep the distance from the rest to the work small.

This bird's-mouth bowl was turned from a small-diameter log.

Turning a Bird's-Mouth Bowl

1. *Mount the blank in the lathe, and turn the outside of the bowl using a ½-in. bowl gouge.*

2. *Turning the bark-covered blank is a highly interrupted cut. Hold the gouge down firmly on the rest with your left hand, and aim the nose of the tool in the direction you wish to cut. Twist the tool with your right hand to stay on the "sweet spot."*

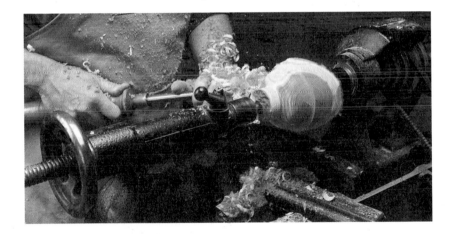

3. *Turn a base for chucking (here, a tenon to grab in a four-jaw commercial chuck).*

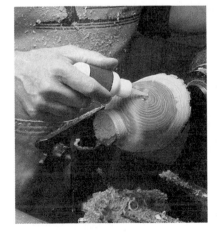

4. *Withdraw the tailstock, and apply cyanoacrylate glue (Super Glue) to the small check that's invariably present at the center of the log. Also apply glue to the bark if you can see it separating from the wood.*

5. *Remove the work from the lathe, flip it around, and chuck the base of the bowl. Begin turning the inside with the bowl gouge (or you might want to use a scraper to start the cut, as shown on p. 97).*

6, 7. *Continue turning the inside, flaring the lip out to match the outside shape.*

8. *Sand and finish the bowl while it's still in the lathe, and then part off. Reverse turn the base of the bowl as explained on pp. 78–82.*

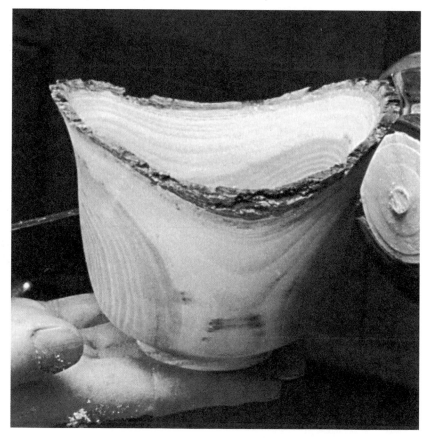

9. *The finished bowl.*

Hollow Forms

Hollow forms—bowls whose interior diameter is greater than the rim diameter—present a particularly pleasing art form. Unfortunately, a lot of novice turners start with such designs and achieve less-than-splendid results. Hollow forms should be attempted only after open forms have been mastered. The secret of hollow forms is to use scrapers. They are essential to the process, because bowl gouges will not get around a corner. As always, when gouges fail, scrapers carry the day.

Although many hollow forms can be achieved by using a good-sized dome scraper, bent tools are necessary for really big hollow forms. Dennis Stewart's Armbrace System offers a bent-tool designed especially for hollow forms (see the photo on p. 90). There are also other bent tools on the market. It is easy, however, to fabricate your own bent scrapers. Good sources of material are old car springs, jack-hammer chisels (new or old), and large screwdrivers—in short, any piece of spring steel. Use a forge or torch to bend the steel to the desired angle.

Because a scraper removes material at a much slower rate than does a gouge, turning a hollow form of any appreciable volume can take a while. You need to take care to ensure that the scraper is always pointed downhill (rolling it to the left—"canting"—in the area near the rim). Chips do not naturally fall out of a hollow form but are trapped within it, so you need to stop the lathe frequently to clear chips. An air hose with a blowgun is very useful for chip removal and saves considerable time. A blast of air clears the chips quickly, but you need to be careful to protect your eyes. Safety glasses alone are not enough. Wear a face shield over your glasses or turn your head.

The presence of chips within the bowl can also make it difficult to judge the wall thickness. Always stop the lathe and remove the chips before gauging the wall thickness. When turning extremely thin walls, a bright light played on the outside (opposite where you are cutting) gives a telltale translucence. For bowls that have bark inclusions and other defects that you do not want to fly away during hollowing, duct tape is a staunch ally. It holds things in place during turning but can be removed later. If the finished form is sufficiently fragile that removing the tape is a problem, soak it with xylol. This petroleum solvent is available at any hardware store and takes all sticky labels and tape off effortlessly.

For large-volume hollow forms with very small openings you can expect to spend more time clearing out chips (an air hose is essential) than scraping. With hollow forms, careful work and patience carry the day.

A hollow-form "ginger jar" by Rude Osolnik.

Turning a Hollow-Form Bowl

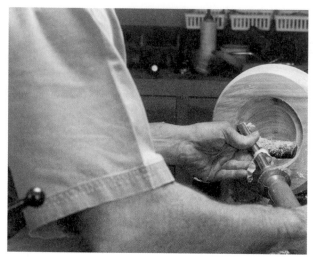

1. *After turning the outside of the bowl, turn the inside to match. Use a bowl gouge to remove the bulk of the interior.*

2. *The last cut possible with the bowl gouge. The bowl is turned to nearly the correct depth (it is best to leave a bit of room to play with) and to the opening of the mouth.*

3. *Because the interior is bigger than the opening, you'll have to use a scraper (here, a large round-nose scraper) to get around the corner.*

4. *The scraper is decidedly canted (rolled to the left) on the rest. The author's thumb is on the flat that would be the top of the tool. Starting at the rim, slide the tool along the wall, working the most at the mid-point to achieve the hollow form.*

5, 6. *Using the Stewart Armbrace tool, increase the hollow of the wall. The bent handle affords good leverage over the scraper hanging downward off the rest so that the burr on the edge drags.*

◼ Tiled Bowls

In chapter 3, I showed you how to piece together a bowl blank from small blocks of wood (see pp. 53–57). But how do you go about turning this odd-shaped blank? It is easy to be daunted by the prospect of turning a

Turning a Tiled Bowl

1. *Mount the tiled bowl blank in the lathe. The blank has been glued to a glue block, which is in turn mounted on a Glaser screw chuck. The gouge indicates the base of the bowl.*

2. *Turn the outside of the bowl. The first cut will be highly interrupted, but because you are always turning face grain it proceeds smoothly.*

3. *Continue cutting with the bowl gouge to create a pleasing exterior shape.*

4. *Once the desired shape has been achieved, you're ready to turn the inside of the bowl.*

tiled bowl when it is first mounted in the lathe. All those corners and gaps look quite intimidating. Actually, turning a tiled bowl is quite easy, because you are never turning against the grain but rather always turning face grain. Control of the bowl gouge is fairly effortless; and once the corners are turned flush, scraping yields excellent results.

5. *Position the tool rest inside the bowl and turn the work over once by hand to ensure that the rest clears at all points.*

6. *Use the bowl gouge to turn the inside of the bowl smooth. Once the worst of the corners are cut smooth, don't be afraid to use a big round-nose scraper to get the shape you desire.*

7. *The interior is almost complete. Cut off and reverse chuck to turn the foot of the bowl.*

8. *The finished bowl.*

Surface Treatments

Although it is hard to beat a well-sanded and finished surface, there are a variety of surface treatments that can add interest to a bowl. Let's take a look at some of these techniques.

Texturing

Texturing is one of the most pleasing and interesting effects available to the bowl turner. Typically, it is in the form of horizontal lines scraped into the surface with a pointed scraper or vertical lines carved into a band (usually at the rim) with a gouge. Texture can also be achieved by sandblasting or burning the surface of the wood.

While creating a rough surface may appear to be easy, doing it well is actually a lot of work. A Vermont turner named Al Stirt taught me one technique: scraping a series of very closely spaced grooves in the surface using a V-scraper. The trick is to grind the scraper to a good burr and touch lightly with the tool pointed downhill at even spacing. Great patience is necessary to keep the spacing fine and even, but the reward is well worth it.

Pyrography Pyrography is just a fancy name for good old-fashioned wood burning. It can take the form of artwork drawn on the inside or outside of a bowl with a wood-burning pen. This may be freehand drawing or geometric shapes. Alternately, random patterns can be achieved by strategically playing a propane torch on a bowl—either on or off the lathe. If on the lathe, you need to clean up the wood chips before lighting the torch, because chips are very flammable. A light burning of

Three bowls by Al Stirt. All three have the outside lightly textured by touching a V-scraper to the work at closely spaced intervals. The middle bowl is further textured in the area just below the rim with vertical carving (created with a carving tool).

Horizontal lines of texture can be created by lightly touching a well-sharpened V-scraper to the spinning work at close intervals.

open-grained woods (such as oak) while they are spinning on the lathe usually enhances the grain and adds color and texture.

You can also burn lines into the surface by grabbing a piece of soft iron wire (sometimes called "stove wire") between two pairs of vise grips and holding the wire against the spinning bowl. A very precise line is burned, forming a mini cove. The effect can be striking.

Sandblasting Sandblasting can be used to achieve a matte effect or to enhance grain. If you plan to restrict the blasting to certain areas, some planning is necessary. Once you have turned the bowl to its near-final form, a good tactic is to use a scraper to turn the area to be blasted slightly lower than the area that ultimately will be sanded smooth. Now sandblast the low area, using the sandblaster like a paint sprayer. Hold the nozzle 8 in. to 12 in. from the work and use overlapping spray patterns until you get an even texture. Remount the bowl in the lathe, and turn the smooth areas down to a height commensurate with the matte areas. You can also etch patterns into the surface of your bowl by using cut-out rubber masks.

A light blasting gives a wonderful matte surface, whereas heavy treatment yields a driftwood-like look. Small, inexpensive sandblasting units that hook to a portable air compressor are available at automotive-supply stores. Cook some play sand in the oven to dry it out, run it through a sieve, load up the sandblaster, and have a blast. Don't forget to wear a safety shield and safety glasses.

Carving

Al Stirt also taught me how to carve turned bowls, which adds an interesting detail. If your initial reaction is, "But I can't carve," don't be put off—you don't have to be Michelangelo to achieve stunning results. Your first attempt may not end up in the Louvre, but after five or six tries, you'll get more than acceptable results.

You don't need a great many carving tools either; one to three tools will do nicely. A 4-mm, 6-mm, or 8-mm #12 sweep V-carving tool is good for creating incised textured bands. (This tool is often called a V-parting tool in carving catalogs.) A couple of #7, #8, or #9 sweep gouges in the 13-mm to 25-mm width range are all that are needed for creating scallops. If carving bowls really strikes your fancy, you might want to invest in an electric-powered carving machine. Most useful is a small electric Automach unit (see the photo below). It allows quick and accurate carving with much more control than driving hand tools with a mallet.

The two secrets to carving bowls are careful layout and building a vise to hold your bowl during carving. It's essential to lay out your design in pencil to achieve even spacing and a pleasing design. A vise to hold the work during carving (hand or electric) is vital for achieving precision. It holds the work rock solid so that the force of your carving goes directly into the work and not into moving it around on the bench or in your lap.

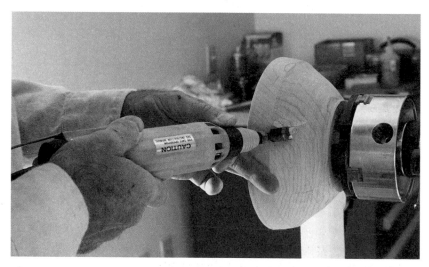

The Automach electric chipping hammer brings speed and control to the carving of bowls.

Vise for Holding Bowls while Carving

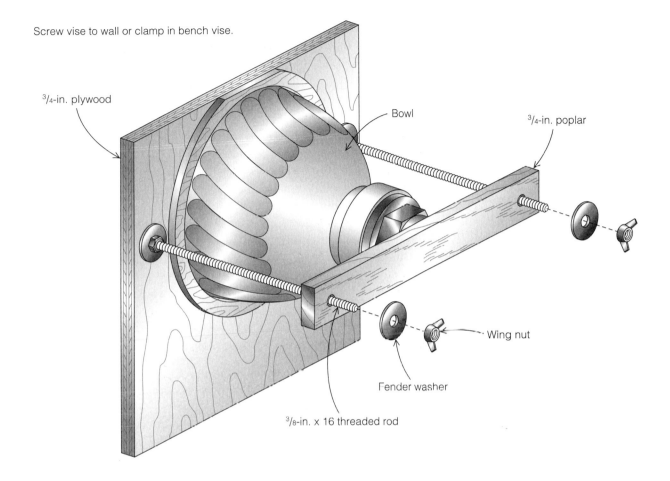

Screw vise to wall or clamp in bench vise.

3/4-in. plywood

Bowl

3/4-in. poplar

Wing nut

Fender washer

3/8-in. x 16 threaded rod

If you carve up to the rim of the bowl, it's almost impossible not to break out the edge badly. Therefore, I turn the rim to final height *after* carving and just turn away the bad breakouts. Even when carving scallops, it's often handy to remount the work in the lathe for cleanup and/or sanding. In short, leave the faceplate or chuck on the bowl until you're certain you've finished turning.

It's definitely easier to carve green wood, but dry wood of a favorable hardness works fine. The advantage to green wood is that any wood can be carved—even hard maple. For dry carving, you'll need to use basswood, butternut, sassafras, or something similar.

Carving a Bowl

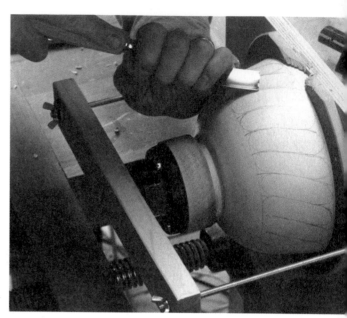

1. *Mount the freshly turned bowl in a shopmade vise, and lay out the carving design (here, a spiral scallop pattern). Use a compass, dividers, tape measure, and the indexing head in your lathe to make sure the elements of the design are equally spaced.*

2. *Make the first trial cut. The grain of the wood or the limitations of your gouges may force you to modify your design slightly to make it work, but your layout will still allow you to keep things equally spaced. Just keep the relationship of the carving to the layout the same on each panel.*

3. *Work alternately in both directions from the initial scallop. It's typical for your carving to improve slightly with each scallop; working this way, you won't end up with the final scallop being vastly different from the initial scallop.*

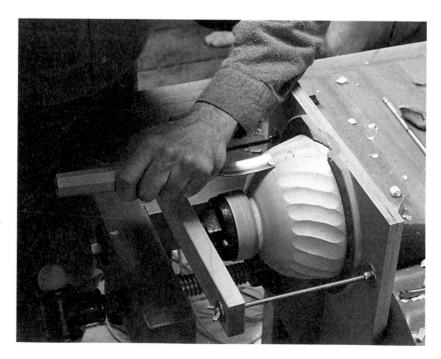

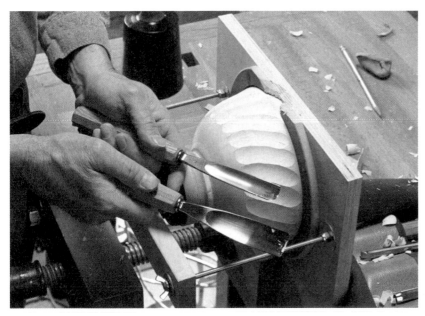

4. *Depending on your design, you may need to use more than one gouge. Here, the tighter sweep at top is for starting the cut, and the shallower sweep below is for finishing off.*

5. *The finished bowl.*

6 Finishing Touches

As a novice turner, you may think your work is done once you've turned your bowl to a pleasing shape. But turning is only half the battle. Still ahead, you have sanding (and possibly buffing), finishing, and maybe even engraving to look forward to. All are covered here, along with some tips on repairing checks, dents, and other minor disasters.

■ Sanding

Sanding can make or break a bowl and is one of the most misunderstood parts of the turning process. Unfortunately, it also a dusty, dirty, and time-consuming operation that's often given short shrift by turners (and in books and articles on turning). Believe it or not, as a general rule of thumb, it will take about as long to sand your bowl properly as it did to turn it. The bad news is that no matter how much your gouge work improves and your turning time decreases, the sanding time will stay about the same. The good news is that there are lots of tricks to sanding, and proper technique pays big dividends. If this job is done right, finishing is a snap—after which you can sit back and admire your bowl.

Good sanding is much more than just holding a piece of sandpaper against the spinning work. It involves using the right grit and grade of sandpaper as well as the right tools and equipment. I use power-sanding equipment for coarser and medium grades of sandpaper and then move to hand-sanding for the finer grades. Let's start with the most overlooked part of the sanding equation—the sandpaper itself.

Sanding is an important part of the bowl-turning process. Sand with the bowl still mounted in the lathe to reduce the drudgery of this task.

Sandpaper

Good sandpaper cuts like a razor-sharp plane; poor quality paper or the wrong kind of paper is like using a garden hoe to finish your work. Sandpaper is made with either a cloth or a paper backing. The thickness and stiffness of either backing material affect how the abrasive grit acts. Thick, heavy backing makes the abrasive particles dig in deeper and cut more aggressively. Cloth backing tends to be stiffer and heavier than paper, and its superior strength makes it better for power-sanding. Cloth backing comes in two weights: X and its lighter, thinner brother J. Paper backings come in A, B, C, D, E, and F weights, with A being the lightest and F the heaviest. I use cloth X papers for initial power-sanding and A, B, or C papers for final sanding.

To reduce the drudgery of sanding, I prefer to do all my sanding in the lathe. But there are some safety issues: It's unwise to hand-sand with a cloth sheet, because it will not rip if it becomes wrapped in the work. Large pieces can trap your fingers in the process, with painful or even tragic consequences. If you must use cloth, cut it into very small pieces, no bigger than 4 in. square. There's less risk when working with paper-backed sheets, because the paper will tear if it gets wrapped in the work. Paper sheets should still be cut into quarter sections, because the smaller size presents less likelihood of getting caught.

The type of abrasive material and how it is bonded to the backing make a world of difference in how the paper cuts. The four commonly available types of abrasive material are aluminum oxide, silicon carbide, ceramics, and garnet. For sanding bowls, aluminum oxide or garnet is best, especially for the finer grades above 120 grit. The abrasive is applied to the backing material in a closed coat or an open coat. Open coat is much better for wood, because there's space between the particles so that swarf (the shavings created by the cutting action of the paper) has a place to go.

The best paper for sanding bowls is stearated, which means that a coating of zinc stearate, a lubricant, is applied to the finished sheet. Wood resins and finishes do not stick as readily to a stearated paper, which is a big plus in bowl work, especially when sanding wet wood.

Grades and grit size   Sandpaper made in North America is graded under the Coated Abrasives Manufacturers Institute (CAMI), and European papers are rated under the P scale dictated by the Federation of European Producers Association (FEPA). The latter is identifiable by the letter P in front of the grit size (for example, P220). A grit size in one system is not exactly equivalent to a grit size in the other, except at 180 grit where they cross. There's also a third system that gives the particle size in microns. It bears no resemblance to the other two systems but is easy to identify because of the Greek letter μ (for micron) after the particle size. Unlike the other two systems, the smaller the micron number, the finer the grit. The chart on the facing page will help you sort out the grading systems. All of my grit recommendations are in the P system.

Whether sanding by machine or by hand, the biggest mistake a beginning bowl turner can make is to start with an abrasive that's not coarse enough. When faceplate turning, there's always some degree of tearout where you were forced to cut against the grain, and you must sand though this to achieve a really good surface finish. It's tempting to start as high as 120 grit, but if you do, you're likely to get big, ugly white spots in the areas of the tearout when you apply the finish. I like to start with 50- or 60-grit paper and sand at this grit for much longer than I think I need to (at least two or three minutes, depending on the wood and on the size of the bowl). This removes all traces of tearout. The second mistake beginners make is to jump grits rather than working up in an orderly fashion. After the 50- or 60-grit paper, I sand progressively with 80-, 120-, 150-, 180-, and 220-grit paper. Skipping a grit wastes time and sandpaper.

The easiest way to sand a bowl is with a power-sanding mandrel mounted in an electric drill. On the left is the Snap-loc system made by Merrit Abrasives. Each sanding disk has a small plastic clutch that snaps into the rubber mandrel. On the right is a system from Klingspor that uses hooks and loops to hold the abrasives on the disk.

ABRASIVE GRADING SYSTEMS			
CAMI	FEPA	Micron	Generic
1500		3	micro fine
		5	
		6	
1200			
		9	
1000			
		12	
800			ultra fine
		15	
600	P1200		
500	P1000		
		20	
400	P800		super fine
		25	
360	P600		
		30	
	P500		
320	P400	35	extra fine
		40	
	P360		
280		45	
	P320		
		50	
240	P280		very fine
		55	
		60	
220	P220	65	
180	P180		
150	P150		
120	P120		fine
100	P100		
80	P80		medium
60	P60		
50	P50		coarse
40	P40		
36	P36		extra coarse

Another important consideration is how fine a grit you should sand to. For a working bowl that is going to see kitchen use, sanding much beyond 150 grit is counterproductive. If it's Christmas Eve, stop at 120 grit; come morning, your mother will love the bowl just as it is. Even better, she'll use it every day rather than putting it on a hallowed shelf with your graduation photo. On the other hand, extra-beautiful wood often demands a mirror polish; I'll share the secrets of achieving one later in this chapter.

The easiest way to sand a bowl is with one of the many power-sanding systems that are on the market today. They get you through the drudgery of the coarse grits in jig time. The sanding mandrel is mounted in a ¼-in. or ⅜-in. electric drill. You need a drill with lots of power and speed, so cordless drills are out. A corded, reversible drill that has a top speed of 1,500 rpm to 2,000 rpm is best. The faster the better! The advantage of using a reversible drill is that it allows you to keep the direction of rotation of the disk opposite the direction of rotation of the lathe, regardless of which half of the disk you use.

Power-sanding

I usually power-sand a bowl at the same speed at which I did the primary turning, which is never faster than 1,100 rpm. Sometimes I even slow the lathe down for sanding, especially for the final hand-sanding. Although it is tempting to speed up the lathe for sanding, this is dangerous and counterproductive. If the bowl is the least out of round (which can happen as a green bowl dries in the lathe), you'll sand only the high spots. And the heat generated by high speed can cause the stearate to fail, especially when hand-sanding.

Power-sanding much beyond 120 grit with the Merrit Snap-loc sanding system doesn't work very well. The heavy X cloth, backed up by the rubber disk, makes the abrasive aggressive. At grits of 150 and higher, the wood becomes more polished, but little swirling scratch marks are left

Adding foam rubber (such as neoprene insulation) to a sanding disk will pay big dividends in the quality of the finish. Glue the rubber to a used disk with contact cement such as Pliobond, and then glue A- or B-weight sandpaper to the foam with a contact cement such as 3M Super 77 spray adhesive.

throughout the surface. These marks are caused by dirt and oversized particles that have been forced into the work because the backing for the abrasive was not resilient enough to ride up and over them.

It is easy to modify the Merrit system to eliminate this problem. Simply take one of your expended sandpaper disks and glue a piece of foam rubber to it with contact cement. The foam rubber should be between ¼ in. and ⅜ in. thick. Over the years, I have used old wet suits (for scuba diving), a camping pad for sleeping on the ground, and my current favorite: neoprene insulation that goes around 1-in. water pipes. Suitable material is not hard to find. I usually make up six or eight padded disks so that I have plenty on hand.

Now glue A- or B-weight sandpaper (which I cut from standard sheets) to the foam rubber. I used to favor garnet sandpaper; but these days I use Klingspor PS33, which is a stearated, open-coat aluminum oxide, B-weight sandpaper. The best glue is photo-mount adhesive, which is available in spray cans at art supply stores. Spray both the foam and the back of the sandpaper, wait a minute or so, and press the foam-covered disk onto the sandpaper. Finally, use scissors to trim the sandpaper about ⅛ in. proud of the disk.

You are now ready to sand to what I call a gallery-level finish—one that reflects light and is good enough to put in an art gallery. The foam backing makes the sandpaper work in a less-aggressive fashion, and a polish is quickly obtained. Sand with 150, 180, and 220 grits. Sanding higher than 220 is best done by hand or with cloth buffs. I use the foam-padded disks over and over. If the paper is cold, it's hard to remove but once warm from sanding it will peel back off of the foam. Simply sand with the pad for a few seconds to get it warm. Peel the sandpaper off and glue on some more.

Hand-sanding

Hand-sanding a bowl is pretty straightforward, but there are a couple of things to watch for. I use the same Klingspor PS33 B-weight paper as I use for power-sanding. I tear it into quarter sheets, and then fold the pieces in half. Wearing a tight-fitting leather glove (like a golf glove) when sanding can save you some painful burns. Slowing down the lathe also helps, because too high a speed destroys the stearate coating (and the glue) and quickly clogs the paper. If your paper dulls quickly, try a lower speed. Don't just hold the paper in one place but rather move it briskly from side to side, trying as much as possible to constantly bring new areas of paper in contact with the work.

On complicated bowl designs there is often an area (such as an undercut rim) where power-sanding is impossible, and you must hand-sand. In the lucky event that the entire bowl can be power-sanded, I still like to give a final hand-sanding to bring the sanding scratch pattern into a uniform direction and give a more pleasing look to the bowl. Even workaday bowls that I power-sand to only 120 grit get a quick final hand-sanding at

Power-Sanding a Bowl

1. *To sand the outside of a bowl, sweep the sanding disk up and slightly across the work to remove most of the tool marks. Flex the rubber pad a little (this takes a good deal of forward pressure on the drill).*

2. *Switch to a foam-backed disk to produce a finely polished surface.*

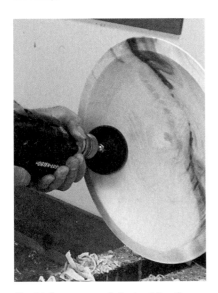

3. *It's best to sand the inside of a bowl with the drill running forward (clockwise rotation). The area just below the lip of the bowl is the hardest to sand, and it's where tearout really shows. Sand this area well with a coarse grit before moving to a finer abrasive.*

4. *Avoid sanding at the very center of the bottom for very long, because it is easy to sand a dimple in this area. Using light pressure, let just the edge of the disk touch the center and then move away.*

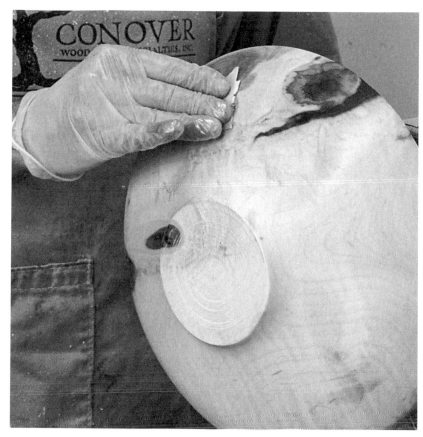

Hand-sand with a small piece of sandpaper with the lathe running. The author wet-sands with mineral spirits as part of the finishing process.

120 grit. Always start hand-sanding with the same grit used for the last power-sanding.

A final trick is wet-sanding. For green wood, using water with a wet-dry sandpaper will give amazing results. Wet-dry sandpaper is available in most hardware stores and is generally a silicon carbide closed-coat abrasive on a B- or C-weight paper. Place a pan of water under the workpiece and constantly dip the sandpaper during the sanding process. You'll have to slow down the lathe unless you have plans to take a shower.

The downside of wet-sanding is that the water prevents the bowl from drying out, which impedes finishing. If you want to apply finish in the lathe, the wood has to dry out and be given a final sanding to smooth the grain raised by the water. (Letting the bowl run at the maximum safe speed for its size will eliminate most of the water through centrifugal force.) A second way to wet-sand is to use wet-dry sandpaper and mineral spirits. It's my preferred method, and one which I incorporate into the finishing process (discussed later).

A good way to buff the inside of a bowl is with a buffing wheel mounted on a mandrel in an electric drill.

■ Buffing

On very close-grained woods, such as maple, buffing will bring the wood to a true polish. A polish is established when the surface reflects light. Power-sand the bowl to 220 grit, and then buff with cloth buffs and stainless-steel compound. I buff in two ways. One is to use a buffing wheel mounted on a mandrel held in an electric drill (like the sanding mandrel), and the other is with a normal tabletop buffer. The drill-mounted buffer is best used with the lathe running to polish the inside of the bowl and the outside adjacent to the rim. The tabletop buffer is best for the bowl's foot and the area adjacent to it. This is, of course, done off the lathe.

Drill mandrels for holding buffing wheels are available at hardware stores and from most woodworking catalogs. You want a cushion-sewn buffing wheel, which is softer than a spiral-sewn wheel. It gets into tight spaces better and gives a higher polish. The mandrel is threaded for a washer and nut to hold the wheel in place. It is best to cut the threaded portion of the mandrel off just over the nut, file the rough edges smooth, and tape the mandrel end and nut with duct tape. Even so modified, you must be careful not to touch the bottom of the bowl with the mandrel end or the nut, or you'll end up with a serious dent. I have found stainless-steel compound to be the best buffing agent; it is available at good hardware stores.

Buffing is a pretty simple technique. Just hold the whirling buff against the spinning bowl. Use moderate pressure (enough to just deform the buff a bit), and keep the buff constantly moving. Apply compound frequently.

For buffing off the lathe, the bowl must be constantly rotated on the buff. I generally work in one-third turns. It's important never to allow the bowl to remain stationary under the wheel; otherwise, it will burn the work or buff a notch in it. I start the bowl rotating before touching the wheel and remove the wheel before I stop the bowl.

▪ Making Repairs

No matter how fine your turning skills, there will be times when you'll need to make some repairs to your bowl during the turning process. Wood is an unstable material, and it doesn't always behave the way you anticipate. The wood may crack, a dead knot may fall out, or a piece of the rim may break out. In this section I'll explain how to deal with checks, defects, and dents.

Checks

It is not uncommon for checks, or small cracks, to appear during the turning process; they can range from microscopic hairline cracks to large fissures. Checks can almost always be easily fixed on the fly with cyanoacrylate glue. The brand I use is Satellite City. This glue can be found at model shops and good woodworking supply houses. It comes in three viscosities: water thin, medium, and thick. A catalyst (or accelerator) is also sold, which will set any of the three viscosities in seconds.

Water thin, as the name implies, is the consistency of tap water. It has powerful capillary action and will flow into the minutest of fissures and checks. Whenever you encounter a check, simply flow a bit of water thin onto it, and the glue will be sucked up. If the check runs through the bowl, reapply until you see glue come out the other side. Spray a bit of catalyst on the glued area, wait five minutes, and the check will be arrested. For bigger checks— where there is an actual gap—water thin glue followed by medium and even thick glue, if necessary, will fix the problem.

Defects and dents

Cyanoacrylate glue can also be used to patch a hole left by an errant tool, a dead knot, or a bark inclusion (a place where the tree grew around its own bark). It's a good idea to prime the defect with water thin glue first and then fill with medium or thick glue, depending on the size of the crater. Dust from turning can be dribbled into the glue and then mixed with a wood splint. Apply more glue and catalyst to accelerate drying. How good mixing wood dust with the glue will look depends entirely on the wood. With some woods, it looks natural; but with others, it will be obvious and out of place. On some woods, the glue alone will look quite natural. It is helpful to glue slips of paper on the low side of big break outs to form dams, keeping the glue from simply running through a defect.

Use cyanoacrylate glue to repair checks; dead knots; and, as shown above, bark inclusions. Apply the glue and then spray with the catalyst (right).

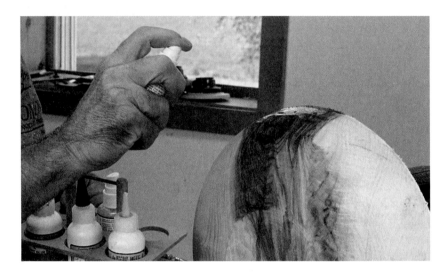

Great care should be exercised when using cyanoacrylate glue, because it will glue skin in seconds. It will glue your fingers together or to the work. Avoid skin contact and wear safety glasses and a respirator (or have plenty of ventilation). It is good to keep a bottle of cyanoacrylate glue solvent handy in case you do glue your fingers. It will dissolve the glue fairly fast. In a pinch, acetone will also work.

Five-minute and one-hour epoxies are also good for filling large defects. I like to use Duro brand, which is sold in a double syringe, because it mixes so easily. It will fill large voids and is easy to mix with wood dust and even pigment. If you are concocting the perfect patch, the one-hour open time makes life less hectic. Remember there are no mistakes, only new design opportunities and that the difference between an amateur and a professional is that the amateur spends a lot of time pointing out his or her mistakes.

◼ Finishing

Finishing is the icing on the cake for your bowl. Unfortunately, it also telegraphs the quality of your sanding job; your final finish, no matter what kind you decide to apply, will be no better than the surface you apply it to. Finishing accomplishes three ends in bowl turning. First, with green woodturning, finish provides a vapor barrier that prevents the end-grain areas of a bowl from drying substantially faster than the face-grain areas—a phenomenon that increases checking. Any finish will prevent rapid water loss in the end grain so that the entire bowl can dry evenly and check free.

The second function of a finish is to protect the bowl from the rigors of daily use, be that kitchen life or simply occasional handling for admiration. Needless to say, some finishes protect better than others, and a perfect finish would be hard as steel, flexible as rubber, and stay clear forever. If you ever find such a finish telephone me—collect. The third function of a finish is to enhance the beauty of the wood. As previously stated, how well a finish does this depends largely on the sanding job that went before.

Nontoxic finishes

Another wrinkle in the finishing conundrum is toxicity. If the bowl is to be used for food service, you don't want the finish to transfer poison to your food. I know of only three absolutely nontoxic finishes. The first is walnut oil, which is often served on salads and can be purchased at any health food store or good grocery. Walnut oil will dry but not very hard or very fast: It takes at least a month to dry anywhere near hard. There is also a finish sold under the name "Preserve," which is advertised to be non-toxic. The manufacturers of Preserve claim it's a blend of nut oils and has

Apply finish to the bowl right on the lathe before cutoff. Simply wipe the finish on with a small piece of cloth or your hand.

For a truly nontoxic finish use walnut oil. Preserve is a commercially available nontoxic finish that is a blend of nut oils that is supposed to dry faster and harder than does straight walnut oil.

better drying qualities than does straight walnut oil, although I have found it to be about the same.

Applying nut oil is simplicity itself. Just wipe the finish on with a small piece of cloth or your hands. Do it right on the lathe before cutoff. Nut oil also wet-sands beautifully, because it dries so slowly. Set the lathe to moderate speed and hand-sand with a small piece of paper. Although logic would say to use a wet-dry paper, I have had excellent luck with Klingspor PS33 sandpaper. The abrasive dulls long before the paper backing gives up the ghost from the oil. Keep the paper wet by adding oil frequently.

I place a small pan of oil for dipping the sandpaper just under the bowl. The dust from sanding will mix with the oil and create a wood filler that further enhances the look. Hold a handful of shavings against the spinning bowl to remove the excess finish, and you are done. Further coats can be applied off the lathe, but you will need to wait three weeks to a month while they dry before recoating. For maintenance, recoat as necessary.

The third nontoxic finish is Behlen's Salad Bowl Finish. Sources at Behlen tell me that Salad Bowl Finish is actually a varnish formulated from natural resins. Because the vehicle (the liquid that delivers the resins to the work) is toxic, Salad Bowl Finish requires 72 hours of drying time before it becomes nontoxic.

Salad Bowl Finish is best applied with a small square of cloth and can be used for wet-sanding. Because of the heavy viscosity of the finish, I use mineral spirits to keep the sandpaper wet. As with nut oil, I have had no trouble with Klingspor PS33 paper breaking down because of the mineral spirits. When dry, Salad Bowl Finish is hard, clear, and waterproof. I have used Salad Bowl Finish extensively but have not had good success with its longevity. Within about two years, it becomes yellow and gummy, especially if it has been in food service. Maintenance is a real chore, because you first have to remove the failed finish. In most cases, turning a new bowl is faster.

Antique oil finish

My favorite bowl finish is Minwax antique oil finish. It is available in a variety of pigments, but I use clear. It is not certified nontoxic, but it dries to a hard clear finish that withstands the rigors of kitchen life. Food oils do not cause it to break down, so maintenance is just a matter of a thorough degreasing and sanding in some more oil. The main cause for toxicity concern is heavy metals that are used as dryers in oils and varnishes. Because the finish dries hard, these metals are encapsulated in the finish and the chance of them getting in my salad is minimal. In other words, food mainly sits in bowls. For something like a cheese platter, where there was going to be a lot of cutting on the surface, I would elect to use nut oil.

I apply antique oil finish in exactly the same way I apply nut oil, except that I wear disposable latex gloves— it saves having to wash my hands with lacquer thinner to remove the dried finish. A word of caution when working with this finish: It has a tremendous affinity for oxygen and dries quickly—hence it's a good candidate for spontaneous combustion. Any rags that are used to apply the finish should be disposed of properly.

Wipe on the oil with a small rag and let it dry 10 to 20 minutes, depending on the temperature. The higher the temperature, the quicker the drying time. When the oil is tacky, sand it in with the lathe running at a slow speed (see the photo essay on p. 126). Keep the sandpaper wet with mineral spirits. Apply another light coat of oil and wait until the finish is tacky. Now grab a large handful of wood shavings and, with the lathe running, wipe off the excess oil. I grab chips in each hand and apply equal pressure on the inside and outside of the bowl. Run the lathe as fast as is safe for the size of your bowl (but never faster than 1,100 rpm). Let the finish dry for 15 to 20 minutes and then cut off the bowl.

I often find it necessary to apply additional coats of finish off the lathe to many of my bowls. I hand-sand each coat with progressively finer wet-dry sandpaper and, once tacky, wipe it with a clean paper towel. For a gallery-level finish, I power-sand in the lathe to 220 grit, apply the first coat of oil in the lathe, and then hand-sand with 220-grit paper to unify the sanding scratch direction. Off the lathe, I apply two more coats of antique oil finish, sanding with 320-grit and then 400-grit wet-dry paper. I allow 24 hours of drying time between coats. If you can spare the faceplate, you can leave dry wood bowls mounted and do all of the sanding and finish-

Very little material is needed to finish a bowl. Because partially full cans of finish oxidize quickly, poring a new can into small bottles saves a lot of money.

Finishing a Bowl

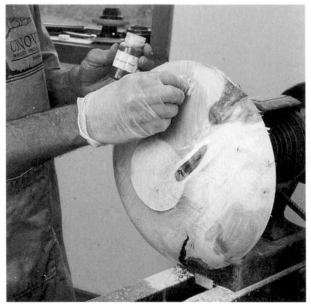

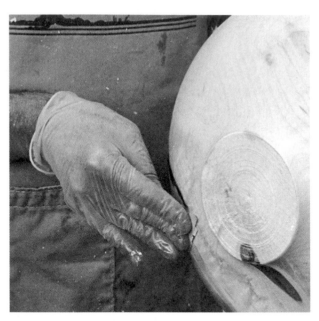

1. *With the bowl still in the lathe, wipe on the finish with a small rag. Here the author is applying antique oil finish.*

2. *When the oil is tacky, sand it in with a small piece of sandpaper. Lubricate the sandpaper with mineral spirits.*

3. *With the lathe running, wipe of the excess oil with a handful of wood shavings.*

ing in the lathe. However you do it, the result is a bowl your local art museum might be happy to honor in their gallery.

Other finishes

Many people finish their bowls with mineral oil, but I have found that it attracts dirt and needs constant repeat applications to maintain. Similarly, wax gets gummy with food oils, and I would not like it in my salad. For bowls that are intended for display only, any finish is fine. Finally, there is the option of no finish at all: Use will provide the finish. As long as the bowl was turned from clear wood, it is unlikely to check in the drying process.

 # Engraving

Marking the base of your finished bowl in some way is a nice touch. Inscriptions can range from just your initials to a lengthy epistle. I generally write my name, the date, and the type of wood the bowl was turned from. On bowls I give as gifts, I often write something commemorating the occasion. I think the date is particularly important, both historically and as a benchmark to see your progress as a turner. There are various ways to engrave the base of your bowl.

Engraving tools

Vibro engravers are available at most hardware stores. They are intended for engraving metal but work fine for bowls. Most have a control that adjusts the length of the engraving point's stroke. You want to set the tool for a short stroke for engraving bowls. Other than that, you use this tool just like a pencil—well sort of. It has to be used with a light touch, as though you were writing with a fountain pen. The tip tends to follow the wood grain, so it takes a bit of getting used to. Flowing script is hard to achieve. Although vibro tools are cheap, permanent, and mark in any wood (before or after finishing), the writing is hard to read in some lights. It takes a glancing illumination to see the engraving. They do not leave what my grandfather called "a fine copperplate hand."

Wood burning is another option. Wood-burning irons give a permanent marking that is legible in any light. Like vibro engravers, wood-burning irons have to be used with a light touch, otherwise they tend to follow the grain. Cheap irons cost less than $20, but they are not easy to write with, because you have to grip them a long way from the tip. Wood burning must be done before finishing; and unless the heat is just right, the marking has a fuzzy edge to it.

Better wood-burning irons work by induction, like a quick-heating soldering iron. A good induction wood burner has a control unit that is wired to the pen, which is about the size of a large fountain pen. A dial on the control unit sets a wide range of heats, and tips are interchangeable.

Tools for marking bowls include (from left) a vibro writer, a wood-burning iron, lettering pens with India ink, and technical pens.

Induction wood burners are a joy to write with, because they are used just like a pen. The only drawback is that they cost between $100 and $200.

My personal favorite is a lettering pen and waterproof black India ink. The nib holder (costing about $2.50) and the nibs (around 50 cents each) are sold separately and are available at any art supply store. Lettering pens are available in a dazzling variety of styles and sizes. For micro-fine detail, try a crow-quill or a (slightly broader) hawk-quill nib. These pens take a smaller holder than normal nibs. For bolder writing try lettering nibs.

To hold ink, a new nib needs to be soaked in lacquer thinner to remove the rust-preventative coating. Then break in the nib by putting it in the holder and writing on a fine Arkansas stone for a minute or two. This will make the tip write smooth and scratch free. Technical pens (one type is the Rapidograph) are also very good. They handle waterproof India ink but can sit filled without use for only about three weeks before clogging. Soap and water remove liquid India ink but use denatured alcohol for dried ink. A good cleaner is one-third alcohol, two-thirds water, and a splash of dishwashing detergent.

Marking should be done just after final-sanding the bottom of the foot, but before applying any finish to this area. In most woods, ink will bleed along the grain lines, producing fuzzy writing. This is easily overcome by applying a thin coat of white shellac with a small rag just after final-sanding the bottom of the foot. The shellac will dry in just a few minutes. Engraving on shellac over sanded wood is like writing on fine paper. Once the ink is dry, you can put an oil finish over the entire area, and there will be no sign of the shellac. India ink has shellac as a base so if you put another coat of shellac over the ink do it very quickly after the ink has dried thoroughly. Don't rub!

Felt-tip pens are another popular choice for engraving bowls. The problem is that their color fades quickly—even the ones labeled as permanent. In the art world, *permanent* means that an ink will withstand 12 launderings and still be readable. *Lightfast* refers to an ink's resistance to fading, but *archival* is the term used for a color that will last indefinitely. Light quickly fades felt-tip markers. Black India ink meets archival standards, and it will usually say so on the bottle.

Signing a Bowl

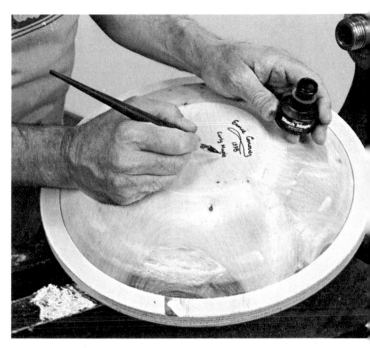

1. *Wipe on a thin coat of white shellac after final-sanding the bottom of the foot.*

2. *Sign and date the bowl using a lettering pen and waterproof India ink.*

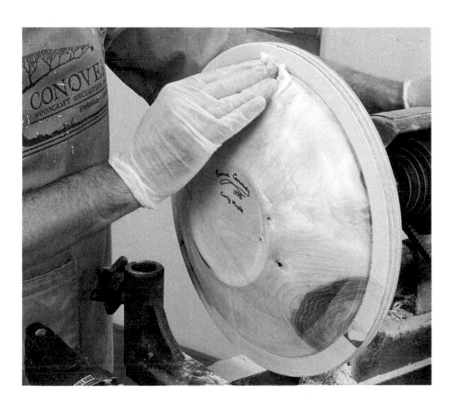

3. *Apply an oil finish over the marked area and the rest of the outside.*

7 Spinning Pewter

Metal spinning is the art of forcing a metal disk down over a form (or chuck), which is revolving in the lathe. Many common everyday items are spun metal. One of the best examples is spun-metal reflectors used extensively in the electric lighting industry. Others include aluminum cookware and, of course, bowls. Commercially, special heavy-duty spinning lathes are used, but spinning can also be carried out on a standard wood lathe.

With the right tools, you can spin a pewter bowl on a standard wood lathe.

Pewter for Spinning

A variety of nonferrous metals can be spun, including gold, silver, copper, brass, aluminum, and pewter. All, except pewter and dead-soft aluminum, have a tendency to work harden during spinning and consequently require frequent annealing. Work hardening is a change in the crystalline structure of the metal caused by the great force applied during the spinning process. The metal becomes hard, brittle, and cracks radially if not annealed at regular intervals. Annealing of nonferrous metals entails heating to cherry red and plunging in water—just the opposite of ferrous metals.

Pewter is immune from work hardening, is easy to work, and is a material people perceive as valuable. Therefore, it is the perfect material to learn to metal spin with. If you are on a tight budget, you might consider dead-soft aluminum as a less expensive learning material. Aluminum bowls, however, are just not the stuff heirlooms are made of.

The main constituent of pewter has always been tin, but in the seventeenth, eighteenth, and early nineteenth centuries, it often contained a small percentage of lead. Early on it was realized that lead was not a good substance to have in contact with food. Britannia metal (and queen's metal) was most probably developed sometime after 1850 in Sheffield, England. Britannia metal is an alloy composed of 92% tin, 7% antimony, and 1% copper. Queen's metal has a bit of silver added as well. Modern American pewter has about the same alloy composition as Britannia metal.

Modern lead-free pewter and Britannia metal are safe, durable metals that can sit side by side with silver at Lady Astor's tea party. Because standards are voluntary, it is important when purchasing pewter or Britannia metal to specify that you want lead-free metal. The best source I have found for pewter is A. J. Oster Alloys Inc., 50 Sims Avenue, Providence, RI 02909-0257 (800-289-3797).

Buying pewter

Don't be surprised to face a $75 to $100 minimum charge when ordering pewter. Pewter is sold by a "gauge" system known variously as the American wire or the Brown & Sharpe standard. Appendix 2 on p. 149 gives the old gauge sizes and their decimal equivalents. When ordering pewter, it is best to specify the size in decimals, because there is much confusion connected with the old gauge system. Although it is best to *buy* pewter in decimals, pewter smiths still *talk* in gauges so you really have to know both systems. Ask your supplier about rolling surcharges, because you will often find it is cheaper to buy a thickness that is a few thousandths of an inch thicker or thinner than the gauge specification. For instance, 16 gauge is 0.0508 in.; but if the pewter is ordered at 0.050 in., there is no surcharge. Appendix 2 will also help you figure the weight and cost of a given blank. Expect to pay $12 to $16 per pound.

What Size Blank Do I Need?

Figuring what size disk of pewter you need to spin a given form can be problematic. Because the metal stretches a bit during the spinning process, you fortunately almost always end up with too much metal. The excess is easily trimmed away, and in fact several trimmings are necessary during the spinning process anyway.

The easiest way to figure the diameter of a blank is simply to stretch a string or flexible steel tape measure from the center of your chuck to the rim. A second method is to draw the design out on paper and measure from the center to the rim in the same manner as the stretched string. This will give you the radius of the blank. In most cases, you'll end up with a little more metal than you need.

To calculate what size pewter blank you need, simply stretch a flexible tape measure (or length of string) from the center of the chuck to the rim. Multiply by two to get the diameter.

Tools and Equipment

Metal spinning can be carried out on almost any lathe; but for serious spinning, a heavy lathe with a massive headstock, tailstock, and tool base is desirable. For spinning, the bigger the lathe the better. But if you own a small lathe, don't fret—you can still spin metal. You are simply limited to thinner material and smaller pieces. On many lathes, the tool base has a tendency to slide sideways along the bed owing to the high lateral pressure placed on it during spinning. Often the clamping mechanism cannot be tightened sufficiently (even hitting it with a mallet) to immobilize the tool base. The solution is to clamp a narrow board to the bed on either side of the tool base with C-clamps.

Chucks

Spinning entails forcing a metal disk down over a form, which is revolving in the lathe. The form is properly called a chuck, and it is the negative form of the item you plan to spin. Think of a chuck as the air inside one of your finished wood bowls. Very satisfactory chucks can be faceplate turned from a durable hardwood, such as maple.

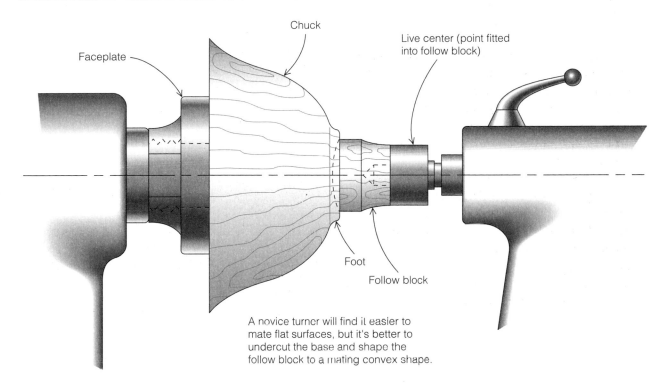

Faceplate

Chuck

Live center (point fitted into follow block)

Foot

Follow block

A novice turner will find it easier to mate flat surfaces, but it's better to undercut the base and shape the follow block to a mating convex shape.

If you do much spinning, you'll want to invest in some extra faceplates because you won't want to remove the faceplate from a chuck you have working perfectly. If you must remove the faceplate from a chuck, try engraving a number and filing a notch in the edge of the faceplate. Pencil the number and a line (opposite the notch) on the chuck. This will give you the same orientation when remounting so centering will be optimal. It's best to rub paraffin or Fels Naptha soap on a finished chuck to provide some lubricity between the metal and the chuck.

It's desirable to incorporate a "foot" into a chuck, as shown in the drawing above. Once you have the metal blank centered on the chuck, the first act is to "catch" the foot. That is, spin the metal down over the ridge that forms the foot. Now the blank will stay centered throughout the rest of the spinning operation, because it is trapped on the chuck by the foot and the follow block.

Follow block

The follow block is simply a block of wood that is turned to a perfect fit with the base of the chuck. It holds the pewter disk against the chuck throughout the entire spinning operation. A well-designed follow block is drilled or scraped out to be a press fit over the point of the live center in the tailstock and is shaped to mate perfectly with the base area of the chuck and to be about ¼ in. in diameter less than the diameter of the foot. Like the chuck, the follow block should be turned from a durable hardwood. Tailstock alignment is critical to the follow block working properly. When advanced by the tailstock ram, it must center on and fit perfectly with the chuck.

For your first tries at spinning, scrape the base of the foot dead flat and do the same with the follow block. Later you may want to make the base of the chuck slightly concave and the follow block a mating, slightly convex shape (as shown in the drawing on p. 133). Because the two must mate perfectly, this scheme is a bit more complicated, requiring repeated trial fits. The advantage is that the finished bowl will have a concave base (just as with a wood-turned bowl) and will not rock on uneven surfaces.

Spinning rest

Much different from a normal woodturning tool rest, a metal-spinning rest is a T fabricated of heavy steel sections. There are two metal pins that can be moved to several locations along the top surface of the T. The pins afford fulcrum points against which the turner can lever the tools and back

Metal-Spinning Tool Rest

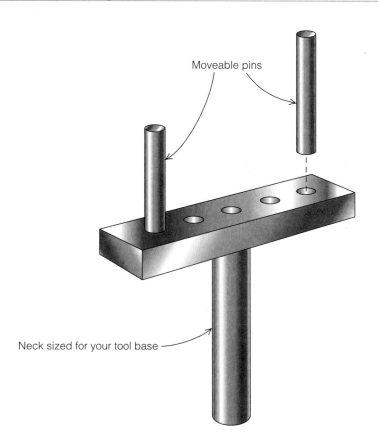

Moveable pins

Neck sized for your tool base

stick. In the past you had to fabricate (or have a machine shop make) a spinning rest yourself. Fortunately, they are being made these days by Sorby and can be purchased from anyone who sells the Sorby line.

Tools

Spinning tools are considerably different from normal turning tools. A good spinning tool has a hardened, polished tip that lays the metal down without marring it, a stiff shank that will not flex under the high lateral forces applied during spinning, and a stout handle for good purchase. As with rests, we once had to make our own tools. Fortunately, pewter can be spun with wood tools made in the shop from hickory. My father made his first set out of sledge-hammer handles that he bought at a hardware store, and you can do the same. Various spinning tools and the specifications of shopmade wood tools are shown in the drawings below and on the following pages. I have listed the American nomenclature for these tools, but because Sorby is the only maker supplying spinning tools for the wood-turning market, I have also included the British terms (in parentheses).

Spinning tools need to be kept well polished, because the surface spun by the tool will be no better than the surface finish of the tool itself. This is true of the wooden tools as well. You can buff wood, and I always buff my tools (wood or metal) with stainless-steel compound on a cushion-sewn wheel before the start of a spinning. For more about metal finishing and polishing see "Buffing" (pp. 146–147).

Forming tool (hook burnish)

The forming tool is used for the initial laying down of the metal over the chuck. Its broad contact area moves a wide area of metal. It is an easy tool to make from wood.

COMMERCIAL FORMING TOOL

SHOPMADE FORMING TOOL

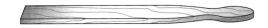

$^{1}/_{2}$ in. x $^{3}/_{4}$ in. x 18 in.; hickory

Spoon (spoon burnish)

The spoon takes its name from the piece of kitchenware that we stir coffee with. It has a highly polished surface, which is a large radius, so it is perfect for final smoothing of the metal to give a regular polished surface. Technically, this is not a polished surface but rather a burnished finish, which is where the British name for the tool comes from. Burnishing is the act of improving the surface quality of metal by rubbing it with a very smooth and ultrahard piece of steel.

COMMERCIAL SPOON

SHOPMADE SPOON

1¼ in. to 1½ in. dia. x 18 in. (rounded at end); hickory

Pointed tool (fingernail burnish)

The pointed tool is used for detailing work, such as coves and beads. It's the tool to reach for any time you need a hard edge or a small detail.

COMMERCIAL POINTED TOOL

SHOPMADE POINTED TOOL

1 in. dia. x 18 in.; hickory

Back stick (steady)

The back stick is used for initial centering of the blank. Mostly it is used in combination with the forming tool to support the metal and keep it from wrinkling during a lift. Before Sorby came out with their spinning tools I never knew a back stick to be anything but wood. The name certainly implies wood, and it is easy to make.

COMMERCIAL BACK STICK

SHOPMADE BACK STICK

¾ in. x 1 in. x 18 in.; hickory

As its name implies, the lip rolling tool is used to roll over the lip of the bowl.

Lip-rolling tool

I learned about this improvised tool from a spinner named David Jones in Millersburg, Ohio. Most old texts on spinning show the spinner using a pointed tool and a back stick (or two back sticks) in conjunction with one another to roll the lip. When I saw David using this tool I thought, "Why didn't I think of that?" It's incredibly easy to make, because it is essentially a pointed hickory dowel with a kerf sawn in it.

SHOPMADE LIP-ROLLING TOOL

$^1/_4$ in. to $^3/_4$ in. dowel (depending on gauge)

Diamond trimming tool

During the spinning process the metal flows outward much like rolling out a pie crust. Occasional trimming is necessary to remove the excess metal and to bring the blank back into round. This is the job of the diamond trimming tool. It can be made from a square section of tool steel, though a diamond-point turning scraper works fine for the purpose.

COMMERCIAL DIAMOND TRIMMING TOOL

Lubricants

A lubricant is necessary to keep the tools from galling, or wearing away, the metal during the high pressure applied by the spinning process. The lubricant needs to have high pressure and temperature lubricity and be easy to remove after the process is completed. Tallow is a good lubricant but hard to wash off. I learned to use Fels Naphtha soap from Rude Osolnik. It is easily crayoned on and is a good lubricant.

An even better lubricant is Murphy oil soap in gel form. (It also comes in liquid form, but you need the gel.) Murphy oil soap has excellent lubricity and eats up heat but washes off easily. Simply use a paintbrush to swab the surface of the blank with the oil soap. I have always wondered if using this soap is a codicil to Murphy's law that nullifies it.

Castrol industrial stick wax, sold by Highland Hardware, is an industrial lubricant specifically for cutting, threading, tapping, and spinning metal. It works well and washes off with a strong laundry detergent. There's a warning on the label that the lubricant may cause eye and skin irritation, although it's never bothered me.

Before spinning the bowl, you need to apply a lubricant to both sides of the pewter disk.

◼ The Dynamics of Spinning

The dynamics of metal movement during the spinning process is intriguing. The pewter goes through dramatic changes under the pressure of the tools, acting more like a plastic than a metal. But, when you think about it, it has to, because you're asking a flat disk of metal to become a hemisphere. This means the metal is stretched at the foot area, but has to shrink (get smaller around the diameter) for the rest of the way up to the lip of the bow. The metal has to go somewhere and this is why you usually end up with extra metal at the lip.

If you have ever watched potters, they move the clay up in the same way when they "throw" a pot. They support the clay with one hand on the inside, just as we support the metal with a back stick, and they form the clay with their other hand on the outside of the bowl, just as we do with the forming tool.

The metal "moves" ahead of the tool much like a wave comes into a beach. This is why spinners speak of "moving metal." It actually forms a bulge ahead of the tool, as shown in the drawing on the facing page (Step 1). For this reason, it is necessary to spin back toward the foot after every lift toward the rim. Otherwise, you'd end up with all of the metal at the rim and severe thinning in the lower areas. By alternately lifting metal toward the rim and then spinning back toward the foot we keep the metal near its starting thickness, and everything goes well. Again the clay analogy works here. If potters did not move the clay back down toward the base of the pot, they would end up with all of the clay at the rim. Therefore, they alternate lifting the clay with pushing it back down to the base.

Low Lifts and High Lifts

When talking about bowl height, pewterers refer to "low lifts" and "high lifts"; the latter is much more difficult to spin than the former. The terms refer not so much to the absolute height of the article to be spun, but rather to how much the metal has to be stretched upward (and inward) to create the desired form. It is more the ratio of the base to the height of the form being made. Fortunately, bowls fall into the low-lift category. Objects like drinking tankards, pitchers, and coffeepots are high lifts. In fact, coffeepots entail spinning the metal smaller at the upper part than the base diameter.

High forms require a series of cone-shaped chucks, called break-down chucks, to stretch the metal into the desired form for final spinning. Each cone has a base that exactly matches the base of the final chuck. A "segmented" chuck, also called a puzzle chuck, is employed to spin high-lift closed forms. After spinning the closed form over the segmented chuck, a center core can be withdrawn. Then the segmented periphery of the chuck can be withdrawn in pieces through the opening left by the removal of the central core. This chapter deals with only low lifts in the spinning of bowls.

How Metal Behaves ahead of the Tools

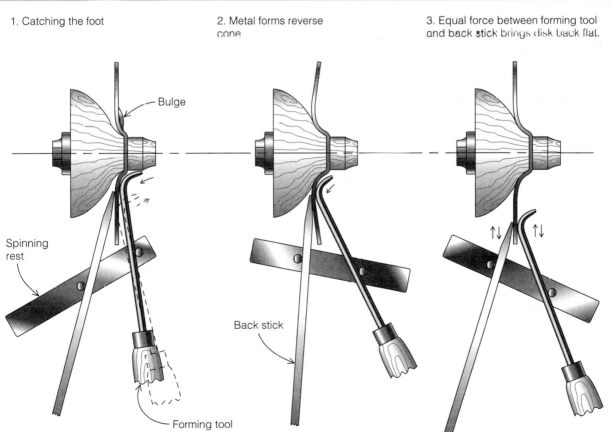

1. Catching the foot

2. Metal forms reverse cone

3. Equal force between forming tool and back stick brings disk back flat.

Bulge

Spinning rest

Back stick

Forming tool

Spinning Safety

There are a number of safety concerns when spinning metal, the first of which is speed. Spinning is never carried out at speeds much in excess of about 1,200 rpm. Your lathe also needs to be able go down to about 600 rpm (or even slower) to accomplish some spinning operations. Spinning at high speed is dangerous! Although 1,200 rpm may be dandy for a 6-in. to 10-in. disk, larger diameters demand lower speed. The bigger the diameter, the lower the speed.

A second concern is touching the sharp edge of the blank. At speed, the edge of the disk is essentially a motorized utility knife. Great care should be taken not to touch the work until the lift is finished and the edge is trimmed and either rolled or the sharpness broken with abrasive paper.

Eye protection is mandatory. Wear safety glasses with side shields, or a face shield—or both. Finally, extreme caution should be exercised with the use of abrasive cloth, steel wool, and Scotch-Brite cloth. It is convenient to do much of the finishing and polishing of a spun piece on the lathe, but a nick in the edge will catch abrasives (especially steel wool) and wrap them up in the lathe. If you're using a large piece, your fingers can be dragged with the abrasive. Always break up abrasive materials into small pieces, no larger than 4 in. square. If they do get hung up in the work or the chuck, at this size they will not drag your fingers with them.

A second problem is that the metal that has not yet been spun down to the chuck will form a reverse cone, as shown in Step 2 of the drawing on p. 139, if you don't straighten it out. This is where the back stick comes into play. It is used in conjunction with the spinning tool you happen to be using (probably the forming tool at this stage) and provides a support for the metal before it is spun down to the chuck. Equal forces are applied to the back stick and the spinning tool, much as you would pick something up with chopsticks. Any time the metal starts to form a reverse cone, it is spun back straight again, as shown in Step 3 of the drawing on p. 139. This is done by moving the tool, with the back stick on the opposite side, out to the rim. Failure to use a back stick properly usually results in wrinkling of the metal, which usually means the blank ends up as scrap.

Rolling an Edge

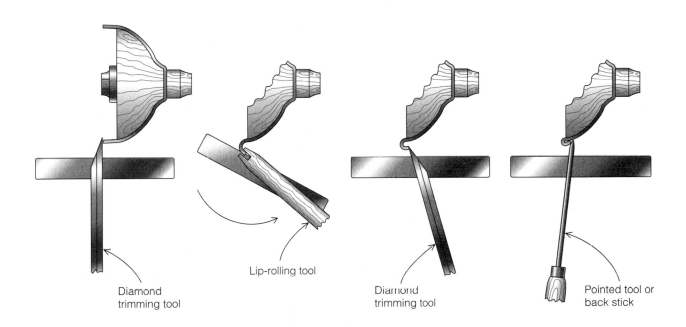

1. Trim the edge.

2. Roll the edge.

3. Trim the edge a second time.

4. Roll the metal down to the side wall of the bowl.

Diamond trimming tool

Lip-rolling tool

Diamond trimming tool

Pointed tool or back stick

Once the metal is spun down to the entire chuck, it's time to trim it. You now have two choices: Simply cut the rim off square and break the sharp edges with abrasive paper, or roll the edge. A rolled edge adds a finished look and strength to the bowl and is easy to do. For heavier gauges of pewter a hard edge works well too. Take your choice. If you are going to roll the rim, then trim the radius about ¼ in. proud of the rim, as shown in Step 1 of the drawing above. Now use the rolling tool to partially roll the metal around (Step 2). A second trimming is now necessary (Step 3). Finally, using a pointed tool or the back stick, lay the metal down tight to the side wall of the bowl (Step 4).

Spinning a Small Bowl

1. *Install the chuck and follow block on the lathe. (For chuck dimensions, see the drawing on p. 145.)*

2. *Gently pinch the pewter disk between the chuck and the follow block, using light tailstock pressure. Start the lathe at low speed (600 rpm or less). Lightly touch the outside edge of the disk with the back stick and, at the same time, lower the tailstock pressure slightly. Once the disk centers, firmly tighten the tailstock pressure.*

3. *Position the spinning rest and then use the forming tool to spin the metal down over the ridge that forms the foot. Support the opposite side with the back stick.*

4. *Use the back stick and the forming tool to perform the lift. Draw the metal into a wrinkle-free cone (toward the chuck) by pressing it against the back stick with the forming tool and sliding both tools simultaneously toward the rim.*

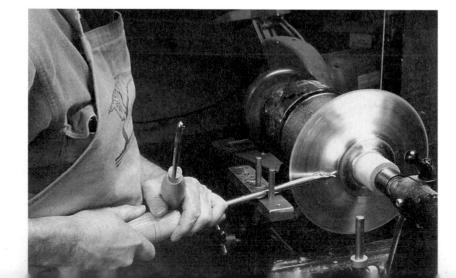

5. *Use the forming tool to spin the metal down to the chuck.*

6. *The first trim. Use a diamond trimming tool or a V-scraper to trim the disk round (but well outside the diameter of the chuck).*

7. *Lubricate the edge, and then use the lip-rolling tool to start rolling the lip. Note the trimmed-off edge of the disk in the foreground.*

8. *With the edge of the disk trapped in the kerf, swing the rolling tool to form the lip into a U shape.*

9. *The second trim. Take off just enough to make the edge true.*

10. *Roll the lip down to the side wall with the forming tool.*

11. *With the lathe set at 1,000 rpm to 1,200 rpm, make slow, even sweeps with a spoon burnish to smooth the metal. Use firm pressure, and work alternately to the base and to the rim.*

12. *Remove the tool rest, and polish the outside surface of the bowl, first with emery cloth and then with Scotch-Brite abrasive cloth.*

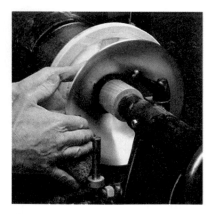

13. *Turn the bowl around, secure to a wood chuck with double-sided tape, and finish the inside.*

14. *The finished bowl.*

Start with a 10-in.-dia. disk
(16 to 22 gauge).

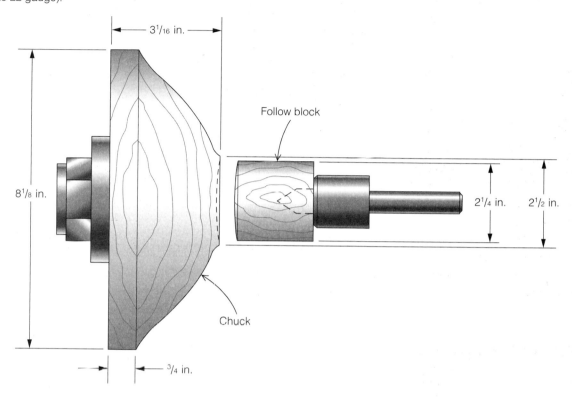

Follow block

3$^{1}/_{16}$ in.

8$^{1}/_{8}$ in.

2$^{1}/_{4}$ in.   2$^{1}/_{2}$ in.

Chuck

$^{3}/_{4}$ in.

Metal Finishing

The secret of professional-looking pewter lies as much in metal finishing
as in the actual spinning. This is just the same as with wooden bowls: If
you don't sand and finish properly, all your work is for naught. Pewter
designs work with a wide variety of surface treatments, from a brushed
look to a mirror finish. Let's look at how you can make your finished
spinning look just right.

The process of metal finishing removes minor imperfections from the
surface of the metal and gives the entire spinning a uniform surface quality. *Uniform* surface quality is the key here; whatever you choose as a finish, it needs to be uniform. Current tastes seem to favor a brushed finish
in which fine abrasives are employed to impart small, unidirectional
scratches to the surface. It is advantageous to do as much of the metal
finishing on the lathe as possible. Fortunately, this makes the production
of unidirectional scratches with abrasives easy.

A polish is obtained when the scratch marks left by the abrasive are
exceedingly small. At some point the scratch pattern can become random

with no detriment to the look of the finish. A mirror polish is obtained by using successively finer grades of abrasive until the scratch marks become smaller than the wavelength of visible light.

Finishing a pewter bowl

I usually start with a small square of fine emery cloth (a cloth-backed abrasive for use with metal, which is available at most hardware stores). The first thing I attack after spinning is the rim (whether rolled or square). After removing the tool rest, I use a small square of emery to carefully break all sharp edges and remove all burrs—anything that might cut my fingers. I now work the entire outside of the bowl right down to the foot. Next I go to Scotch-Brite abrasive cloth. Although 000 steel wool will work fine, I prefer Scotch-Brite: It has less tendency to get wrapped up in the work and leaves a nicer brushed finish. If a finer finish is desired, pumice and common mineral oil on a small square of felt leaves a very nice finish.

Finishing the inside of the bowl can be done on the lathe as well. The best tactic I have found is to mount a wood disk of an appropriate diameter on a faceplate, scrape out a recess that matches the foot of the bowl, and then secure the bowl in the recess with double-sided tape. Then the inside is finished the same as the outside. The easiest method for doing the very bottom is to first withdraw the tailstock and follow block. Then hold a piece of fine Scotch-Brite against the base of bowl, keeping it on the chuck; start the lathe at a very slow speed, and let it run for a couple of seconds. Snap-loc disks are available from Merrit with a Scotch-Brite facing. Armed with an electric drill you can spin the Scotch-Brite disk against the bottom to yield a unidirectional brushed finish.

Buffing

A buffer can also be handy for off-the-lathe polishing. Charged with the correct wheels and/or compounds, a buffing wheel can give you anything from a brushed look to a mirror polish. Buffing is the technique of using cloth or felt wheels, revolving at moderate speed and charged with abrasive compound, to improve the surface finish of metal. The abrasive compound is usually a wax/grease and abrasive mixture. Sold in stick form, it is crayoned on the revolving wheel. Small jackshafts designed for building a buffer are available at industrial hardware stores and from mail-order tool catalogs. They have a ½-in. or ⅝-in. arbor, which fits readily available 4-in.-, 6-in.-, and 10-in.-diameter cloth wheels and are best powered by a fractional horsepower 1,725 rpm motor.

A second way to make a small buffer for pewter polishing is to mount a buffing wheel in the lathe itself. The same small arbor that we used for the inside of a bowl with a ¼-in. or ⅜-in. shank is perfect. Mount the arbor in a drill chuck in the headstock spindle of your lathe.

Buffing wheels and compounds   Buffing wheels are available in two types: spiral-sewn and cushion-sewn. The spiral-sewn wheel is better for coarser compounds when aggressive cutting action is desired, whereas the cushion-sewn wheel is better for final polishing when gentle cutting action and a mirror finish are required. Scotch-Brite flap wheels are available at industrial hardware stores and are great for brushed finishes at the buffer.

Buffing compounds are proprietary in formulation and tend to be packaged by the purpose for which they are intended. Therefore, compounds are sold for brass, steel, stainless steel, and so on. For buffing pewter, I have found that Dico compound E5 emery gives a fine brushed finish and removes minor surface imperfections, and SCR stainless or rouge gives a mirror polish. Dico compounds and buffing wheels are made by Divine Brothers in Utica, New York, and are available in most good hardware stores. Equivalent compounds are made by Formax Company of Detroit, Michigan, and are sold at all Sears stores.

I keep a spiral-sewn wheel charged with E5 emery on the left side of my buffing arbor and a cushion-sewn wheel charged with SCR stainless or rouge on the right side. After burnishing with the spoon, I buff *lightly* on the left wheel; then if I want a mirror finish, I move to the right wheel. When buffing you must *always* buff off the edge. Buffing into the edge could send your spinning crashing into the floor. The key word here is *lightly.* Heavy buffing with any degree of pressure will round over the edges and wash out details.

I often use a 4-in. wheel to buff the inside of a spun bowl. Just as with wood bowls, you want to put duct tape over the arbor end and nut to prevent them from marring the surface if they inadvertently touch the work. Pewter will mar easily, so the best tactic is to watch the arbor end and not let it touch the work at all—duct tape or not.

Use a buffing wheel charged with compound for the final polishing of a pewter bowl.

Appendix 1

TILE ANGLES AND LENGTHS											
Number of segments	6	7	8	9	10	11	12	13	14	15	16
Cutting angle in degrees	30	25 3/4	22 1/2	20	18	16 1/3	15	13 7/8	12 7/8	12	11 1/4
Desired diameter (in.)	Tile length (in.)	Tile length (in.)	Tile length (in.)	Tile length (in.)	Tile length (in.)	Tile length (in.)	Tile length (in.)	Tile length (in.)	Tile length (in.)	Tile length (in.)	Tile length (in.)
4	2	1 3/4	1 1/2	1 3/8	1 1/4	1 1/8	1 1/16	15/16	7/8	13/16	3/4
5	2 1/2	2 3/16	1 15/16	1 11/16	1 9/16	1 7/16	1 5/16	1 3/16	1 1/8	1 1/16	1
6	3	2 5/8	2 5/16	2 1/16	1 7/8	1 11/16	1 9/16	1 7/16	1 5/16	1 1/4	1 3/16
7	3 1/2	3 1/16	2 11/16	2 3/8	2 3/16	2	1 13/16	1 11/16	1 9/16	1 7/16	1 3/8
8	4	3 1/2	3 1/16	2 3/4	2 1/2	2 1/4	2 1/16	1 15/16	1 3/4	1 11/16	1 9/16
9	4 1/2	3 7/8	3 7/16	3 1/16	2 3/4	2 9/16	2 5/16	2 1/8	2	1 7/8	1 3/4
10	5	4 5/16	3 13/16	3 7/16	3 1/16	2 13/16	2 9/16	2 3/8	2 1/4	2 1/16	1 15/16
11	5 1/2	4 3/4	4 3/16	3 3/4	3 3/8	3 1/8	2 7/8	2 5/8	2 7/16	2 5/16	2 1/8
12	6	5 3/16	4 9/16	4 1/8	3 11/16	3 3/8	3 1/8	2 7/8	2 11/16	2 1/2	2 5/16
13	6 1/2	5 5/8	5	4 7/16	4	3 11/16	3 3/8	3 1/8	2 7/8	2 11/16	2 9/16
14	7	6 1/16	5 3/8	4 13/16	4 5/16	3 15/16	3 5/8	3 3/8	3 1/8	2 15/16	2 3/4
15	7 1/2	6 1/2	5 3/4	5 1/8	4 5/8	4 1/4	3 7/8	3 9/16	3 5/16	3 1/8	2 15/16
16	8	6 15/16	6 1/8	5 1/2	4 15/16	4 1/2	4 1/8	3 13/16	3 9/16	3 5/16	3 1/8

Appendix 2

PEWTER DISK WEIGHTS													
Pewter weighs 0.2701 lb. per cubic inch avoirdupois.*													
Gauge	22	21	20	19	18	17	16	15	14	13	12	11	10
Decimal equivalent	0.0253	0.0285	0.0320	0.0359	0.0403	0.0453	0.0508	0.0571	0.0641	0.0720	0.0808	0.0907	0.1090
Disk dia. (in.)	Disk weight	Disk weight	Disk weight	Disk weight	Disk weight	Disk weight	Disk weight	Disk weight	Disk weight	Disk weight	Disk weight	Disk weight	Disk weight
2	0.34	0.39	0.43	0.49	0.55	0.62	0.69	0.78	0.87	0.98	1.10	1.23	1.48
3	0.77	0.87	0.98	1.10	1.23	1.38	1.55	1.74	1.96	2.20	2.47	2.77	3.33
4	1.37	1.55	1.74	1.95	2.19	2.46	2.76	3.10	3.48	3.91	4.39	4.93	5.92
5	2.15	2.42	2.72	3.05	3.42	3.84	4.31	4.85	5.44	6.11	6.86	7.70	9.25
6	3.09	3.48	3.91	4.39	4.92	5.54	6.21	6.98	7.83	8.80	9.87	11.08	13.32
7	4.21	4.74	5.32	5.97	6.70	7.53	8.45	9.50	10.66	11.97	13.44	15.08	18.13
8	5.50	6.19	6.95	7.80	8.75	9.84	11.04	12.40	13.92	15.64	17.55	19.70	23.68
9	6.96	7.84	8.80	9.87	11.08	12.45	13.97	15.70	17.62	19.79	22.21	24.94	29.97
10	8.59	9.67	10.86	12.19	13.68	15.38	17.24	19.38	21.76	24.44	27.42	30.79	37.00
11	10.39	11.70	13.14	14.74	16.55	18.60	20.86	23.45	26.33	29.57	33.18	37.25	44.77
12	12.37	13.93	15.64	17.55	19.70	22.14	24.83	27.91	31.33	35.19	39.49	44.33	53.27
13	14.51	16.35	18.36	20.59	23.12	25.98	29.14	32.75	36.77	41.30	46.35	52.03	62.52
14	16.83	18.96	21.29	23.88	26.81	30.14	33.80	37.99	42.64	47.90	53.75	60.34	72.51

Weights in ounces avoirdupois. To convert to pounds avoirdupois, divide by 16 (oz. per lb.).

Index

Card-Making
Techniques from A to Z

Jeanette Robertson

Photos by Michael Hnatov

STERLING

New York / London
www.sterlingpublishing.com

DEDICATION

To Aunt Edith, Uncle Roy,
Grandma Rose, and Mother Viola
for nurturing my creativity

ABOUT THE AUTHOR AND ARTIST

Author and artist Jeanette Robertson began making handmade cards even before she went to grade school. She earned an Associate's Degree in Textile Design at the Fashion Institute of Technology and designed fabric patterns for various New York textile companies. Later she began selling her watercolor art to major greeting card companies.

Her love of patterns is evident in her handmade cards. "The use of pattern with texture and color is more fun than a challenge," Ms. Robertson says. She enjoys playing with the seemingly infinite combination of possible patterns and works toward inventing fresh new designs.

Ms. Robertson lives in Upstate New York with her husband Norman and their golden retriever.

Designed by *Rose Sheifer Graphic Productions*
Photos by *Michael Hnatov Photography*

STERLING and the distinctive Sterling logo are registered trademarks of Sterling Publishing Co., Inc.

Library of Congress Cataloging-in-Publication Data
Robertson, Jeanette, 1950 Oct. 15–
   Greeting cards from A to Z / Jeanette Robertson ; photos by Michael Hnatov.
     p. cm.
  Includes index.
  ISBN-13: 978-1-4027-2351-3
  ISBN-10: 1-4027-2351-2
 1. Greeting cards. I. Title.
  TT872.R63 2006
  745.594'1—dc22

10 9 8 7 6 5 4 3 2 1

Published by Sterling Publishing Co., Inc.
387 Park Avenue South, New York, NY 10016
© 2006 by Jeanette Robertson
Distributed in Canada by Sterling Publishing
C/o Canadian Manda Group, 165 Dufferin Street
Toronto, Ontario, Canada M6K 3H6
Distributed in the United Kingdom by GMC Distribution Services,
Castle Place, 166 High Street, Lewes, East Sussex, England BN7 1XU
Distributed in Australia by Capricorn Link (Australia) Pty. Ltd.
P.O. Box 704, Windsor, NSW 2756, Australia

Printed in China
All rights reserved

Sterling ISBN-13: 978-1-4027-2351-3 (hardcover)
        ISBN-10: 1-4027-2351-2

Sterling ISBN-13: 978-1-4027-5375-6 (paperback)
        ISBN-10: 1-4027-5375-6

For information about custom editions, special sales, premium and corporate purchases, please contact Sterling Special Sales Department at 800-805-5489 or specialsales@sterlingpublishing.com.

Contents

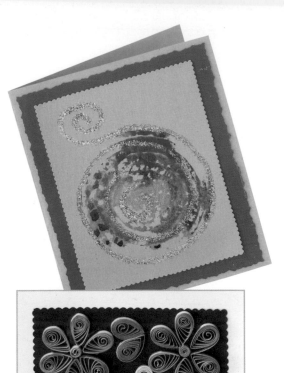

Introduction

In an age of fast food, fast cars, speedy computers, and impromptu e-mails, it's nice to sit down to carefully create a handmade card for a friend, colleague, aunt, sweetheart, child, parent, or someone dear. Making a handmade card shows how much you care. What says "I've been thinking about you" more than something crafted by your own hands and heart?

But not all card creations require slow time or artistic wizardry. In the few minutes it takes to fire up your computer, you can fashion a simple one-of-a-kind card.

The card-making techniques in this book range from the inexpensive (just use recycled materials found around your home) to the extravagant and can even include little gifts like baubles and beads. Whether you're a first-time or a seasoned card crafter, you'll discover fresh techniques that will inspire you to make up a card that's just right for the receiver. We've organized them from A to Z.

After you've chosen a particular technique and studied the finished cards, check the supply list before you begin. Be sure that you have all the necessary materials so that you don't have to stop midway and dash out to the store or a neighbor's house to find just what you're looking for.

We've included tags to identify "quick and easy" card-making techniques as well as other hints. We've also designed cards in a variety of styles. Since you'll have complete control of the creative process, you'll be able to define the style and finished appearance of the card. Depending on the materials you choose and how you put the card together, you'll be able to create cards that are elegant or simple, playful or serious, frilly feminine or handsomely masculine. It's up to you. Our examples are only intended to inspire you.

To make these cards uniquely your own, you could create your own rubber stamps rather than going out to buy them. Rubber stamps would allow you to make multiple cards that look a little alike or that have your personal signature, as it were.

Most of the A-to-Z techniques here allow you to decide how big or small you want the card and decorative elements. For selected cards, when you might need a little more guidance or when dimensions could influence design, we give measurements. If you keep a few standard envelope measurements in mind, that may help if you intend to mail the card. Otherwise, you can craft your own envelope. We'll show you how. Do keep in mind that the post office may charge more for square or unusual sizes of cards, so be sure to ask them or add extra postage if necessary. We advise that you mail the more delicate cards in padded envelopes for extra protection.

Card-Making & Card-Giving Hints
MATCHING CARD DESIGNS WITH RECEIVERS

If you want a handmade artsy card, create broccoli, potato, or onion prints; use snippets of various colors of tissue paper, decorative paper, or calligraphy to create a paper quilt. If you want to remember the 1960s, try a tie-dyed card. If you want to commemorate anniversaries, try framed cards or accordion photo displays. If you'd like to express a little wildness, try an outrageous card with oddities collected from around the house, wild animal stripes or spots, silly feathers, postage stamps, and cockeyed papers. For a formal appearance, use foil or vellum, make a black-and-white card, or use calligraphy or fancy computer-font initials.

For masculine cards, try wood texture; strong, dark colors; sporty objects, images, and decals; favorite photos; conservative stripes; necktie, fish, or car shapes; elements from nature, like bark and twigs; tag-shaped cards; wire or metallic embellishments; zigzag photo cuts; raffia; or squeegee prints.

For feminine-looking cards, try lace; doilies; cutouts; Victorian styles; silk flowers; ribbons; tissue, delicate, and flowery inclusion papers; filigree; baroque styles; and pastels.

For teenage girls, try shaped cards like flip-flops or a glittery telephone, rhinestone cards with personal initials (usually just the first name here), foam appliqués, silk flowers, favorite photos, pet themes, accordion folds, eraser-stamped cards and envelopes (invite teens to help you make them), hangings, inexpensive jewelry, lace, and tissue paper.

For teenage boys, try textures like wood or wool, magnets, sporty images, window cards, favorite photos, and computer-aided graphic designs.

For kids, try shaped cards, like teddy bears; textured cards, like our woolly creature; three-dimensional cards with foam appliqués or raised standout elements; kid die-cuts, alphabets, windows, and cutouts; or oversized cards.

For those with limited vision, try oversized cards or cards with texture. Be sure to make the greeting grand and easy to read. Also work on contrasting colors so that any image or message can be easily seen.

The elderly may appreciate more traditional cards, but you probably know what your great aunt or grandfather likes. Keep in mind that the reading glasses are likely to come out when they sit down to look at your card. Mostly they'll appreciate (young tykes might not) the effort you took in creating something personal, just for them.

For free-form fun, try splatter, squeegee, or sponge prints. When you're in a hurry, make quick-and-easy cards by adding stickers, decals, or appliqués. Or recycle parts from old cards into a new one. A snip here and

there with deckle scissors can also create a fast but pleasing effect. Die-cut cutouts also can dress up an otherwise simple card.

For crafters, try yarn, quilt pins, quilted cards, button adornments, and colorful printed fabrics as well as felts, linens, and woolly and silky textures. Don't forget that brown paper bags make good, natural recycled material, whether for envelopes or elements of card décor. Ordinary tags (the kind used for prices and all sorts of things) can also become crafty-looking design elements.

For a challenge, try silhouettes, scherenschnitte, or paper quilling.

Cards that are their own gifts can include jewelry (small charm, ring, bracelet, or necklace); colorful paper clips; a lottery card inside a pocket; framed photos; a hanging, like a suncatcher or "stained-glass" window; kids' artwork; refrigerator magnets; bookmarks; or a gift pack of greeting cards.

Sympathy card designs best express elegant simplicity and dignity. Include the words "In Sympathy" or write your own heartfelt message. Embossed cardstock; vellum or linen papers; floral, tree, or leafy images; subdued designs; and pastels, whites, creams, and lavenders work nicely here. Avoid busy designs.

To make multiple cards, consider screen prints, vegetable prints, color photocopies of finished cards, printouts of computer-aided designs, silhouettes, ready-made cardstock with embossed designs, or using templates, patterns, or stencils. You could also make large sheets of paper with bubble-wrap, squeegee, splatter, salt, or sponge prints and cut the handmade printed paper into smaller cards.

Don't forget to fashion your own envelope, too. Make border designs with an eraser-stamp, use die-cuts and insert a contrasting colored paper underneath, try linings that coordinate with the card, cut flaps with deckle scissors, or write the receiver's name in calligraphy.

CARD-GIVING HOLIDAYS & OCCASIONS

You know all the usual card-giving holidays—Christmas, Valentine's Day, Mother's Day, Father's Day, Easter, Halloween, Thanksgiving, New Year's, St. Patrick's Day, Kwanza, Passover, and Chanukah—as well as the every-day-card occasions—birthdays, anniversaries, get-wells, friendship, sympathy, graduations, bar mitzvahs. And you've sent or received invitations and announcements for new babies and weddings, enclosed gift cards and tags, or written thank-you cards.

Around the world, festivals celebrate frogs and fish; the moon; animals, kites; snow; tiny paper boats floating with candles or sidewalk luminaria; and more. Imagine how delightful they could be for card-making. Why not April Fool's Day with its pranks and May Day with its rites of spring?

Just for fun, make up your own celebrations. Did your friend buy a new car? Make a card with car decals and a road map. To celebrate Aunt Edith's new puppy, make a card out of some stickers and include a gift certificate for dog food. Your friend began her own catering business, so wish her good luck with a card covered with food stickers, doilies, and miniature forks and spoons. Aunt Polly has just won a prize for her roses; congratulate her with a card featuring tiny silk roses tied with blue ribbon.

Get funky and send out cards for purple hair, pierced ears, a nose job, got a new boyfriend, your son's hard-rock band, got a dent in my car and my husband didn't kill me, Sherie and Avis made sandcastles at the beach, six-year-old Roy just baked his first cake, three-year-old Evan swallowed a button. You get the idea.

Naturally, you won't neglect tried-and-true announcements: Nicki moved into her new house, Toloa won a horse contest, Barbara's dog won the best-behavior award, Ellen took first place in a craft show, Susan finally sold that antique buggy, Kara has graduated from college, we retired and moved South, Kate is getting married, our folks celebrated their 50th wedding anniversary, Geryle has a new job, and more. To acknowledge such occasions, you could fashion, for instance, a house-shaped card, a gold medallion with a ribbon, embossed announcement, dog prints, a mortar made from black felt, images in gold foil, newspaper clippings of job ads arranged with colored-paper clippings, or a photo of your grandparents in a handmade frame card.

Since you'll be able to fashion quick cards yourself, you can honor selected friends when the appropriate month, week, or day arrives. Here are just a few: Black History Month (February), Women's History Month (March), Read-a-Book Month (December), National Firefighters' Week (week when September 11 falls; Canada), Nurse's Week (May 6–12), Administrative Professionals' Day (Wednesday of last full week in April), National Teachers' Day (Tuesday of first full week of May), or Grandparents' Day (first Sunday after Labor Day). Earth Day (April 22 or celebrated on the vernal equinox) and Arbor Day (varies by country and region) are celebrated across the globe.

Don't forget to write on the back of the card that it was hand-crafted by you. How could Sherie, Avis, Aunt Edith, and Norman resist loving you all the more?

You'll find some sources we've used on p. 160.

Accordion Folds

ACCORDION CARD PHOTO GALLERY

keepsake

Create a keepsake accordion photo gallery of your favorite pets or people. These make nice Christmas, anniversary, birthday, graduation, and family reunion gifts.

Here I use a sheet of 11 × 17-inch cardstock and cut it in half lengthwise. In Europe and other countries, long cardstock may vary from these measurements. Make adjustments accordingly. If you have long scrap paper, it's nice to first test your accordion size(s) before using good cardstock.

MATERIALS

extra long cardstock base (11 × 17 inch or about 28 × 43 cm)

paper cutter or sharp scissors

decorative paper

deckle scissors

two-sided tape

text

photographs (pets, family, or friends)

- Cut a long cardstock base in half lengthwise. For best results and a clean cut, use a paper cutter. The finished measurement will be about 5½ inches (14 cm) wide and about 17 inches (43 cm) long.

- Fold this cardstock accordion style. Four faces each about 4½ inch (10.8 cm) wide work pretty well. To achieve clean folds, you can score the cardstock.

- Use a decorative paper, with a theme if you wish, on the front of the card. For this project, I chose pet paw tracks.

- Inside the card are decorative holiday papers forming a simple frame for the photos you plan to mount. Cut all papers with deckle scissors slightly smaller than the four new card faces between the folds.

- Tape the decorative papers to the card with two-sided tape.

- On top of the decorative paper, tape the photos with two-sided tape.

- On small deckle-cut strips of paper, add the names of the pets or people. Or create these names with a computer printout on nice paper and then cut the names into small deckle-edge strips or nameplates. With two-sided tape, center the names below the pets or folks pictured.

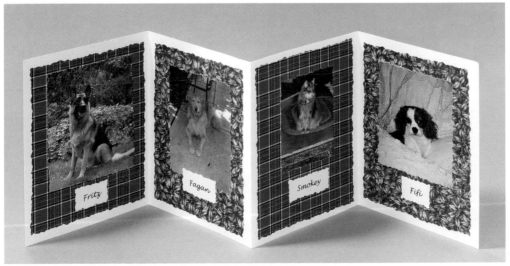

ACCORDION-FOLD INSERTS
challenging

Cards with accordion-folded inserts are multidimensional; the result is impressive. The recipient usually won't expect the surprise that's inside.

This card has assorted sizes and designs of hole-punch cutouts. It's made for a votive candle to sit in its glass container inside the open card. When the candle is lit, you'll see an array of dancing dots. Avoid fire hazards; do not leave the room when the candle is burning.

MATERIALS

ruler	long cardstock
pencil	legal-size paper for insert
craft knife	text
glue stick or two-sided tape	scoring tool
cutting mat	hole punches (assorted)

- To make the accordion-folded paper insert, use legal-size paper. Cut the paper to measure 5 X 12 inches (12.5 X 30.35 cm).

- For this to work correctly, you'll need an even number of folds; we use six folds here.

- Place the paper on a cutting mat. With a ruler and a pencil, measure and mark every 2 inches (5 cm) at both the top and bottom of the 5-inch (12.5-cm) sides. Then use the ruler and a scoring tool to carefully score the areas marked.

- Fold along the scores in and out to create zigzags (viewed from the edge) or an accordion.

Accordion folds for insert.

Firmly holding accordion-fold insert.

Bulldog clip holding accordion fold insert with punched decorative holes.

- Holding the assembly firmly with one hand, cut holes in horizontal rows with different sizes of hole punches. For design variations, you can make the "rows" wavy.

- After you complete punching holes in the entire length of the assembly, you can open the folded paper.

- Cut cardstock to 5 X 10 inches (12.5 X 30 cm). Score the center-fold area and fold. The card will be 5 X 5 inches (12.5 X 12.5 cm).

- You're now ready to attach the accordion insert to the card. Position the folds so that the accordion is inside the card. Make sure to fold the first and last section of the accordion in such a way that the backs of these sections face the inside of the card. Apply glue with a glue stick on one inside fold of the accordion.

- Carefully slip the first fold onto the cover and press the fold so that it adheres to the front edge of the cardstock. Repeat this process for the back of the card. (See photos of finished card.)

HINT: Test the fold position by simply sliding the accordion insert over the card before applying glue. Using ready-made text or text you have created on your computer or by hand on colored paper, you can glue the cutout text to the cover of the card.

IDEAS: Cut musical notes into the accordion for a musician, stars for an astronomy buff, flowers for the gardener, letters for a teacher, or frogs for that princess. Use stickers.

VARIATIONS

For fun variations, consider these ideas. Make a deeper accordion, include lots of designs and fun items, follow a theme, or use a paper print. Follow the directions above and instead of cutting holes, glue on photos, stickers, text, decorative paper scraps, or whatever you like. With a longer accordion insert, you can make more folded panels; just be sure to use even numbers of panels (and an odd number of folds). Attach decorative paper to the cover with a glue stick.

After you finish decorating your accordion, follow the same directions above for attaching the accordion to the card. If you place a bulky item over a fold, you may need to rescore.

Alphabet
quick and easy

The alphabet can serve as decoration or the theme of a card. Here the letters themselves, whether from a typewriter, computer, handwritten script, or elegant calligraphy, become the focus. You can choose letters that are significant or simply spell out a message.

A quick-craft method is to use brads attached to the front of the card. We've found some here with letters that happen to match our sort of typewriter-key print background paper. We've added deckle-cut papers to fill it out.

MATERIALS

cardstock base or stiff decorative paper

colored or decorative paper

two-sided tape

deckle scissors

brads

one-sided tape

● Begin with cardstock or a stiff decorative paper. If your cardstock is plain, cut out decorative paper and attach it to the cardstock with two-sided tape.

● Cut strips from colored or decorative paper into ragged strips with deckle scissors.

● Secure the open brads on the back side of the "cover" cardstock with one-sided tape or package tape. So that the card looks good inside and to secure the brads, cover your work with another decorative or solid-colored paper lining on the verso side of the card face. Adhere the decorative paper to the cardstock with two-sided tape.

● Mail the finished card in a padded envelope.

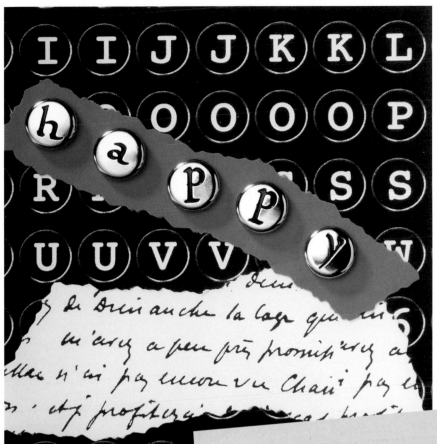

Appliqués
quick and easy

If you find yourself in a pinch for a last-minute card, you can create a quick card with just cardstock and appliqués.

Oops, you forgot that birthday or you wanted something to go with that gift you bought months ago for the cousin you'll be visiting tomorrow. Driving to a store can be inconvenient or take up precious time. Keep a supply of appliqués in your craft supply box. With a nice cache of appliqués, you'll be able to instantly craft a card to fit the many occasions that may arise.

MATERIALS
cardstock base

decorative paper

appliqué

two-sided tape

deckle scissors

optional embellishments

- Use ready-made cardstock base or cut your own cardstock.

- With deckle scissors, cut a decorative paper so that it's slightly smaller than the cardstock dimension. Adhere the decorative paper to the cardstock with two-sided tape.

- Again use two-sided tape to adhere the appliqué or appliqués to the decorative paper. If the appliqué comes with an adhesive backing, you will not need to add tape.

- If you have an appliqué message like "Congratulations," also add that to the decorative paper with its own adhesive backing or two-sided tape. As you wish, you can create your own banner message or simply write it inside the card. Or use brads.

- Mail finished cards in a padded envelope, as necessary.

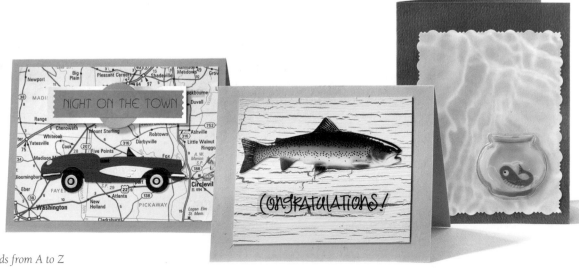

Booklet Cards

easy • multiple uses

> Booklet cards work nicely for photos or vacation shots or mini-journals.

MATERIALS

cardstock base	ribbon
decorative paper	brads
deckle scissors	scoring tool
paper (with or without lines)	ruler
paper cutter	two-sided tape
hole punch	embellishments (optional)
computer text	travel brochure photo
stickers	two-sided tape

- Begin the journal card with a ready-made cardstock. With deckle scissors, cut the decorative paper slightly smaller than the card face.

- Find one or more photos from your travel brochure. Cut them out with deckle scissors. (How many photos you need depends on how many card booklets you want to make.) Adhere the photo to the card face with two-sided tape.

- Borrow text from the travel brochure, create text on your computer, or write it with a calligraphy pen. Secure the text, cut to size, and adhere it to the card with two-sided tape.

- To make pages for the card journal, measure the total inside dimensions of the card. If your card measures $8^{1/2}$ x $5^{1/2}$ inches (21.5 x 14 cm), for instance, cut papers slightly shorter by about $^{1/2}$ inch (1.25 cm) on both sides. So paper for inside pages would measure 8 x 5 inches (20 x 12.5 cm). When folded, each page will be 5 x 4 inches (12.5 x 10 cm).

- Four paper sheets will give you eight pages to write on after they're folded. Five folded sheets will give you ten pages. For a one-week vacation, four sheets (eight booklet pages) is just right.

- Make good clean cuts with a paper cutter. Score and fold the sheets of paper pages and put them into the card fully open.

- With a hole punch, punch two holes through all layers. If this is too hard, punch holes in each layer separately, but be sure that the holes line up.

- Thread a 1/2-inch or thinner ribbon (allow about 2 feet or 60 cm) through the holes a few times to secure the pages to the card cover and tie a bow outside the card at the fold.

BRADS OR FASTENERS

Instead of ribbon and punched holes, you can secure pages to the card with brads or fasteners.

After inserting folded pages inside the card, close the card booklet "cover." With a hole punch or small nail, bore a hole through all layers of cardstock and paper near the fold and about 1 inch (2.5 cm) from the top. Be careful to keep your fingers out of the way.

After making your first hole, insert the brad and open its prongs on the back of the card. Still holding the layers firmly, make a second hole near the fold and about 1 inch (2.5 cm) from the card bottom. Insert the second brad and secure it.

To make the booklet easier to open when writing, score the card cover. Position a metal ruler near the fold, just beyond the brad, and use your scoring tool to score only the card cover.

HINT: You can also use lightweight card-stock sheets for the inside pages and cut them at the same size as the card cover. You can feature photos, messages, or other things inside the multipage card. Secure the pages with colorful raffia, ribbon, cord, or yarn.

Bookmark Cards

quick and easy • gift

What could be more delightful than receiving two gifts in one card? On the outside of the card is a bookmark and inside the card is a gift card to a bookstore or a new library card. Most large chain bookstores sell gift cards in different denominations. The recipient will both enjoy the book and use the bookmark you made.

Of course, if you wish, you can insert a magnetic gift card from another kind of shop, but books works well with the theme.

MATERIALS

cardstock base	hole punch
cardstock for bookmark	gift card
decorative paper	two-sided tape
ribbon	stickers

- Make a long card out of cardstock.

- Using decorative cardstock, recycled cards, or recycled gift tags, make a bookmark slightly smaller than the card cover.

- Center the bookmark over the cover of the card, and using a hole punch, punch a hole through both items.

- Thread a ribbon through the holes and tie one knot. Allow the ribbon to dangle a little.

- Inside the card, adhere the gift card to the card with stickers on all four corners of the card. They will keep the card in place. You won't want to glue or tape the back of the store gift card to the paper card if the store gift card has a magnetic strip.

Borders

BORDER LAYERS
quick and easy • fun

Borders can be created very easily by just layering decorative papers. Use contrasting colors and patterns, monochromes, or combine both techniques to make a visually appealing design.

Laugh 'til it hurts!

MATERIALS

patterned cardstock base

two-sided tape or glue stick

text

deckle scissors

decorative papers

ruler

pencil

- Use a patterned cardstock base.

- Going through scrapbook paper leftovers, you may find pretty patterns and colors. I picked out a ready-made greeting.

- Use two or more decorative papers in different sizes and layer them one on top of the other. (The card in the photo uses two.)

- To create borders, measure and mark rectangles of the desired size (each can be about 1/2 inch or 1.25 cm smaller than the other) on the back side of the decorative papers; cut out the rectangles with deckle scissors. Remove the rectangles. What remains will be framelike borders.

- With two-sided tape or a glue stick, adhere the largest border to the card face first, and then each smaller one on top. All layers create borders.

- Finally, with two-sided tape, attach a greeting.

ERASER-STAMP BORDERS
quick and easy • hand-printed

Follow directions for making an eraser-stamp from an oridinary pencil eraser on p. 46. I've shaped a square design from my eraser. By changing ink-pad colors you can make the design more interesting and colorful.

MATERIALS

cardstock base

preprinted text greeting

eraser-stamp

ink pad (several colors)

two-sided tape

- Begin with a cardstock base.

- Create a text greeting or recycle one from an old greeting card. Fasten the greeting to the center of the card with two-sided tape.

- Use an eraser-stamp loaded with ink from an ink pad to randomly print your design all around the outside edge to create your first border.

- Change ink-pad colors and create a second border around the text area by randomly stamping the design about 1/4 inch (0.63 cm) from the text box.

PAPER-BAND BORDERS

Borders just dress up a card cover like few things can. I like them because they can be simple or complex, dazzling or plain. It's up to you.

MATERIALS

cardstock base

decorative or colored paper

computer text or other text

glue stick or two-sided tape

deckle scissors

ruler

eraser-stamp print (optional)

- Begin with cardstock base.

- Measure bands of paper about ½ inch (1.25 cm) wide, and on the underside of the decorative or colored paper, draw a light pencil line so that you'll know where to cut. With deckle scissors, cut out the four bands of paper.

- With a glue stick or two-sided tape, adhere the paper bands to the card face about ¼ inch (0.63 cm) in from the edge.

- Create text on your computer or write it by hand. If you're feeling creative, snip and fray the edges of the paper with scissors. Scissors fringe cuts can be about ¼ to ½ inch (0.63 to 1.25 cm) deep. Attach the text to the card with a glue stick or two-sided tape; be careful not to tape or glue the fringed parts.

Broccoli Prints
multiple cards

Broccoli may have always been an ordinary vegetable to you, but it is very pretty when used as a stamp.

Stamp ink or paint can be used to make the prints. The best bonus about broccoli stamps is that you can make multiple cards from a single slice of broccoli. Make as many as you want. If you vary the colors and embellishments, you won't tire of the design.

MATERIALS

base cardstock

fresh broccoli

kitchen paring knife

kitchen cutting board

ink pad, watercolor, or acrylic paints

artist's paintbrush

embellishments

- Using a sharp kitchen knife, carefully cut a section of broccoli lengthwise.

- Dip the broccoli in an ink pad or, using an artist's paintbrush, cover the cut flat side of the broccoli with watercolor or acrylic paint.

- Firmly press the length of broccoli to the cardstock. Carefully remove the broccoli from the cardstock.

- You may repeat this process as many times as you like.

- Embellish as desired. I've used a hole punch and inserted raffia that's tied into a bow in the front of the card.

- Discard the broccoli when you're finished. And naturally, wash your hands well before sitting down to a meal…of something else.

Bubble-Wrap Prints

BUBBLE-WRAP CARDS
handmade

Dress up the bubble-wrap prints by using deckle scissors, text appliqué, and contrasting cardstock or papers.

MATERIALS

cardstock

bubble-wrap printed paper (see p. 25)

deckle scissors

glue stick or two-sided tape

text appliqué or decal (optional)

- Choose a cardstock base.

- Cut a piece of bubble-wrap printed paper with deckle scissors, slightly smaller than the face of the card.

- With deckle scissors, cut out a smaller piece of contrasting colored paper. Make it about $1/2$ inch (1.25 cm) shorter than the bubble wrap on both sides. It could be about $1 1/4$ inches (3.25 cm) high.

- With a glue stick or two-sided tape, adhere the bubble-wrap printed paper to the front of the card (the cardstock base).

- Adhere the smaller contrasting paper to the bubble-wrap printed paper with a glue stick or two-sided tape.

- If desired, affix a greeting appliqué or decal to the paper. If you do not have a decal or appliqué, you can also use a greeting printed out from your computer in a pleasing font or one that you write by hand.

BUBBLE-WRAP PRINTED PAPER
easy • allow time

Everyone buys products cushioned in packages with bubble wrap. I like to use the smaller bubbles for hand-printed paper. If you play with colors, you can get wonderful results. This texture is easy to create, but allow time for the paint to dry. I bet your recipient will be trying to guess exactly how you created such an interesting design.

MATERIALS

cardstock base or heavy drawing paper

watercolor paint

artist's flat paintbrush (1 to 2 inches or 2.5 to 5 cm wide)

water

bubble wrap

- Be sure to use heavy drawing paper or cardstock.

- When using watercolor paint mixed with water, you must work quickly to achieve a successful result. Randomly brush paint onto the paper.

- Quickly cover the wet painted paper with the bubble wrap, bumpy bubbles down. Press firmly. Take a heavy book and put it on top of the dry side of the bubble wrap. The weight will put pressure on the bubbles, aiding the creation of the print.

- After a few hours or the next day, remove the book and bubble wrap.

HINT: If you're afraid that you'll get paint on the book or other heavy object, slip it inside a large freezer-type zipped plastic bag.

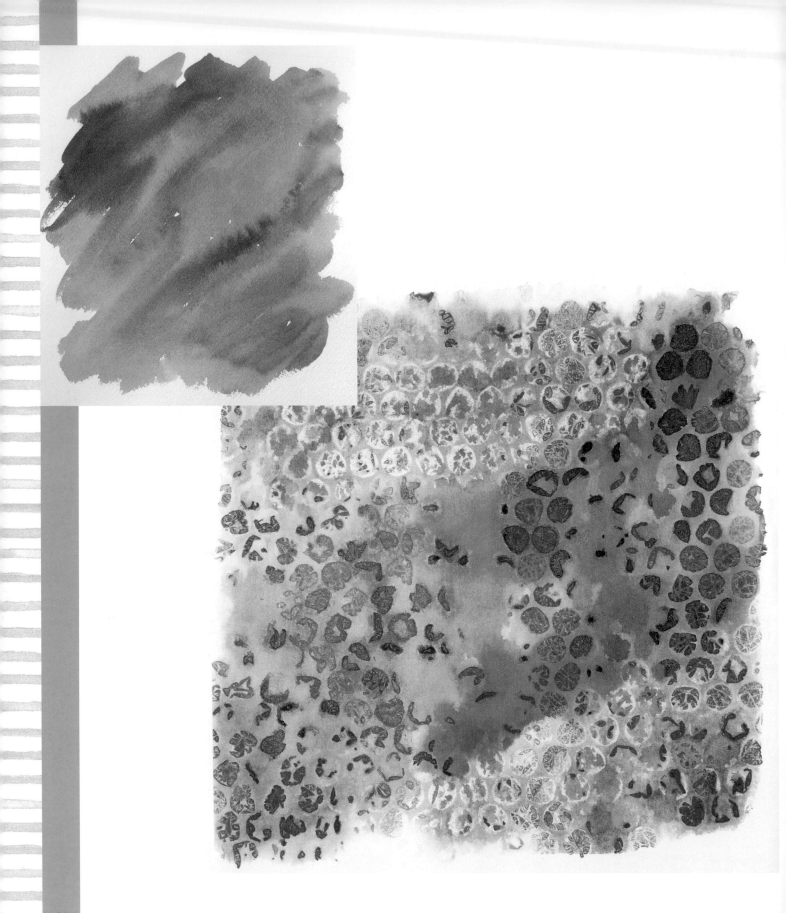

Greeting Cards from A to Z

Buttons
off-the-wall • recycled

Sometimes it's fun to be a little silly. If you're like me, you have an assortment of buttons that go only with clothing you've discarded long ago. I like to collect them and recycle them into my card-making projects.

MATERIALS

colored cardstock base

decorative paper

deckle scissors

two-sided tape

assorted buttons

hard-bonding glue

hole punch

ribbon

- Use a cardstock base.

- Cut decorative paper with deckle scissors into a rectangle slightly smaller than the face of the card. Adhere it to the cardstock with two-sided tape.

- Arrange buttons in various colors and sizes on the decorative paper. When you achieve the desired design, put a little spot of glue on the decorative paper and press down on the button. Attach the remaining buttons the same way.

- Allow the glue to dry thoroughly.

- With a hole punch, make two small holes close together near the fold of the card.

- String ribbon through the holes and tie the ribbon in a bow on the front of the card.

- Mail the finished card in a padded envelope.

Clip Art
quick and easy • computer-aided • multiple cards

Clip art can be found nearly everywhere. Many computer software programs have it, and bookstores sell clip-art books (Sterling has many) that are public domain, which means that they're not copy-righted. Many pieces of clip art found in books, such as Dover's, date from the 19th century and so lend that flavor. Some books include more contemporary images. Computer clip art has a wide variety of themes. Be sure that what you're using doesn't have any copyright or trademark issues.

MATERIALS

clip art

glue stick or two-sided tape

colored or textured card-stock base

decorative paper (optional)

deckle scissors

photocopier

rhinestones, sequins, or other embellishments (optional)

hard-bonding glue (optional)

- Select clip-art designs that appeal to you.
- Cut out the designs and adhere them to cardstock or decorative paper with a glue stick or two-sided tape.
- Make a photocopy of the card on a colored or textured cardstock.
- If you wish, embellish with rhinestones or sequins, using hard-bonding glue to adhere the stones to the card.
- If you use embellishments, mail the finished card in a padded envelope.

Computer-Aided Photo Cards

computer-aided design • multiple cards

You don't have to be an artist to be able to create appealing cards. Inexpensive computer programs can achieve spectacular results. You don't even have to be especially computer savvy to fashion unique cards.

These instructions are for a PC; those for a Mac will be similar.

Adobe Photoshop is the most sophisticated and popular image and photo-manipulation software, used by professionals and amateurs alike. Adobe Photoshop Elements is a less expensive, simpler version. Other software programs can do many of the same things, and many new computers, whether Macs or PCs, come bundled with photo software.

Layout software, like Quark XPress and Adobe InDesign, also allow you to manipulate images in simple ways with color boxes, silhouettes, contorted dimensions, wrapped text, and more.

MATERIALS

cardstock base

digital or print photo and photo scanner

computer

photo manipulation software

computer color printer

laser paper

- On your computer, double-click the Adobe Photoshop or other photo icon.

- On your File menu, click Open and go to the desired folder and photo file. Or if you have a photo on a CD, go to the disk drive on your computer to open the CD where you've stored a photo or other picture that you want to work with. (On a Mac, the CD icon will appear on the desktop.) Double-click the file to open it or simply click "open" after you've selected the appropriate file from your photo file list.

- Before you do anything to the photo or other image, save it under a new name. You do that by clicking on the File menu, and selecting "Save as." You can even save it in a new folder. That way you'll keep the original photo clean in case you don't like your results and want to start fresh.

- Go to Filter on the menu bar. When the Filter menu bar drops down, you'll have lots of options. You can blur, stylize, sharpen, and do lots of things. Play around and see what effects you like.

- See examples of how you can alter a photo that shows a row of deck chairs on p. 31. Our photo software computer options created colored pencil, cutout, stained glass, ocean, pallette knife, and poster edges.

- After you find what you like, click on OK. Save the image.

- Click on the File menu and then click the Printer Setup option. Choose the paper size and orientation you want to print. For orientation, the portrait option gives you more height than width, and the landscape option allows more width than height.

- Choose the size and number of altered photos you want to print.

- Click on Print (or OK).

Original

(Filter, Artistic) Colored Pencil

(Filter, Artistic) Cutout

(Filter, Texture) Stained Glass

(Filter, Distort) Ocean Ripple

(Filter, Artistic) Poster Edges

Cutouts

fun • challenging

If flowers will make you smile...

...then here's a bunch so smile a lot

Cutouts in the cover or face of the card partially reveal what's inside the card. These cutouts can be in many small shapes or be themselves large windows to reveal an image or message inside. (Also see Windows on p. 151.)

MATERIALS

cardstock base

craft knife

cutting mat

flowers photo

computer or handwritten text

green marking pen

two-sided tape or glue stick

- Begin with cardstock base.

- On the inside of the card, adhere a photo of flowers using two-sided tape or a glue stick.

- On the card cover, with the card open, cut the shape of a flower in the middle of the card. When the card is closed, part of the floral photo should show through the cover's cutout or window. If you wish, cut a hole or window where the flowers on the photo will show. With a green marking pen, draw a stem and leaf on the cover coming out of the cutout flower.

- Write one to three cheerful lines with computer or handwritten text. Have one part of the text on the cover of the card and use the rest inside the card. For a little more interest, instead of cutting the text paper, tear it by hand, and adhere it to the card with a glue stick.

Decals
quick and easy

In most craft, art, and stationery stores you'll find a wealth of decals and decorative papers to use for card-making.

    If your recipient has a hobby or occupation, decals are most likely available with the appropriate images or themes. Most decals are self-sticking, which makes your job easier. The fun is selecting decals and decorative papers to mix and match.

MATERIALS

cardstock base

decals

decorative paper(s)

glue stick or two-sided tape

deckle scissors

embellishments (optional)

- Use a contrasting or coordinating card base, or cover the card-stock base completely with decorative paper.

- Cut a piece of decorative paper with a paper cutter or craft knife if you want a straight edge, or use deckle scissors if you'd prefer a decorative edge.

- Adhere the decorative paper to the cardstock with two-sided tape or a glue stick.

- Adhere decals to the decorative paper using a glue stick or two-sided tape if the decals are not preglued.

- Embellish as desired.

- Mail delicate finished cards in a padded envelope.

Deckle Edges

quick and easy

Depending on what you do with your scissor cuts, deckle edges could work for a jagged Halloween message, rounded scallops for a fancy and lacy valentine, watery waves for a bon voyage, egg-and-darts for an Art Nouveau appearance, kid cuts for a child's birthday, or an odd assortment of cuts for humorous cards.

A simple vertical or horizontal cut along one edge of your paper may be all you need. Deckle edges, depending on the kind and the materials you use, can make any card go from plain to fancy, simple to formal, or just-OK to something on the wild side.

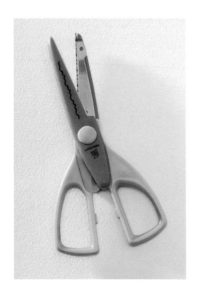

Here are a few hints.

- Most deckle scissors have a "repeat" pattern. When making a long continuous cut, it is best to match up the repeat. If the pattern is random, there won't be a problem.

- Cut the front right edge of the card with deckle, revealing the usual straight card edge below.

- It's OK to use any paper, foil, or cardstock as long as the deckle scissors can make a clean cut. Very thin foil or rice paper will not cut well. Corrugated stock would not be suitable. Drawing a light pencil line would help guide your cutting.

- Cut your paper or cardstock in a position in which you are comfortable. I usually hold my paper off my work table. You may be more comfortable cutting on the table. Aside from straight cuts, you can be creative and cut at angles, curves, random shapes, circles, measured, or freestyle. The creation can be as simple as cutting one edge, or you can get carried away and make lots of cuts with different deckle edges all on one card.

Decorative Papers
quick and easy

You can quickly and easily create a card using simply a cardstock base and decorative paper or even leftover wrapping paper. A quick cut with deckle scissors and you'll have the card face ready for your message.

MATERIALS

cardstock base

decorative paper or wrapping paper

deckle scissors

two-sided tape

embellishment (optional)

message (ink on paper or computer-generated)

- Begin with cardstock base.

- Using deckle scissors, cut a square or rectangle of decorative paper or wrapping paper a little smaller than the card face.

- With two-sided tape, adhere the decorative paper to the front of the card.

- Carefully position and adhere your message to the decorative paper with two-sided tape.

- Add any embellishments desired.

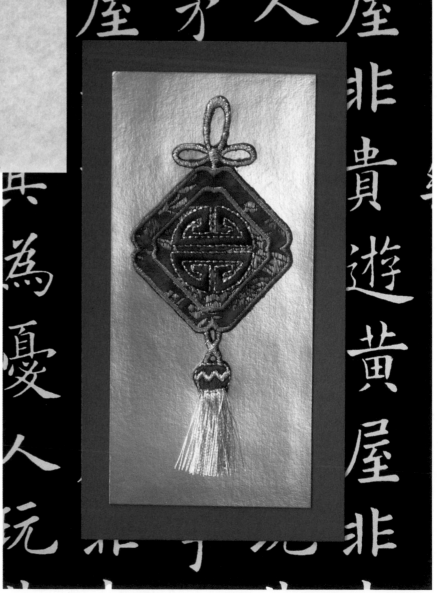

Die-Cuts

quick and easy • elegant simplicity

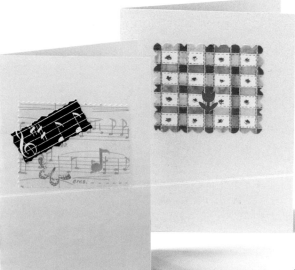

Combine the use of die-cuts with fabulous colored cardstock and decorative papers, and you have a winning card design. Or you can use dramatic black-and-white cardstock. Your friends and family will be impressed. This is one card that a home computer and printer cannot make!

Die-cuts are inexpensive and can be found in arts and crafts stores. They punch small decorative holes in paper and cardstock. You'll find many designs to choose from, such as music notes, flowers, butterflies, snowflakes, hearts, and more. Corner die-cut devices usually have built-in guides to help you correctly position the paper or cardstock.

MATERIALS

cardstock base

decorative or colored paper

die-cut

deckle scissors

two-sided tape or glue stick

embellishment (optional)

- Use a ready-made cardstock or cut your own.

- Cut decorative or colored papers with a deckle edge into rectangular or square shapes.

- Use a die cut to make the desired design in the paper rectangles or squares. Adhere the decorative paper to the cardstock with a glue stick or two-sided tape. Layer one or more papers on the cardstock. You'll want to use contrasting colors so that the die-cut or cutout appears clean and clear against the second color background.

- Embellish as desired.

Embossed Cards

EMBOSSING PROCESS
moderately challenging

Embossed cardstock is readily available; you can make attractive cards very quickly with it. Although making your own embossed cards is a little more challenging, the results are well worth it. You'll need to buy a stencil, cardstock, and stylus. When using a stencil, a light box is usually necessary to work on your design.

Or simply find an embossing kit with all the tools you'll need contained neatly in one box. A kit eliminates the need for a light box. An embossing kit also makes it easier to line up desired motifs. For this card, I've used a kit.

MATERIALS

cardstock base

paper

embossing kit or tools (stencils, stylus, working surface, pegs to hold stencils)

letter and other embossing stencils

light box (optional)

two-sided tape

glue stick

- Begin with letter stencils.

- Using the guidelines that are on the embossing stencil, place the cardstock upside down over the reversed stencil. A reversed stencil will have the letters upside down also. The reason for this is that when you rub the stylus in the motif, the embossing will come out correctly when finished. The embossing is pushing the cardstock or paper forward and away from you. When turned around, the embossed surface will be raised.

- Position the cardstock or paper over the first letter you want to work with. Once in place, use your stylus to firmly press down on the image in the stencil. Work around the edges and then move to the middle of the letter.

- When finished, move the cardstock to another letter and repeat the first process. Use the guidelines to keep the letters in line. Or you can put the letters at an angle for a different look.

- After you complete the letters, add a border.

- Change the stencil and use one with lines, designs, and borders. A wavy line was used in this design. When I finished the bottom line, below my letters, I moved the cardstock to position the wavy line above the letters.

- After doing all this, I wanted to add a little more pizzazz. So I used a stencil with dots. I kept moving my cardstock to position the dots along the wavy lines.

LAYERING WITH EMBOSSED CARDSTOCK

- Use a colorful cardstock base.

- With regular or deckle scissors, cut colorful embossed cardstock slightly smaller than the cardstock base. Adhere the embossed cardstock to the cardstock base with two-sided tape or a glue stick.

- Arrange appliqués on top of the embossed cardstock if desired.

Using a stylus to emboss a shape onto cardstock.

HINT: You can create an elegant card made with ivory-colored cardstock and just embossing.

MONOGRAM WITH COLOR EMBOSSING
moderately challenging

This isn't your grandmother's monogram. Take a classic monogram and turn it modern with the "in" colors of the year. This design uses hot pink, orange, and lime. Add a little die-cut and deckle edge for a little more zip to the design.

MATERIALS

cardstock base

colored paper

embossing kit

die-cut motif

two-sided tape

glue stick

deckle scissors

hole punch

paper cutter

● Using colored paper, emboss the word LOVE into one colored paper. Follow the embossing directions on p. 38.

● Cut out the word with deckle scissors. This piece measures 1¹/₂ x 3¹/₂ inches (about 4 x 9 cm).

● Using a second colored paper, emboss a decorative line. A wavy line was used here. The parallel lines are spaced about 2 inches (5 cm) apart. Cut out this paper on a paper cutter to measure 2¹/₂ x 4 inches (6 x 10 cm).

● With two-sided tape, adhere the LOVE paper to the wavy-line paper.

● Adhere the assembled papers askew to a base cardstock that's about 5 x 4¹/₄ inches (12.5 x 11 cm). Use two-sided tape.

● Using a flower die-cut, cut out two flowers in paper.

● With a hole punch, cut a center hole in the flowers. Adhere the flowers to the cardstock with a glue stick.

READY-MADE EMBOSSED FRAME CARD
quick and easy

Embossed cardstocks are sensual to the touch. The raised design is usually the same color as the cardstock, while the embossed surface reflects light and shadows. Your cards can be elegant or fun, depending on what you do with your creativity.

Embossed designs go nicely with other card-making techniques, too. Embossed cardstock makes an attractive frame for art or a photo.

MATERIALS

embossed cardstock base

art or photo

scissors or deckle scissors

two-sided tape or glue stick

one-sided tape (optional)

● Choose a cardstock with a subtle embossed design.

● Cut out a piece of art or use a photograph for the center of the card. If you wish, cut a deckle edge on the art or photo.

● With a glue stick or two-sided tape, adhere the art or photo to the embossed cardstock.

HINT: You can also use an embossed mat or frame and adhere it to the cardstock with two-sided tape or a glue stick. First tape the photo or artwork facedown to the back of the mat or frame. Then mount the photo and frame on the cardstock with two-sided tape.

Envelopes

DIE-CUT ENVELOPE FLAPS
quick and easy

Die-cuts come in a variety of shapes. You'll find stars, flowers, leaves, geometric shapes, hearts, snowflakes, shamrocks, and much more. The smaller die-cuts will allow you to suggest constellations of stars or a mini-snowstorm. Larger ones may be easier to manage and suit kids' projects. You could choose the child's initial(s) or a simple boat, plane, car, cat, or dog.

MATERIALS
envelope
die-cut(s)
colored paper
one-sided tape

- Holding the envelope steady, punch your die-cut design into the envelope's flap.

- On the inside of the flap, cover the newly punched hole(s) with contrasting colored paper cut to size. Using one-sided tape, adhere the paper to the envelope's flap.

- When you close the flap you'll see a cutout with colored paper showing through.

HINT: Experiment with the effects of individual die-cuts on inexpensive test paper (we use photocopier paper or even newsprint) before committing your design to an envelope. Of course, a single die-cut window added to an envelope (or indeed a card) may be all you need.

HANDMADE ENVELOPES
challenging • fits any card size

Since you're fashioning your own card, you may have odd sizes that don't quite fit existing envelopes. Here's how you can create your own envelope to fit any card size.

MATERIALS

paper for envelope

ruler

pencil

craft knife

cutting mat or cardboard

two-sided tape or glue stick

decal, sticker, or melted-wax sealing tools (optional)

- For an average-size card, you'll need at least a 12 X 12-inch (30 X 30-cm) sheet of paper. To make an envelope for a really large card, you may need to use paper that comes on a roll or find another thin (not as heavy as cardstock) oversized paper. Directions here will suit an envelope that fits on large scrapbook paper

- Measure with a ruler and mark the areas for the card, top, bottom, and side flaps with your pencil. See the diagram and note particulars below. You'll be drawing light pencil lines that you'll then cut out.

- Keep in mind that the area reserved for the card needs to be a little larger than the card itself. Allow extra space at the top and on one side: 3/8 inch (1 cm), or about the thickness of a pencil.

- Make the bottom flap shorter than the card by about 3/4 inch (2 cm), or the width of your thumb.

- Make the pointy V-shaped top flap half the height of the card area.

- For the smaller side flaps, measure parallel to the envelope sides about 3/4 inch (2 cm) or the width of your thumb. Draw a light pencil line from top to bottom.

- With your craft knife, cut along your drawn outline of the envelope. (See the solid line in the diagram.)

- Score the rectangle or square area reserved for your card on the marked and printed side. (See the dotted line in the diagram.)

- To make folding and gluing easier, clip a little angle off the **side flaps'** four corners. Fold in the sides and apply glue or two-sided tape. Then fold the **bottom flap** up and secure it with two-sided tape or glue.

- We want a **pointed top flap**. Find the center of the top flap (top, outer edge) and mark it lightly with your pencil. Measure up from the card area (see dotted line in diagram) on each side of the top flap 1¼ inches (3 cm), or about the width of two fingers, and mark these spots. To create the pointed flap, using a craft knife and ruler, cut away from the left side to the center point and from the right side to the center point. And you're done.

- If you'd prefer a more decorative top flap, cut the edges forming the point with deckle scissors.

- Insert the card into the finished envelope. Fold the top flap down. Secure the top flap with a decal, sticker, glue, or two-sided tape. If you want it to be fancy, use melted-wax seal with the desired impression.

HINTS: Remember that less weighty envelopes and cards are less expensive to send abroad. If you don't want to make a V-shaped flap, you could use 8½ x 11-inch (21.5 x 28 cm or A4) paper to create an envelope with a square or rounded flap.

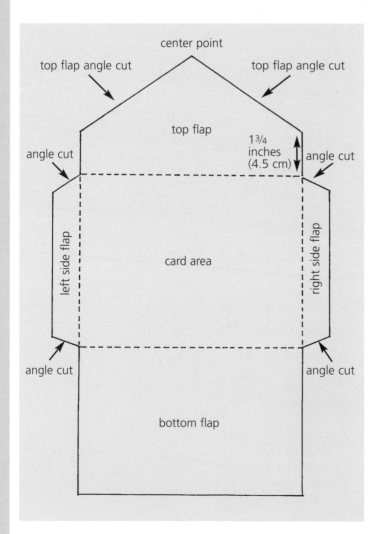

LININGS FOR ENVELOPES AND FLAPS
recycled paper

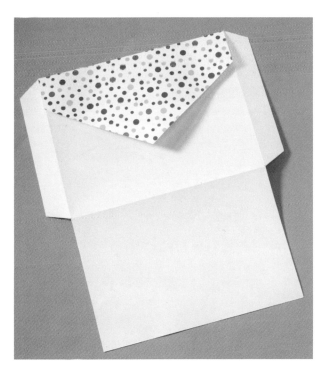

- Select a V-shaped flap envelope that will fit your finished card.

- With deckle scissors, cut V-shaped decorative papers to fit the flap.

- With a glue stick, completely cover the underside of the decorative papers.

- Place decorative paper on the inside of the envelope flap, making sure that it's smooth. Make sure that the flap is dry and that no excess glue oozes out. Cut the edge of the decorative-paper flap with deckle scissors.

LININGS FOR ENVELOPES

The procedure for lining envelopes begins with a flat, not-yet-folded envelope. Simply use a glue stick to adhere the decorative paper to the flat, unfolded envelope paper, then fold, shape, and create the envelope as you normally would. Another option would be to use decorative paper that's printed on one side and plain on the outside. (See Handmade Envelopes on pp. 43–44.)

Eraser-Stamps

quick and easy

MAKING THE ERASER-STAMP

From an ordinary pencil eraser, we can create our own inky "stamps." Try using your eraser-stamp with one or more ink stamp pads (having different colors is nice); you'll be all set to have fun.

MATERIALS

pencil with clean "new" eraser tip
craft or X-acto knife

- Cut a triangle, square, hexagon, circle, or other shape into an unused pencil eraser. Or use the eraser as-is for a dot motif.

- With a sharp craft knife, carefully cut away from the eraser tip what you do not want printed. For the triangle, make one clean cut down from the top of the eraser on each of the three sides, turning the eraser for each cut. Slice down to the metal band. Remove excess eraser parts.

  - One way is to cut vertically down the eraser from the top and then remove the excess by cutting in, horizontally, near the metal band from the side.

- Another way is to insert the knife back into the three cuts and twist the knife blade away from the center and toward the eraser's outside edge.

- As you become more practiced, you'll be able to make more shallow cuts in the eraser (see drawing), which will give your eraser stamp more stability.

HINT: Avoid using old, hard, and brittle erasers. They do not easily absorb or transfer ink.

CAUTION: Craft or X-acto knives are very sharp. To protect your hand from cuts, make a cardboard shield about 4 inches (10 cm) square. Cut a small hole in the center and slide the pencil through it. Hold the pencil underneath the shield while you use the other hand to cut and shape the eraser.

USING THE ERASER-STAMP

You'll figure out lots of ways to dress up cards with eraser-stamp borders and other geometric images.

White envelopes are fine, but even a little bit of color can be fabulous. Make a bold design statement by embellishing your envelopes with unique stamped designs that you've created. Dress up that padded envelope, too.

MATERIALS

eraser-stamp

ink stamp pad(s)

cardstock base or plain paper

plain or padded envelope

- After you've made your pencil eraser-stamp, you can begin printing. You may want to practice a little on scrap paper or newspaper.

- Dip the eraser in an ink pad and then press it firmly onto the card or envelope. Use multiple colors or metallic ink for variety.

- What's great is that the eraser-stamp will last a long time.

HINTS: Play with random printing. You can also make stripes, plaids, waves, lines, and other patterns with eraser prints. Let your children have a go at it, too. Use other shapes on another card or envelope. The more the merrier. You may want to avoid stamping in the area on the envelope where you'll put the postage stamp; some inks may prevent the stamp glue from sticking completely.

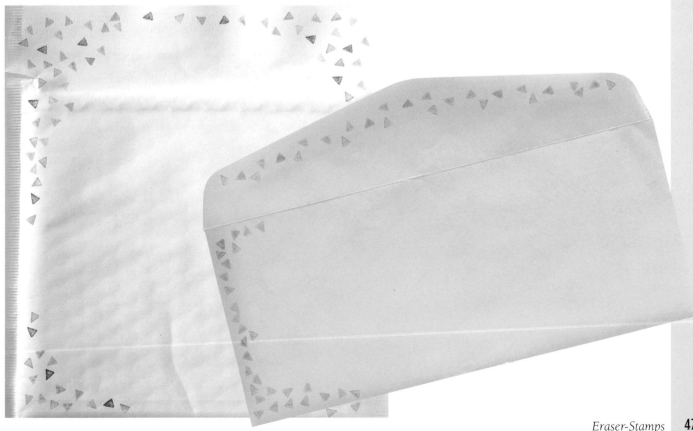

Flowers
feminine

Combine silk flowers with decorative paper to create a lovely feminine card for a female friend, cousin, sister, mom, aunt, or grandmother.

MATERIALS

silk flower

raffia or ribbon

cardstock

decorative papers

two-sided tape or glue stick

hole punch

deckle scissors (optional)

● Select a pretty colored cardstock.

● With deckle or other scissors, cut a contrasting piece of decorative paper slightly smaller than the front of the card.

● With a glue stick or two-sided tape, adhere the paper to the front of the cardstock.

● Cut a second decorative paper slightly smaller than the first paper, and adhere it with a glue stick or two-sided tape to the first decorative paper. If you wish, you can use deckle scissors on decorative paper.

● Use a hole punch to make two small holes near each other on the front of the card where you want to secure the small silk flower or silk flowers bouquet.

● Thread raffia or ribbon through the holes and tie small silk flower(s) to the card.

● Finish with a bow.

● Mail the card in a padded envelope.

Foam Appliqués

quick and easy

Foam appliqués can be found at most craft shops. They're usually self-sticking. Match the appliqués with appropriate decorative paper, and you'll have a winner. I've used a beach towel and flip-flops to suggest a lazy summer theme. For another I chose a cat and dog with suggestive paw prints. The third card shows embossed cardstock with subtle swirls echoed in the foam-appliqué swirls and the dragonfly appliqué.

MATERIALS

cardstock base

decorative paper

foam appliqués

glue stick

deckle scissors

tag (optional)

brads (optional)

- Use a firm cardstock (embossed, if you wish) when working with foam appliqués because they're thick and a little heavier than most paper and other objects you'd want to glue to the cardstock.

- Find decorative paper with a theme that complements the appliqué. (You could try handmade salt paper.) Using deckle scissors, cut the decorative paper slightly smaller than the cover of the card.

- Adhere the decorative paper to the front of the cardstock with a glue stick or two-sided tape.

- Position the foam appliqués on the decorative paper, remove the paper backing, reposition them, and press down, making sure that they stick securely. If you wish, add a tag, securing it with brads.

- Mail the finished card in a padded envelope.

Formal-Dress Cards

sophisticated • black and gold

Just as a little black dress or indeed a tuxedo with tails appears elegant and sophisticated, black greeting cards can, too. Ordinary paper will not do here; we'll need something unique. A little bit of gold paper or gold foil will enhance the look. We've also added a little rice paper. This will surely bring appreciative sighs. Send this card for that formal or fancy-dress occasion.

Rice paper, often handmade in a variety of designs, can be found at most arts and crafts stores.

MATERIALS

black cardstock base

deckle scissors

two-sided tape

gold paper

handmade rice paper

gold ink pen (optional)

- Begin with a black cardstock base.

- With deckle scissors, cut the cover of the card slightly shorter than the back of the card.

- Keep your deckle scissors handy by cutting gold paper slightly larger than the piece you've removed from the front of the card.

- Adhere the gold paper to the inside bottom edge of the card using two-sided tape.

- Cut another piece of gold paper for the front of the card and put it aside.

- Cut or tear off a piece of rice paper.

- Adhere the rice paper to the cover of the card with two-sided tape.

- Using two-sided tape, place the reserved gold paper on top of the rice paper.

- Write your greeting on the inside of the card with a gold ink pen. If you choose not to use the gold ink pen, you could instead paste white paper on the inside of the card so that you'll have a place to write your message in ordinary ink. You can give that white paper a deckle edge as well to create a more elegant look.

- Top this off with an envelope with a gold-foil interior; you'll find one in a stationery store. If not, make your own (see Envelopes).

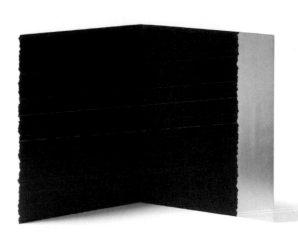

Frames

MAKING YOUR OWN FRAME
challenging

If you want to start from scratch, you can make your own frame in desired proportions or sizes. For sharp, clean cuts, we advise using a metal ruler, X-acto blade, and a cutting mat.

MATERIALS

metal ruler

pencil

triangle tool or
T square

colored cardboard or
stiff paper for frame

cutting mat or card-
board (to protect
work surface)

craft knife (or X-acto
knife)

● Decide what size you want the frame to be on the outside.

● Using your triangle or T square and a pencil, draw a right angle on the colored cardboard.

● You now have two straight sides.

● Measure one side to be the long side of the frame and put a pencil mark along the line.

● Measure the other side and put a pencil mark at the end of the dimension you want.

● Using one side of the triangle, align the edge closely along one of the lines and at the pencil mark you drew.

● Draw a line for the third side of the frame.

● Line up the triangle to the other line at the pencil mark and draw the fourth side of the frame.

● When you've determined the outside dimension, you can cut it out with your craft knife.

● With your ruler, measure 1 inch (2.54 cm) in from each side and draw a pencil line.

● Using your craft knife and ruler, cut out the hole of the frame.

● Do all your cutting on thick cardboard or a craft cutting mat to protect your work table.

FRAME TEMPLATE

Although you can use ready-made frames and photo borders to create cards, it's nice to make your own frames from scratch. Give that special photo a good turn by fashioning your own individual frame. Draw on a theme that coordinates with the photo.

If the photo tells a big fish story, for instance, your frame could be embossed or otherwise decorated with imaginary lures, fishes, boats, or fishing lines.

● The template measures 5 x 7 inches (about 12.5 x 17.8 cm). Photocopy the template to adjust it to the desired size. After you've figured out what size you want, make a template out of thin cardboard. Use this cardboard template as a pattern for future projects. With a pencil, trace the pattern onto the cardstock, and with a craft knife, cut out the frame and hole. Be sure to cover your work table with heavy cardboard, a cutting board, or a craft mat to protect it from damage.

PHOTO-FRAME CARDS
quick and easy

You want to send a photo to a friend or family member, but you'd like to dress it up. Many card and photo supply shops sell ready-made photo frame cards. You'll find them in standard sizes to fit 3 × 5-inch or 4 × 6-inch photos or the appropriate centimeter equivalents (roughly 7.5 × 12.5 cm or 10 × 15 cm). Many are designed for holidays or special occasions.

MATERIALS

photo-frame cards

photo

- Slide your photo into the slot provided to accommodate a photo. The photo should fit snugly in place. Glue or tape should not be necessary.

- Write your own personal greeting inside the card. Many holiday cards come with printed greetings.

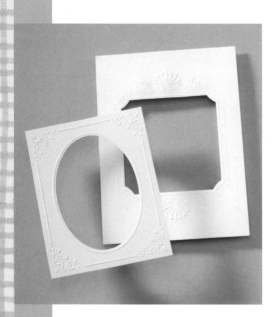

DOILY FRAME

MATERIALS

frame-card base

frame template

square or rectangular
doily

photo or print

two-sided tape

one-sided tape

scissors

craft knife

metal ruler or triangle
tool

stickers (optional)

- Use your own template to make the frame-card base or use
  a ready-made frame-card base.

- With a square or rectangular doily, cut out the decorative
  lacy edge with a craft knife and ruler.

- The doily will need to be larger than the hole of your frame to allow for trimming. Work with a metal ruler and a sharp craft knife on heavy cardboard or a cutting mat to protect your work table. Cut along the decorative edge of lace all around the rectangle or square. Cut two opposite diagonal corners and separate. Position over the frame and trim excess length.

- Use two-sided tape to adhere the lacy doily to the frame card.

- Turn the frame over and adhere a photo or print to the back of the frame using one-sided tape.

- Apply stickers to the front of the frame if desired. You can overlap the stickers with the photo or print.

Cut doily with a craft knife and a ruler or triangle tool.

FOIL-FRAME CARDS

Ready-made blank foil cards, some with frames, can be elegant. They're found in craft or office supply stores. Share your favorite photo with friends or recycle an old greeting card inside a foil frame.

MATERIALS

foil photo-frame card or foil-edge cardstock

photo or recycled card

two-sided tape

deckle scissors (optional)

● Select a ready-made foil photo-frame card.

● Position the photo or recycled greeting card in the opening of the foil card and secure it with two-sided tape if the frame is not constructed so that it will hold it in place.

HINT: Foil can become a decorative element in card-making. Use it as a shaped snippet, layer, or frame. Depending on its weight, foil can be delicate to work with.

Gift Pack of Greeting Cards

multiple cards • feminine

I enjoy making four cards that are all the same and then packaging them as a gift. They are especially good for hostess gifts. This project is made with hydrangea paper and silk-flower embellishment. I used hydrangeas because they're the favorite flower of the recipient. You can choose a flower for this gift card that's your friend's favorite.

MATERIALS

cardstock

decorative paper

deckle scissors

two-sided tape or glue stick

raffia

silk flower

- Start with a cardstock base.
- Using deckle scissors, cut a floral decorative paper.
- Adhere the paper to the cardstock with a glue stick or two-sided tape.
- Make four cards all the same.
- Stack four envelopes and stack the four cards on top of the envelopes.
- Wrap the bundle with raffia.
- Place a silk flower in the knot of the raffia and tie a bow.
- Mail the finished card pack in a padded envelope or take them with you when you visit your friend.

Gift Tags

VARIATIONS
quick and easy

Gift tags are usually smaller than greeting and note cards. That's of course because they're usually attached to a gift, big or small. They can be simple or highly decorative. Here we show a variety of gift tags; some include envelopes.

Assorted gift tags

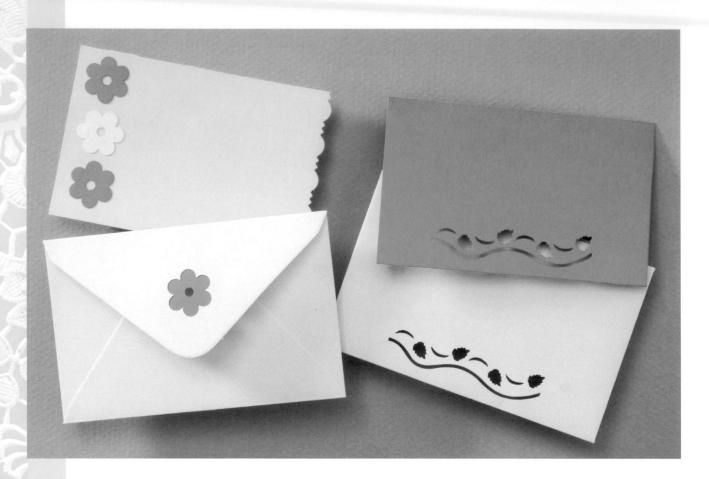

DIE-CUT GIFT TAGS AND ENVELOPES

MATERIALS

cardstock or cardstock
scraps

tiny envelope(s)

die-cut

colored paper

glue stick

deckle scissors

hole punch

one-sided tape

- Use a colorful cardstock cut to the desired size. To make the simple gift cards or gift tags a little more dressy, cut one of the edges with deckle scissors.

- Using a flower design die-cut, cut out a flower in a different color paper than that of the cardstock itself. If you wish, you could make several flowers, each in a different color for a little bouquet.

- Cut a small hole in the center of each flower with the hole punch.

- Adhere the flowers to the cardstock by using a glue stick on the back of the flower(s).

- With a die-cut, cut out a flower on the flap of the envelope.

- Cut a small piece of colored paper and tape it to the inside of the envelope flap so that it shows through your cutout.

GIFT TAGS FROM SCRAPS

If you have many pieces of cardstock scraps left over from larger projects, don't let them go to waste. Recycle them. Make small gift tags. Dress them up with embellishments.

MATERIALS

cardstock scrap(s)

recycled gift tag

deckle scissors

raffia

rhinestone(s)

two-sided tape

hard-bonding glue

hole punch

- Cut a cardstock scrap to size.

- Using deckle scissors, cut an old gift tag.

- Adhere the gift tag to the cardstock with two-sided tape.

- Make sure the card is flat on your work table.

- Using hard-bonding glue, dab a very small amount of the glue onto the back of the rhinestone.

- Place the rhinestone in the corner of the gift tag. Do the same with all four corners.

- Let the glue dry according to the instructions.

- Punch a hole in the upper left corner of the folded card.

- Thread raffia through the hole and tie a knot. Leave enough raffia to tie it to a package.

GIFT TAGS WITH GLITTERY STICKERS

Use stickers to create a wonder gift tag. This project uses a glitter sticker and will dress up any gift.

MATERIALS

cardstock

glitter sticker

hole punch

ribbon

deckle scissors

- With deckle scissors, cut your cardstock to the desired size for the gift tag.

- Place the self-sticking glitter sticker on the cardstock gift tag.

- Using the hole punch, punch a hole in the upper left corner of the card. Be sure to punch all the way through the front and back covers of the card.

- Thread a ribbon through the hole and tie a bow.

- If you want to attach this card to the ribbon of a package, loop the card's ribbon through the ribbon on the package and then tie the final package-ribbon bow.

GIFT TAGS WITH STICKERS

MATERIALS

cardstock

recycled cards or stickers

yarn

two-sided tape or glue stick

deckle scissors

hole punch

- Cut a small card base from cardstock.

- Cut an old card, calendar, or other image using deckle scissors. Cut the image slightly smaller than the cover of your card.

- Adhere the old card or calendar image with two-sided tape or a glue stick.

- Using a hole punch, punch a hole in the top left corner of the folded card. Let the hole go through the cover and back of the card.

- Thread decorative yarn through the hole and tie a knot. Leave enough yarn to tie the tag to a gift.

Glitter

pizzazz

Is there anything with more pizzazz than glitter? You can add glitter to almost anything and it can look—depending on the color scheme and other elements—feminine and fancy, glitzy, or jazzy.

MATERIALS

cardstock base

die-cut

deckle scissors

decorative paper

colored paper

glitter

glue pen

two-sided tape or glue stick

- Begin with a cardstock base.
- With deckle scissors, cut out an interesting shape of colored paper.
- Adhere the colored paper shape to the cardstock base with two-sided tape or a glue stick.
- Cut out decorative paper with deckle scissors. Punch a die-cut design into the decorative paper.
- With two-sided tape or a glue stick, carefully position and adhere the die-cut decorative paper on top of the colored paper.
- Make designs on the card face with a glue pen. Quickly sprinkle glitter onto the glue and let dry a few moments.
- Shake off the extra glitter onto a paper and funnel it back into the container. There's no point in wasting glitter; you may want it for another project.

Hangings

BUTTERFLY "STAINED-GLASS" HANGING
challenging • gift

Many printed vellum designs work nicely with suncatchers and other hangings. This design is a stained-glass pattern. The design of red stained-glass butterflies contrasts with the blue parchment cardstock base. The stylized butterfly shape is easy to cut with a craft knife. Hang this in a window when it's snowing outside to remind you of the joys of summer butterflies fluttering in the breeze.

MATERIALS

long cardstock (not folded)	hole punch
parchment cardstock	ribbon
glue stick	ruler
craft knife	cutting mat
stained-glass vellum pattern	paper cutter
blue marker	pencil
black marker	tracing paper
computer or handwritten text	light box (or sunny window)

- Cut out a long piece of cardstock on your paper cutter. The finished card measures 5 × 8½ inches (12.7 × 21.5 cm); it will be flat and not folded.

- Cut the vellum slightly smaller than the cardstock.

- With a pencil, draw a butterfly on tracing paper. After you've drawn the size and shape you want, go over the lines with a black marker so you can see them when transferring the design to the cardstock.

- Use a light box or sunny window to trace the design onto the cardstock with a pencil.

- Cut the design out with a craft knife on a cutting mat (to protect your work table and to ensure clean cuts).

- After your butterfly cutouts are finished, adhere the vellum to the back side of the cardstock that has pencil markings. Use a glue stick to cover the cardstock so that it bonds with the vellum.

- By hand or on your computer, write the words butterfly in different languages. Cut the printouts into geometric shapes with a craft knife and ruler. Attach them to the card face with a glue stick.

- Draw the butterflies' antennae with a blue marking pen.

- On the top center of the card, punch a hole with your hole punch that's about ½ inch (1.25 cm) into the cardstock.

- Thread a ribbon through the hole and tie a bow. The card can now be hung in the window from the ribbon.

HINT: This flat card does not require a back unless you'd like to add one to cover your work. If you add a decorative paper back, be sure to cut out the appropriate windows for the butterflies so that the sun or light can shine through.

Treat the finished suncatcher as a postcard that's mailed in an envelope.

SUNCATCHER
challenging • gift

Your friend will be able to hang this suncatcher in a window to enjoy for a long time. The length of this suncatcher card should be double the width.

I love beads and prisms in a sunny window because I enjoy watching the dancing rainbows they cast on my walls.

MATERIALS

corrugated cardstock (not folded)

craft knife

cutting mat or heavy cardboard (to protect table)

printed vellum

one-sided tape

two-sided tape

computer or handwritten text

hole punch

solid-colored cardstock (not folded)

deckle scissors

scissors

brads

string of beads

raffia

ruler

pencil

- With a craft knife, cut out from the corrugated cardstock the desired card shape and hole. Use heavy cardboard or a cutting mat to protect your table.

- Cut the decorative vellum a little larger than the hole in the corrugated cardstock. Tape the vellum to the back of the card with one-sided tape. Do not let the tape show in the hole.

- Write text by hand (here's where calligraphy would come in handy) or on your computer in a pleasing type font. Cut out the printed message with deckle scissors.

- Using deckle scissors, cut out solid-colored cardstock a little larger than the text. Adhere the text to the cardstock with two-sided tape. Fasten the text assembly to the front of the corrugated card with brads in each corner.

- With a hole punch, make two holes on the top corners of the card. Thread raffia through the holes and tie a bow. The raffia can be hung on a hook in a window.

- On the back side of the card, run a row of two-sided tape near the bottom edge of the card.

- Hang a short string of beads across the bottom of the card. Press the band of beads onto the two-sided tape. Cover this with one-sided tape to secure the beads.

● Mail the finished card in a padded envelope.

HINT: If the back of the light-catcher card will be visible as it sways in the breeze, cover the back of the card with decorative or plain paper cut to size and secured with two-sided tape. Of course, you'll need to make a cutout in the decorative paper for the light-catching window in the corrugated card. Use the template again as needed.

Initials
quick and easy

Here's something personal. Create an elegant card that bears your friend or family member's initial (first or last name). Of course, the surname initial creates a more formal card. The style of the initial and its placement will also make a difference as to whether it's formal or fun.

Rhinestones will be glitzy, but elegant script or calligraphy plus a more sedate background will make the cards appear more formal.

Make the initial large or small, depending on your taste and overall design.

MATERIALS

ready-made decorative cardstock

decorative or solid paper

decorative calligraphy or computer-printed initial

deckle scissors or regular scissors

two-sided tape or glue stick

rhinestone (optional)

hard-bonding glue

- Using a ready-made card will save time.

- Create fancy calligraphy with a calligraphic marker or calligraphy pen.

- Or instead, choose a fancy type font from your computer type manager. Make it really big, say from 26 to 72 points or larger. (The letter M on the card shown is 55 points, but apparent point size can vary with the type font.) Print it out. You may find that you need to enlarge it on a photocopier machine. Adjust the initial's size for the appearance and design you want for the given card.

- With deckle or other scissors, cut out the initial from the computer printout. Cut a rectangle or square around the initial. Or, if you wish, make a silhouette; cut around the outline of the initial itself. (If you're using calligraphy paper, adjust the size of the calligraphy paper by cutting away any excess.) Adhere the initial to decorative or solid paper with two-sided tape or a glue stick.

- Adhere the assembled pieces to decorative cardstock.

- Put a little dab of hard-bonding glue on the bottom of a rhinestone. Position the rhinestone on the card. Let dry.

- Mail the finished card in a padded envelope.

OPTION: You could also use two or three initials. If you use three, make the initial for the last name large and the other two, on either side of the large initial, about two-thirds or half as big.

HINT: If you enlarge calligraphy on a photocopier it will not appear as crisp. You can reduce but not enlarge calligraphy, for best results. Usually we advise that you not reduce it by more than 25 percent.

Ink Prints
fun

Bottled ink comes in vivid colors; it's easy to use. If you've been saving somewhat flat seashells, such as scallop shells, for a special project, try this.

MATERIALS

heavy cardstock or watercolor paper

artist's large paintbrush

artist's small round #4 to #6 paintbrush

2 shallow plastic or foam cups

deep blue ink

turquoise ink

hard-bonding glue

seashells

- You can use the ink right out of the bottle, but if the neck of the bottle is too narrow or you don't want to contaminate it, pour a small amount of ink into a shallow plastic or Styrofoam cup (without wax) or other nonfood dish you can discard or easily wash. You'll want a separate shallow cup for each ink that you use.

- If you're using watercolor paper rather than heavy cardstock, measure the watercolor paper and cut it to the size of card desired. Or you can keep it flat and cut out the card after you finish your ink print but before you attach the seashells.

- Make a large rectangle with deep blue ink on the face of the heavy cardstock or watercolor paper, using an artist's large paintbrush. Let the ink dry.

- Paint waves of deep blue and turquoise inks with a small round (#4 to #6) paintbrush. Let dry.

- Use hard-bonding glue on the seashells and adhere to the card. Let dry.

- Mail the finished card in a padded envelope.

HINT: Try different colors of ink and designs. You can glue various found objects to the ink-print card.

Invitations

quick and easy • computer-assisted

If you're sending invitations for an event or party, you'll want to make a card that will impress the recipient. Work with a theme if you can.

You can work with type in Microsoft Word, Quark XPress, Adobe InDesign, and other word document or layout programs as well as in Photoshop or other computer photo options, if you've installed the software. Of course, the more sophisticated you are at using a computer, the less help you'll need here.

MATERIALS

cardstock base

two-sided tape or glue stick

deckle scissors

clip art

computer

computer printer

paper for computer printout

- Choose a cardstock base that will enhance the colors in the clip art.
- Cut out the clip art using deckle scissors. Adhere the clip art to the card face with a glue stick or two-sided tape.
- In your computer, choose a good, readable type font and point size. Write the what, where, when, and other details for your invitation. Print out the text on the desired paper.
- Cut out the text printout with deckle scissors.
- With two-sided tape or a glue stick, adhere the text to the inside of the card.

BOOKMARK INVITATION
computer-aided • gift

How about having an invitation with a surprise inside? This invitation to a book club has a book-mark attached to it. It's plain and simple.

If you're really savvy at using your computer, you won't need help here.

MATERIALS

raffia

cardstock base

cardstock for bookmark

clip art

hole punch

computer

computer font library (optional)

computer printer

● Use a cardstock that your computer printer will accept to create a bookmark that also acts as an invitation.

● Create the invitation text on computer, using an attractive type font in an appropriate size.

● Try out a few different colors that coordinate with the cardstock. Some, like yellow or pale colors, can be hard to read, and reds can be jarring. Dark blues and dark greens usually work nicely.

● Don't mix too many fonts on a single card; the result can be chaotic and difficult to read.

● Use clip art to support your theme. In this case, the invitation is for a book club; members will be reading a book about the Adirondacks.

● Make two holes in the card face, near the top, and string raffia through it. Attach the bookmark to the cover of the card with the raffia, either tied behind on the inside of the card or into a nice bow on the front of the card.

HINT: You can also make a regular invitation with all details inside the card and attach a bookmark to the card face.

Jewelry

CHARM FOR BRACELET
average complexity

Jewelry, even inexpensive costume jewelry, can make a nice gift when attached to a greeting card. Depending on the baubles and beads, it can make a dazzling card presentation. Use decorative papers and a little foil or metallic ribbon to enhance shiny, glittery jewelry.

MATERIALS

2 colors of corrugated cardstock

plain cardstock base

Mylar stars on tiny metallic string

thin wire

thin nail (for punching a hole)

rubber cement

clear package tape

charm (or other small piece of jewelry)

- Set aside the cardstock base.

- Cut a piece of corrugated cardstock to fit the front of the card on the plain cardstock base.

- Tear by hand a second piece of corrugated cardstock of a different color to make irregular edges. This will be a decorative base that will also reveal the first layer of corrugated cardstock.

- Generously use rubber cement on the front of the first corrugated cardstock where you plan to place the second torn piece of corrugated cardstock. Then generously use rubber cement on the bottom of the second, torn corrugated cardstock. Let both dry. This is called dry mounting.

- After the rubber cement is dry (in about 30 minutes), carefully position the top corrugated cardstock on the bottom corrugated cardstock. In the photo, you'll see that the grain on the bottom cardstock was positioned vertically while the grain for the second, torn corrugated cardstock piece was horizontal. Be careful. After the two glue-covered surfaces meet, they cannot be removed.

- Punch two tiny holes through the front of the card near the middle. I used a thin nail to make the hole, but other found tools, like a pushpin, could do the trick.

- Pull a thin wire through the holes and twist it around the small ring on the charm (normally used for attaching it to the bracelet). Make the twist on the back side of the charm; this will help secure the charm to the cardstock.

- Wrap the Mylar stars or other adornment around the entire card and secure them to the back with package tape.

- Using the dry-mount method, apply rubber cement to the front of the plain card-stock and the back of the corrugated paper you have already assembled. Let dry.

- Carefully place the two pieces together. When they've bonded, they cannot be pulled apart. You'll be able to hide your work.

- Mail the finished card in a padded envelope.

WITH THIS RING
quick and easy

When my husband proposed to me, he created a card of several pages. Inside he wrote a poem. On the front of the card, he tied an engagement ring with a ribbon. Even if you cannot write a poem or other little ditty, you can make a lovely card.

MATERIALS

colored cardstock base

colored paper

foil paper

decorative paper

deckle scissors

two-sided tape or glue stick

ribbon

ring (costume or fancy)

● Use a colored cardstock base.

● With deckle scissors, cut a square or rectangle of contrasting-color paper smaller than the card face. Adhere the paper to the front of the card with two-sided tape or a glue stick.

● Cut a narrow band of foil paper with deckle scissors. Adhere the narrow band to the card with two-sided tape or glue stick.

● Cut out decorative paper (last layer) with deckle scissors into a square or rectangle shape. Place this paper on top of the band, carefully centering it. After deciding where you want it, use two-sided tape or a glue stick to adhere it to the paper(s) on the card face.

● Punch two small holes in the card with a thin nail. Thread a ribbon through the holes and tie a ring on the card. Finish with a bow in the front of the card that secures the ring. On the reverse side (verso) of the card face, tape the back of the ribbon to ensure that it stays in place.

● Mail the finished card in a padded envelope, or, better yet (especially if it's precious), deliver it in person.

HINT: A whimsical piece of jingly jewelry could be nifty for a daughter, granddaughter, or niece's gift. Adjust the formality of the card to suit the recipient. Choosing the right decorative paper will make a difference.

Keepsakes

KEEPSAKE WITH CHILDREN'S ARTWORK
quick and easy • recycle • kid-friendly

The kitchen refrigerator may be the gallery for your children's art, but what do you do when you take the artworks down? You could recycle the art to make a card and send it to grandma and grandpa.

Here's a nice rainy-day project for children. Precut white or any color of drawing paper to a size that would fit on a standard card face. Then let children begin drawing or painting with their favorite tools.

MATERIALS

child's artwork
cardstock base
scissors
two-sided tape
embellishments (optional)

● Using ready-made cardstock is a fast way to make this card.

● Adhere the child's artwork to the card with two-sided tape.

● Each finished card will have its own personality.

HINT: For more fun, let the children use glitter, sequins, and other embellishments.

KEEPSAKE OF EVENT
quick and easy

Remember that wonderful evening you had going out with your favorite friend? Make a keepsake card as a thank-you to send to your friend with memorabilia that suggests the tone of the event and the evening. The card in the photo helps me remember a night at the theater that I shared with a friend.

MATERIALS

cardstock larger than the postcard

postcard (home or away)

ticket

restaurant clipping

decal

theatre program clippings

two-sided tape

deckle scissors

● Begin with a cardstock that's slightly larger than the local postcard. It will serve as a sort of frame.

● With two-sided tape, adhere the postcard to the front of the cardstock.

● Cut up the program that came with the play. Use photos from the play, your ticket stub(s), an ad from the restaurant where you ate, and some decals or other memorabilia. Affix each item to the card with two-sided tape.

KEEPSAKE WITH OLD PHOTOS
average complexity

Enjoy old black-and-white photos with this keepsake card.

MATERIALS

corrugated or plain cardstock base

decorative or solid-colored paper

old B&W photos

deckle scissors

two-sided tape

packaging tape

handwritten or computer text

raffia

- Begin with a cardstock base.

- With deckle scissors, cut decorative or solid-colored paper slightly smaller than the card face. Adhere the decorative paper to the cardstock with two-sided tape.

- Also with two-sided tape, mount the photos on the decorative paper.

- Add any text you desire with another slip of paper. A computer printout in a fancy font on nice paper would work, or use your best handwriting. You can deckle-cut the edges so that your caption fits below the photos.

- Wrap the card with raffia and tie a small corner bow.

- On the back of the card, use packaging tape to secure the raffia.

Grandma & Grandpa in 1951

Lace

LACE DOILY
quick and easy • feminine

When you're in a hurry but want to send a friend a feminine card, try this trick with a lace doily and an appliqué. To please an avid gardener, you could find a butterfly and flower appliqué. Naturally, all kinds of appliqués could work, depending on the theme you want to establish.

MATERIALS
cardstock base
doily
two-sided tape
deckle scissors
appliqué

● Select a pretty card base. Ready-made cardstock will be quickest.

● On the front of the card, affix a small doily with two-sided tape.

● Cover the center of the doily with an appliqué.

● For a little extra decoration, cut two or three sides of the cardstock with deckle scissors.

LACE FABRIC
feminine

Find a small piece of real lace, perhaps a scrap from a sewing project. Or you could buy a bit of lace from a fabric store. If you can sew, you'll enjoy making this card. If the recipient sews, too, that's all the better.

MATERIALS

white or light-colored cardstock base

long, solid-colored piece of cardstock

deckle scissors

fabric lace

sewing scissors

two-sided tape

brads

die-cut flowers

- Use a ready-made white or light-colored cardstock base or make your own; set it aside.

- With deckle scissors, cut a long piece of colored cardstock so that it's 1.5 times the length of the front of the card. Fold in each end of the colored cardstock so that its total size, with both ends folded in, will be a little less than that of the front of the card. (See the folded finished lavender example in the photo which also reveals a white border, the base cardstock.)

- With deckle scissors, cut the end flaps to a decorative V-shaped point.

- Trim a piece of lace to fit inside the folded cardstock, and adhere with two-sided tape to the colored cardstock.

- Then put two-sided tape on the inside of the V-shaped flaps and seal the flap to the lace.

- Using a die-cut flower shape and a metal decorative brad, punch a hole with the brad through the layers of colored (lavender shown here) cardstock and lace and fasten the brad. Our example uses two flowers and two brads, one for each flower.

- Finally, with two-sided tape, affix the assembled colored cardstock with lace, die-cut flowers, and brads to the light-colored cardstock base you had set aside. It will act as a sort of frame for the rest and show off the deckle-cut border of the folded color cardstock.

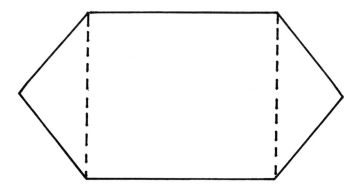

Fold along dotted lines.

LACE TRIM
feminine

A little lace makes cards feminine and fancy, while
reminding us of romantic
valentines, little girl charms,
doting grandmothers, summer
nightgowns, and tea time.

Dress up a card with lace
for a female friend or relative
who needs a pick-me-up.

MATERIALS

ready-made decorative
cardstock

decorative papers

two-sided tape

deckle scissors

lace trim or lace ribbon

packaging tape

sewing scissors

● Begin with a pretty, decorative cardstock base. With sewing scissors
or ordinary scissors, cut one or two short strips of lace trim to fit
the front of the card with a little extra extending on the reverse side.
To secure the lace trim, use packaging tape on the reverse (verso)
side of the card face.

● For the card in the photo, I used 3/4-inch (2-cm) lace ribbon that's
about 8 inches (20 cm) long on a card base that's 4¹/2 x 6 inches
(11.5 x 15.24 cm).

● Over the lace, add a square of decorative paper cut with deckle
scissors. Two-sided tape works nicely to attach the decorative paper
square on top of the lace.

● As a final touch, on top of the decorative paper, place a decorative
motif. Attach it with two-sided tape.

● If you want to hide your work (the taped lace), attach a sheet of
decorative paper with two-sided tape on the back (verso) of the
"front cover" of the card.

Magnets

ART OR TEXT MAGNET

quick and easy • computer-aided

This project is so simple that you could probably do it blindfolded. Use a small art print or recycle a greeting card.

The magnet, about the size of a business card, comes in small packages and can be found in office supply stores.

MATERIALS

cardstock base

art or computer text

scissors

business-card-size magnet with adhesive back

two-sided tape

- On your computer, create rows of text with the word(s) or phrases that suit the occasion.

- Alternate each row with different colors of text. If you have a PC and use Microsoft Word, highlight a row of text with your cursor, then go to the Format menu, scroll down to Font, then in the Font dialogue box change the color under Font Color. You can do this with every other word, every other phrase, or every other line of text, as you wish. Try out a pattern that suits you.

- You could also work with layout software that allows more manipulation of color backgrounds, such as Quark XPress or Adobe InDesign. You'll also have box border and color selection options in those or other computer layout software programs.

- Adhere the "Hello" or other message card tag to the magnet.

- Fasten the magnet to the cardstock base with two-sided tape.

- If you have a Mac, some of the newer models allow you to manipulate type and layout designs as you wish. It's also possible to do this in Adobe Photoshop or in Adobe Illustrator programs, but if you're savvy about those programs, you won't need help here.

- You'll be able to do fancy things like wrapping text or creating calligrams (shapes like apples or hearts made out of calligraphy) or doing other interesting things.

HINT: For fancy borders, you could simply use deckle scissors instead of trying to fashion something in your computer layout program. Colored paper for the printout also will serve instead of a color box generated by a computer program.

ART VARIATION

- Use ready-made cardstock. If you choose one with embossed borders, the finished look will be more decorative.

- Trim a print of the desired artwork to the size of the magnet. Peel off the paper backing to reveal the sticky side.

- Carefully position the art on the magnet.

- With two-sided tape, press the art print and magnet into the front of the card.

PUPPY MAGNET
quick and easy • gift

How cute is this little puppy magnet attached to the card? It's surely cute enough for the recipient to use on the refrigerator door. Of course, you'll want to find a magnet that suits the person receiving your card. You'll want to choose a magnet that isn't too heavy so that it stays adhered to the card.

MATERIALS

cardstock base

decorative paper

small refrigerator magnet

two-sided tape

deckle scissors

- Cut out decorative paper with deckle scissors and adhere the decorative paper to the cardstock base with two-sided tape.
- Affix the magnet to the decorative paper with two-sided tape.
- Mail the card in a padded envelope.

Mesh
quick and easy • *textured*

Dress up paper and stickers with an overlay of mesh in a desired color. You'll find mesh in arts and crafts stores in various colors.

MATERIALS

cardstock base

colored paper

stickers

mesh

scissors or paper cutter

two-sided tape

- Begin with ready-made cardstock base if you're in a hurry.
- Cut colored paper slightly smaller than the front of the card.
- Attach stickers here and there around the colored paper in the desired design. I've used a "Thinking of You" greeting as well.
- Cut mesh to the size of the card face.
- With two-sided tape, affix the mesh over the stickers and any message to the card near the edges of the card face.

Nature's Elements

AUTUMN-LEAVES PAPER PRINTS
quick and easy • multiple cards

In the fall, collect beautiful leaves found on sidewalks and paths. Immediately take these freshly fallen leaves to a photocopy store to make laser color copies. Play with variations by reducing the size, changing the arrangement, or trying out colored paper (whether for the background or the printouts). What results is your own decorative paper for card-making.

MATERIALS

colorful fall leaves

color laser-print photocopier

laser photocopy paper

scissors or paper cutter

cardstock base

two-sided tape or glue stick

deckle scissors (optional)

ribbon or decals (optional)

- Gather freshly fallen, brilliantly colored autumn leaves. You'll want fairly clean, disease-free leaves. (You may want to rinse and carefully dry them on paper towels as necessary. But the less you handle them, the better.) Smaller leaves work best for displaying a pattern of multiple leaves.

- Arrange the leaves face down on a clean color laser-print photocopier bed. Place a sheet of colored or plain paper behind the leaves; it will become the background color. Make a test copy. Try reducing the leaves to 50% or even to 25%. Make another test copy. Rearrange the leaves if you're not satisfied. Change the size of the photocopy to suit your aesthetic sensibilities. Remember that you can in turn reduce a photocopy of a photocopy if you want a very small pattern of leaves.

- If you're in a hurry, use a ready-made cardstock, or make your own. Cut out the photocopy of fall leaves so that it is slightly smaller than the card face.

- Bond the decorative-leaves photocopy with two-sided tape or a glue stick to the card face.

- Embellish as desired with deckle scissors, ribbon, text, or decals. Since nature has its own grace, you may not want to do anything more than display this elegant leafy print.

HINT: Placing the colored sheet background on top of the leaves will help protect the photocopier's lid from any dirt. When finished, clean the photocopy bed with alcohol and a soft cloth or consult the photocopy store attendant for the proper cleaning procedure. (He will probably prefer to do this himself.) Avoid using leaves that might leave a sappy mark.

The photocopy-shop attendant might scream foul, but the leaves won't damage the machine. Clean the photocopy bed properly and avoid using any diseased leaves or scratchy twigs.

BIRCH-BARK PRINT
rustic • masculine

When walking in the woods you may find some wonderful peelings of birch tree bark and some twigs. Strip the thin bark from your own tree and make a color laser photocopy. Making cards from the actual bark is not easy because the bark curls and is difficult to flatten.

An artist friend paints birds directly on birch bark.

You can fashion your own postcard if you have access to white birch bark, but meanwhile here's a card facsimile.

MATERIALS

cardstock base

photocopy of birch bark (or another bark)

paper cutter

solid-colored cardstock

two-sided tape

hard-bonding glue

twigs

hole punch

raffia

scissors

- Make a color laser photocopy of white paper-birch bark.

- Trim the birch-bark photocopy so that it's slightly smaller than the card face. A paper cutter can do this job neatly. Adhere the birch-bark photocopy to the cardstock base with two-sided tape.

- Cut a narrow strip of contrasting cardstock and center it on the card vertically. Adhere the strip to the face of the card with two-sided tape.

- Measure and trim the twigs to the length of the card. Ideally, the twigs should be as flat as possible.

- Lay the twigs on the contrasting strip in the center of the card and pour a few drops of hard-bonding glue in the center. Let dry.

- After the glue is dry and hard, you can gently work with embellishments.

- Punch a hole on both sides of the stack of twigs. You'll want each hole placed very close to the twigs.

- Thread the raffia through the holes and tie a knot in front of the card. With scissors, trim off the excess raffia.

- Mail the finished card in a padded envelope.

Nature's Elements **93**

FEATHERS
quick and easy

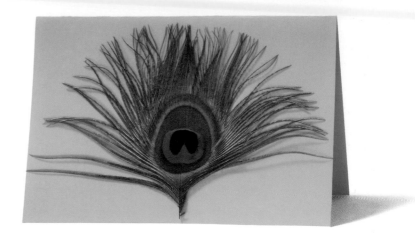

Peacock feathers (you'll need just one) add whimsy and beauty to a card. You could use feathers from other birds, but the peacock feather easily does the trick. If you don't have access to lovely bird feathers, you could also buy feathers at an arts and crafts store.

MATERIALS

cardstock base

peacock tail feather (or other beautiful feather)

two-sided tape

vellum

- Since the "eyes" of peacock tail feathers are very large, you'll need to make a large card with cardstock.

- Using two-sided tape, adhere the tape to the "eye" of the feather. Press down the tape and attached feather onto the cardstock.

- Cover the front and back of the cardstock with vellum, cut to size.

- Use a strip of two-sided tape on the back of the cardstock to adhere the vellum to the cardstock.

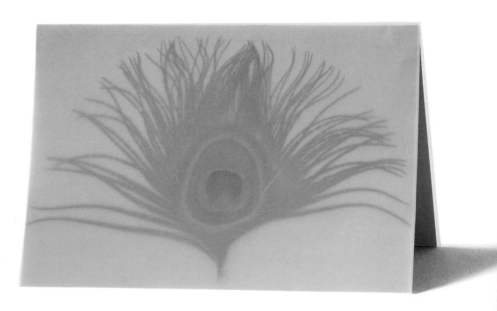

LEAF PRINT
average complexity

Find a freshly fallen leaf or several leaves to create the motif for your card. All kinds of leaves will work nicely: maples, oaks, sycamores, ginkgos, rose leaves, or ferns. Just make sure that the leaf isn't too dry or brittle. You could detach a fresh leaf from its tree or plant, say, when preparing cut roses for a vase.

You'll want to capture with your print not just the outline of the leaf but its vein structure. Experiment with different kinds of leaves and different colors of ink pads.

MATERIALS

one or more leaves

large ink pad

rubber gloves (optional)

photocopy paper or other thin paper

solid colored paper

cardstock base

deckle scissors

decorative papers

two-sided tape

Press the leaf into the ink pad.

Rubbing leaf-impression onto paper with a spoon.

● Press a leaf into a large ink pad. (I've used just one for the card shown.) Rubber gloves will protect your fingers.

- Quickly and carefully position the inked leaf ink-side-down on the colored paper.

- Place a thin sheet of photocopy or other paper on top of the leaf. Rub the top sheet of paper with the curved side of a spoon.

- Carefully lift the top sheet of paper and leaf from the colored paper. You should have an inky image of the leaf with all the veins impressed on the colored paper. You can repeat this process with more leaves if you wish.

- With deckle scissors, cut out the colored paper with its leafy impression(s).

- Cut out a larger square of decorative paper using deckle scissors. Another square or rectangle of decorative paper can be used for the card face. Use deckle scissors if you wish for this bottom layer.

- Stack each layer of paper, with the leaf print on top. Adhere them together with two-sided tape in between.

- For interest, you could arrange your papers slightly askew.

Onion Prints

handmade paper • average complexity

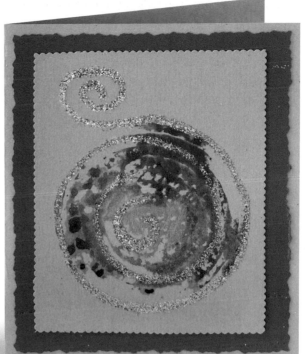

Please don't cry! We'll be using a Vidalia onion to make great paper. Onions make wonderful prints and designs. If you want to enhance the design, you can add glitter or other embellishments.

MATERIALS

colored cardstock base

onion

kitchen paring knife

white or colored paper or cardstock

watercolor paint

small artist's paintbrush

glitter (optional)

two-sided tape or glue stick

glue pen

deckle scissors (optional)

scissors or paper cutter

- Cut an onion down the middle. You can cut the onion from tip to tip or from side to side, whatever you wish. Each pattern will be different.

- Cut out a sheet of white or solid-color paper or cardstock. Use deckle scissors, regular scissors, or a paper cutter.

- With watercolor paint and an artist's paintbrush, brush different colors on the cut face of the onion.

- Firmly press the painted side of the onion face down on the solid-color paper. Carefully lift the onion to reveal the impression. You'll have an onion print that bears the individual onion's many rings.

- Let the print dry.

- If desired, embellish the onion print with glitter by first drawing a design with a glue pen. Then quickly sprinkle the glitter over the glue and let it dry a few moments.

- With a glue stick or two-sided tape, adhere the onion-print cardstock to the face of the colored cardstock base.

- For more interest, use more decorative or colored paper layers.

HINT: If you use glitter, shake off the excess glitter onto a piece of paper, fold the paper, and funnel the glitter back into the bottle. Save your glitter for other projects.

Ornaments

METAL ORNAMENT
quick and easy • gift • holiday

At Christmas, you could send a Christmas card that includes a simple gift ornament. The idea is to remove the ornament from the card and hang it on the Christmas tree or perhaps in a child's room.

Ornaments are not only for Christmas. I'm sure you'll be able to dream up other occasions and find or create ornaments to suit them.

If you don't want to make your own, a metal ornament to suit the occasion can be found in most craft stores.

MATERIALS

metal ornament or handmade ornament

sheet of holiday decorative paper or wrapping paper

scissors or paper cutter

cardstock base

raffia or yarn

two-sided tape

hole punch

- Cut a sheet of holiday decorative paper or wrapping paper slightly smaller than the face of the card.

- Mount the holiday paper to the card with two-sided tape.

- Punch a hole through the top of the card.

- Thread raffia through the hole in the card and the ornament. Tie the raffia. The receiver can untie the raffia, remove the ornament, and hang it with the retied raffia on the Christmas tree or in a child's room.

- Mail the finished card in a padded envelope.

PAPER ORNAMENT
quick and easy • gift • recycled

If you'd like to recycle holiday cards, here's one suggestion. Make a paper handmade mitten or other ornament to hang on a tree or decorate a package.

If you can knit or crochet something tiny to attach to the card, you won't need our suggestions here.

MATERIALS

old holiday card(s)	yarn
scissors	sequins (optional)
cardstock base	two-sided tape
holiday decorative paper	hard-bond glue
paper cutter (optional)	rubber cement

● From an old holiday card, cut out the shape of winter mittens, both front and back. You'll be making a pair (or four pieces total when counting front and back for the mittens). Or make a single large mitten front and back.

● Apply rubber cement to the back side of all the mitten pieces and let them dry. This is a dry-mount method.

● While the glue dries on the mittens, cut out holiday wrapping paper or other decorative paper, slightly smaller than the card face. Tape the decorative paper to the card using two-sided tape.

● Stretch yarn across the top of both mittens when the rubber cement is dry. Keep the mittens fairly close to each other and allow a generous amount of extra yarn beyond each mitten so that you can tie a bow. If you plan ahead, you could make a sort of cuff for the mittens (cut them long, well beyond the wrist) that will hold the yarn just as loops in curtains allow you to hang them from curtain rods.

● Prepare to bond the two pieces (back and front) of the mittens together. This bonding will also help hold the yarn in place. Be careful where you place them, because after bonding the mittens will not separate.

● If you'd like to decorate the mittens, apply a little hard-bonding glue on the front of the mitts and affix sequins to them for added sparkle.

● Cut two small slits near the top of the card face about 1 inch (2.5 cm) apart. Or use a hole punch to make these holes.

● Slide the yarn through the slits and let the mittens hang down the front of the card.

● Tie a bow on the inside of the card. Your receiver will be able to remove and use the mittens ornament.

HINT: If you simply want to make one or more mittens or another ornament that is adhered to the card, you'll probably want to secure the yarn on the back of the card face (verso side) with tape. If you wish, cover the back of the card with decorative paper. Use two-sided tape between that layer and the cardstock.

Outrageous Collection

pizzazz • recycled

Just as you might prepare a feast from refrigerator leftovers, you can create a card from the collection of leftovers in your craft box.

Don't forget items you didn't know what to do with, like netting from supermarket fruit boxes or misplaced buttons. Colors do not have to match. The more outrageous your creation, the more fun the card will be.

This supply list includes what I used to make this card. Gather materials from found objects around your house; they'll dictate how to assemble the individual card.

MATERIALS

cardstock base

(leopard print and zebra print) decorative paper(s)

feathers

star brads

button(s)

silk flowers

sticker(s)

netting

hard-bonding glue

two-sided tape

one-sided tape

- Gather your own collection and create your own card. Here's how I put my concoction of disparate materials together.

- With two-sided tape, I adhered the leopard print to the cardstock base, leaving a little of the cardstock revealed on top.

- I folded a piece of zebra print paper in half and affixed it to the base of the card only with two-sided tape. The folded edge of the zebra paper was kept roughly in the middle of the card.

- I fastened two star brads to the card's two bottom corners.

- I placed a sticker on top of the zebra print. Then I gathered the netting, feathers, and silk flowers and taped them with one-sided tape under the zebra print. To finish off the pocket, I closed up the sides of the zebra paper with two-sided tape.

- I fastened another star brad to the upper end of the card.

- With a dab of hard-bonding glue, I secured the button to the corner of the card.

- Mail the finished card in a padded envelope.

Oversized Cards
challenging

Send a magnificent huge card to that special person who needs to hear from you. Forget about those tiny note cards that you can barely fit enough words on. This card will let you ramble on with lots of things to say. Or write large for someone who has difficulty reading small print. Kids also like them.

Oversized cardstock can be found in photocopy shops, office supply stores, or arts and crafts stores.

MATERIALS

oversized cardstock	cutting mat
floral decorative paper	craft knife
striped decorative paper	stickers (optional)
glue stick	deckle scissors

- The pink cardstock base is 11 x 17 inches (28 x 43 cm). Score and fold it in half. On a paper cutter, trim to 8 x 10 inches (20 x 25 cm).

- The decorative paper has a pink stripe and coordinates with the floral decorative paper we'll use in the next step. Cut out the striped paper with a paper cutter about $1/3$ inch (0.8 cm) shorter than the cardstock cover on all four sides. Adhere the decorative striped paper to the face of the cardstock with a glue stick.

- The large floral decorative paper has flowers that connect to each other. Trim it to fit the card cover on top of the coordinating striped paper. Use deckle scissors to make the edge more interesting.

- Things get a little challenging now. You'll need to decide what flowers to cut around to form a loose border. You'll need to cut around all four sides and then remove the middle that's cut out. Use your craft knife and carefully cut around the flowers on a cutting mat to protect your table.

- When you remove areas in the middle and around the flower shapes, you'll reveal the striped decorative paper beneath. Position the cutout in a desirable way over the striped paper. If it looks good, adhere the large floral border to the card with a glue stick.

- For the design shown, cut out a flower from the leftover paper and glue it in the middle of the striped paper. Also glue stickers of smaller flowers randomly on the striped paper.

Wishing
You
A Great
Trip

Paper Designs

BLACK-AND-WHITE PAPER
elegant • sophisticated

If you make your own hand-made paper, no one will have anything quite like it. Then you can really say about your card, "I made it myself!" We also work with other paper design styles here.

Also find directions for other paper designs: Splatter Prints (p.131), Sponge Prints (p. 132), and Squeegee Prints (p. 134).

MATERIALS

white cardstock base

black paper

hole punch

two-sided tape

handmade squeegee-painted paper

gossamer ribbon

deckle scissors (optional)

- Begin with a white cardstock base.

- Cut a piece of black paper slightly smaller than the front of the card. (You'll find black paper in most arts and crafts stores, often in the scrapbook section.)

- Use two-sided tape or a glue stick to adhere the black paper onto the front of the card. For added interest, place it slightly askew.

- Make textured paper using the squeegee method (see p. 134) and white and black acrylic ink.

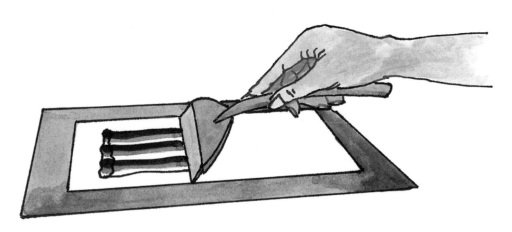

Using a squeegee to pull paint across paper.

- Cut the squeegee-painted paper slightly smaller than the black paper and adhere it to the black paper on the card face with two-sided tape. Set it askew in a direction opposite to that of the black paper.

- With a hole punch, punch two holes into the card face. To maintain the skewed theme, punch them on opposite sides.

- Thread a gossamer ribbon through the holes and tie a bow on the front of the card.

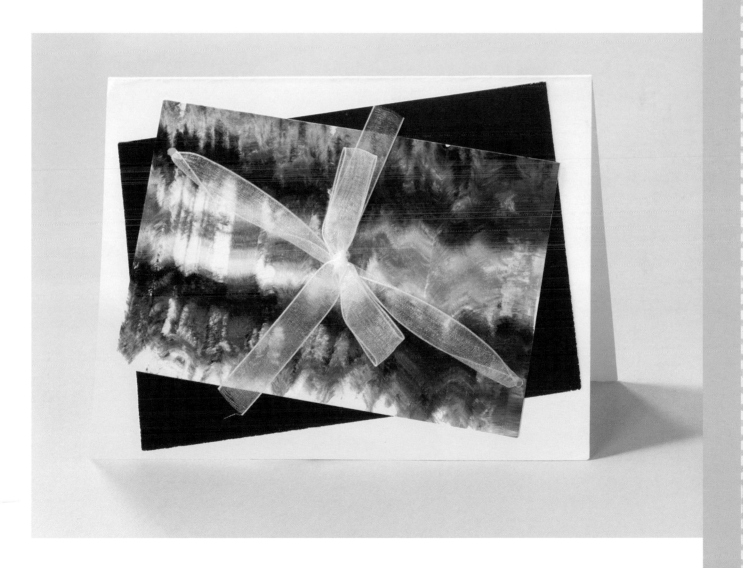

CRACKLE PAPER
time-consuming • rustic • masculine

If you're after a rustic look, this is it. The distressed appearance of old peeling paint has become very appealing today in antique or faux antique home furnishings and decorating. It also works well as the background or foreground for more masculine card designs.

Making crackle paper isn't difficult. It simply requires adequate drying time between each stage, so you'll want to plan a little ahead.

MATERIALS
two-ply Bristol drawing paper

acrylic paint (two colors)

crackle compound

wide sponge brush

wide, coarse brush

- With a wide sponge brush, brush acrylic paint on a sheet of heavy drawing paper. I've used dark gray paint for the first step shown here. Let the paint dry.

- Then brush on crackle compound with a wide, coarse brush. Allow the crackle compound to dry.

- With a wide sponge brush, brush on a second color of acrylic paint. We used off-white as shown in the photo. Let the acrylic paint dry.

- The finished crackle paper will make a nice card. Perhaps you'll want to attach a message or leave it plain, adhere a "found art object," or otherwise create a card to suit the receiver.

PLASTIC-WRAP PAINTED PAPER
painted texture

Although this technique is similar to that of bubble-wrap handmade paper, the textured effect is somewhat different.

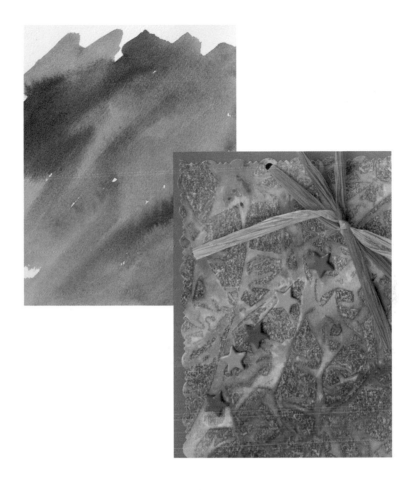

MATERIALS

heavy drawing paper

watercolor paint

artist's flat paintbrush
(1 to 2 inches wide)

water

plastic wrap or plastic bag

HINT: If you're afraid that you'll get paint on the book or other heavy object, put it inside a large freezer-type zipped plastic bag.

- With an artist's wide, flat paintbrush, mix watercolor paint with a little water and quickly brush the paint randomly on the heavy drawing paper.

- Change colors and repeat the process as many times as you wish. But avoid mixing too many colors in one spot since the effect will be muddy.

- While the paint is wet, quickly cover the paint with crumpled plastic wrap or a thin plastic bag. Press down into the paint. Put a heavy object, such as a book, over the plastic to secure it in place and to help create the impression on the paper.

- Let the paint dry a few hours or overnight.

- Remove the book or heavy object and the crumpled plastic wrap.

- If the paper is still damp, allow the paper to dry before using it.

SALT-PRINT PAPER
quick and easy • fun

This decorative paper is simple to make. You also don't have to go far from the kitchen.

MATERIALS

kosher salt

flat cardstock

ink or watercolor paint

- Set a sheet of cardstock on your worktable. Working very quickly, spread liquid ink or watercolor paint onto the cardstock with a paintbrush. Do not let the ink or paint dry.

- While it's still wet, sprinkle a little kosher salt on the wet ink or paint.

- Let dry.

- After the ink or paint is dry, you can brush the salt off the paper.

- Little crystallized spots are left. If you did not get these spots, you probably let the ink or paint dry too much before applying the salt.

- Use this salt-paper decorative cardstock to make a card. You can also cut it into desired shapes and adhere it to another cardstock base.

HINT: Protect the work table with newspapers or plastic before beginning. Ink or watercolor stains can be permanent.

WOOD-TEXTURE PAPER
quick and easy • masculine • rustic

This textured paper has a rugged look that men or woodworkers will appreciate.
Instead of using carbon paper, you could do a rubbing on photocopy paper using a flat, broad crayon in a wood color like sienna on the surface with the raised-texture piece of wood underneath.

MATERIALS

photocopy paper

carbon paper

spoon

small piece of wood
with full grain

HINT: As a next step, you can make a photocopy of this sheet to keep as a master copy. Make additional copies as you need them, using different colors of paper. Of course, you can also change the color of the wood texture on a color photocopier or with your own computer's photo software and a photo scanner.

- Use a small piece of wood with a full, raised grain. Weathered wood is best; painted or sanded wood will not work. It's advisable to use a weathered board that has been outdoors for a few years. Deck planks work well.

- Lay a sheet of photocopy paper (yes, the kind of inexpensive paper you'd normally use in a photocopier) directly on top of the wood.

- Place a sheet of carbon paper, face down, on top of the photocopy paper.

- On top of the two layers place a sheet of photocopy paper.

- Firmly holding down each layer, rub the curved side of a spoon on the top sheet of photocopy paper, going back and forth over the surface. Be sure to rub the entire length and width of the wood, covering as much of the paper as possible or as desired for your finished wood-grain paper.

- Remove the layers to reveal the bottom sheet of drawing paper with the pattern of the wood grain.

Photo-Mat Cards

quick and easy

Almost any well-composed photograph can make a nice card. Photos of children work nicely as gifts for doting grandparents and aunts and uncles. Naturally, your spouse or favorite relatives or friends are great, too. Create an interesting presentation by using embossed mats. You can find these mats at most arts and crafts stores or photo-supply stores.

MATERIALS

photograph

mat to fit

photo

one-sided

tape

cardstock base

scissors or paper cutter

two-sided tape

● Lay the mat (for photo or art) face down on the table. Place the photo face down on top of the back of the mat. With one-sided tape, tape the back of the photo to the back of the mat.

● Cut out cardstock slightly larger than the mat. With two-sided tape, join the cardstock to the mat. Then presto! You're done.

HINT: Many photo frames also come ready-made as cards. The mat essentially provides a frame, although the cardstock also does that as well.

Plastic-Wrap Prints

quick and easy • handmade paper

Under handmade plastic-wrap painted paper (see p. 109), review how to make decorative paper using plastic wrap to create a pattern with any color of inks or paints you choose. If you know that someone loves the color orange, for instance, you can make orange paper. Or you can create the appropriate colors to go with your theme.

MATERIALS

cardstock base

brads (optional)

deckle scissors

raffia

hole punch

plastic wrap

paper

inks or watercolors

decorative papers (optional)

two-sided tape

- Make handmade paper with various colors of paints or inks and plastic wrap to create a decorative pattern. Let it dry.

- With deckle scissors, cut the handmade paper slightly smaller than the face of the card. Adhere the paper to the card using two-sided tape.

OPTION: Cut other sheets of decorative papers to fit your desired design on the face of the card. Attach them with two-sided tape to the face of the card. Or randomly fasten decorative brads through the front of the card. Punch two holes in the card cover, thread raffia through the holes, and tie a bow. Mail the card in a padded envelope.

Pocket Card
quick and easy • gift

While we use a lottery ticket as a gift and theme here, you can create a pocket with your own little gift inside.

MATERIALS

cardstock base

new lottery ticket (gift)

2 lottery forms (for pocket and decoration)

brads

two-sided tape

scissors

Backside of card face

● This card uses a ready-made cardstock base.

● Make a pocket with a lottery form just the right size to hold the fresh lottery ticket. (Test the orientation, size, and shape first with a slip of paper or cardboard, if you wish.)

● Apply two-sided tape to three sides of the pocket and affix the pocket to the card base. Use decorative brads in the four corners of the pocket.

● Cut out other lottery forms to make the pocket more decorative and adhere them with two-sided tape.

● Slip the new gift lottery ticket in the pocket. Remember that it's time-sensitive.

OPTION: Make a pocket card out of other materials and present your enclosed flat, ticketlike gift.

Potato Prints

fun

It's easy to make your own imaginative stamp out of a potato.

MATERIALS

potato

cardstock base

kitchen or paring knife

craft knife

ink stamp pad(s)

ribbon, vellum, eraser-stamp embellishments (optional)

- To create a potato stamp, cut a potato in half with a kitchen knife.

- Using a craft knife, cut away the part of the potato you do not want as part of your design. Leave only the positive design as the print surface.

- Press the design (flat surface) on your potato stamp into the ink stamp pad and then firmly press it onto the cardstock.

- Return the stamp to the stamp pad and repeat the design as you wish on other spots on your card.

- Add embellishments like a ribbon or layer of vellum, or use a pencil eraser-stamp to dot the card as well.

HINT: Draw your design on the cut potato using a soft lead pencil if you think this will help you. Also try using different colors of ink stamp pads.

Potato print variations

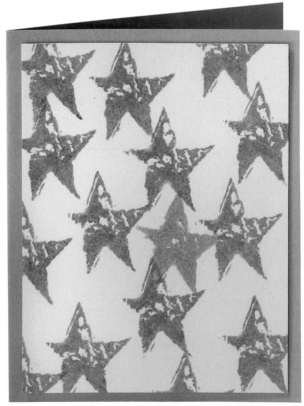

Greeting Cards from A to Z

Quilling
challenging

Quilling is also known as paper rolling, paper scrolling, filigree, and mosaic. The term comes from the feather quill around which thin strips of paper were curled or rolled. Today various other implements are used for quilling.

Some versions of this craft are said to date from ancient China and Egypt. Since it depends on the availability of paper, it was more popularly practiced in Europe in the 1500s. Nuns and later proper young ladies learned the art. They often attached the quilling to the inside of a framed shadow box, and coordinated the backing with the quillwork displayed.

MATERIALS

cardstock base

deckle scissors

quill paper or quill stickers

glue

decorative paper

brads (optional)

two-sided tape

● With deckle scissors, cut out decorative paper.

● Layer decorative paper in various sizes, as desired. Adhere the decorative papers to cardstock with two-sided tape.

● Glue on top of the decorative paper the quilled paper.

● Add brads or other embellishments if you wish.

● Mail the finished card in a padded envelope.

HINT: Today quill kits are available in craft stores or you can find quill decals. Many quillers use acid-free mat board instead of a shadow box. Find a recommended quill glue in an arts and crafts store.

Quilting Pins
average complexity • gift

Here's a special card to send to someone who sews quilts. Decorative papers with a calico design and decorative quilting pins make a wonderful card that's also a gift. The recipient can remove the quilting pins and use them. These pins look like flowers, so a flowerpot motif is just right.

MATERIALS

cardstock base
decorative paper
embossed cardstock
two-sided tape
quilting pins

- Cut out decorative paper to fit the cardstock base. If you can find a quilt print, that's best.

- Adhere it to the cardstock base with two-sided tape.

- Spread the pins in a fanlike design. The pins will be your bouquet of flowers.

- Affix the pins, at the pointed end, to the card with two-sided tape.

- Cut out embossed cardstock in the shape of a flowerpot.

- With two-sided tape, adhere the flowerpot on top of the base of the pins. Extra tape is good.

- Mail the finished card in a padded envelope.

Quilt-Paper Card

quick and easy • recycled

Here we use a variety of small printed decorative papers to create a popular quilt pattern called Around the World. You'll have fun creating your own paper quilt.

MATERIALS

decorative paper

scissors or paper cutter

cardstock base

two-sided tape

craft knife

ruler

- Cut decorative paper slightly smaller than the front of the card. On top of your cardstock base, adhere the decorative paper with two-sided tape.

- From two other decorative papers with different patterns, cut squares. For the card shown, cut three or four 1-inch (2.54-cm) squares from different decorative papers. You can cut your pieces to any size, as long as they're square.

- Beginning in the center of the card, adhere the first square to the middle of the card with two-sided tape.

- Using a different decorative patterned paper, affix four squares to each corner of the first square.

- On the top and bottom of the original square, fill in the gap with two other paper squares.

- If you make a larger card or a square card, continue adding squares.

Recycled Gift Tags & Holiday Cards

quick and easy • recycled

Recycling old holiday cards suggests all kinds of possibilities. You can use all or none of the materials below to create fresh new cards from old cards, tags, stickers, wrapping paper, ribbon, and the works. You can cut down large cards that still have white space inside for nifty gift tags or small cards.

POSSIBLE MATERIALS AND TOOLS

old cards

ready-made cardstock

wrapping paper

decorative paper

gift-tag stickers

photo border cards

scissors or paper cutter

deckle scissors (optional)

glue stick or two-sided tape

die-cuts

computer text

ribbon

brads

● Cards, tags, wrapping paper, even ribbon can be recycled to make new cards. A few cards shown in the photos consist of the front cut from an old card and adhered to a new cardstock base. You could also embellish gift tags and fasten them to new cardstock bases. To make still other cards, you can add your own computer-printout text in a fancy font on the face of the card. Some cards have ready-made borders, and you can make a frame for others. There's really no end to how creative you can be when recycling. Just have fun.

To Avis
From Jeanette

Happy Holidays

To Mom
From Steve

Let It Snow

Someone is thinking
Of you this Holiday

Ribbons
quick and easy

With your home computer and printer, decorative cardstock, and fabric ribbon, you can fashion a card quickly.

MATERIALS

decorative cardstock

computer with selection of fonts

computer printer

fabric ribbon

two-sided tape

scissors or paper cutter

deckle scissors (optional)

hole punch (optional)

● From your computer, choose a nice, decorative font and adjust the font size to fit your greeting on the face of the card. After you've played around with your greeting and are happy with it, print it out. Check the size against the face of the card with a little "white space" around it.

● Cut the text greeting to a size smaller than the card face. If your computer printer doesn't accept specialty paper, you can photocopy your greeting on the new paper and then cut it to the desired size.

● Trim and fold the cardstock.

● Cut a length of fabric ribbon to fit across or down the card. (Ours has a rose design.)

● With two-sided tape, adhere the ribbon to the card.

OPTIONS: Of course you can use ribbons in many ways. Use a hole punch to make holes in a card face so that you can thread the ribbon through it and tie it in front. Or use ribbon near the fold to make a booklet sort of binding.

Scherenschnitte

SCHERENSCHNITTE (The Real Thing)
challenging

Scherenschnitte is the German term for paper cutting, an art found in many cultures. Designs can be highly complex or relatively simple.

To make your own scherenschnitte, you can use an X-acto knife or sharp scissors. Some people prefer to cut around a traced cutout pattern. Most prefer to create scherenschnitte on black paper, later attached to a light or contrasting background, because the black shape helps define the decorative cutwork.

MATERIALS

thin paper (preferably black)

craft knife (X-acto) or sharp scissors

spray adhesive

cardstock base

pencil

cutting mat

- Using thin paper and a pencil, lightly draw a design on the thin paper.

- With a cutting mat under the paper, use a sharp craft knife, such as an X-acto (size 11 blade works well, cut on the very tip only) to very carefully and gently cut out the design. Replace the X-acto blade as necessary when it gets dull.

- When you're finished cutting your design, cover the back of the design with spray adhesive. Be sure to do this in a well-ventilated area. Use a newspaper behind the design to avoid getting the adhesive glue all over.

- Gently lift the paper-cut design and carefully place it on the cardstock base.

- Press down on the design, taking care not to disturb it but ensuring that it adheres to the cardstock.

- Since scherenschnitte is so delicate, you may want to make a photocopy of the paper-cut art to create a card. Keep the "master" for more photocopy cards.

HINT: You can also make your own print from scherenschnitte. It won't have the three-dimensional quality of cut paper, but the effect is lovely

SCHERENSCHNITTE MADE EASY

For an easy paper-cutting project, we can speed up the process with a few tools.

MATERIALS

cardstock base

thin paper

pencil

colored or decorative paper

hole punch

die-cut

deckle scissors

craft or X-acto knife

glue stick

- Begin with thin paper that's slightly larger than the card face. Fold the thin paper in half, taking care that when the design is unfolded (here we've used a heart), it will be oriented in the way you wish. With a pencil, draw the heart or another design (without the scallops) on one side of the folded thin paper. Remember that the fold should be in the middle of the design.

- Cut out the heart or other shape with deckle scissors.

- Using die-cuts and a hole punch, cut out the desired designs within the heart as you would when making a paper snowflake.

- *For the heart design,* carefully cut the design of the tulip on the edge of the fold with a craft knife. Remember that you are only cutting half the tulip. When you open the folded paper, the entire tulip will show.

- Affix the cut paper to the background paper with a glue stick.

- Cut the colored paper with deckle scissors.

- Adhere to the cardstock base with two-sided tape.

- *For the butterfly design,* fold the thin paper in half. Draw your half-butterfly design with a pencil on the folded paper. Use a craft knife, not scissors, to cut it out. Then draw "windows" in the butterfly's wings and use a craft knife to cut them out.

- Adhere the butterfly to colored cardstock or thick colored paper.

Screen Prints (Silkscreen)

challenging • multiple cards

Screen printing (silkscreen) offers exciting effects for making cards. It also enables you to make several cards of the same design. Many arts and crafts stores have screen-printing kits as well as mail-order catalogs. Since all of them vary somewhat from each other, it's best to follow the directions with the kit you purchase. However, to get an idea of the basics, follow these directions.

SCREEN-PRINTING KIT

emulsion and/or film

squeegee

ink

screen with fabric attached

OTHER MATERIALS

degreasing chemical

tape (for securing screens)

masking tape

sink with running water and a hose

heavy Bristol paper

work board (plywood or masonite)

- Design a motif, such as a photo silhouette, and print it in one or more colors. To print a few colors with a variegated appearance, you'll need dollops of a few colors.

- First degrease the screen and get ready to attach the image.

- Using a chemical process with a film stencil or photo-sensitive material, attach the desired design to the screen.

- Get ready to print the design. Lay down a sheet of heavy, smooth-finish Bristol paper (larger than your open-card design) on a work board. Tape all four corners to the work board with removable masking tape.

- Place the screen over the Bristol paper with the fabric facing the paper.

- On the top of the fabric area, not near the design, apply a few dollops of ink.

- Hold your squeegee firmly and run the rubber end of the squeegee through the ink and over your design. Just one swipe will do.

- Carefully lift the screen off, away from your paper. Your image will be there. Remove the masking tape and set the paper aside to dry, about an hour or so depending on climate.

- Now use your squeegee to push the ink back to the top of the screen to be ready for the next printed card.

- When you finish making multiple prints, you must clean the screen thoroughly with cold water from a hose. Do not let a full force of water hit the screen because it can remove or damage the image and screen.

- After the ink dries, fold and trim the card to the desired size. Use a scoring tool and paper cutter for that job.

HINT: Protect your table, carpet, and furniture with plastic sheeting and wear a smock or old painting clothes.

Shaped Cards

fun • adults • teens and kids

Shaped cards can draw on many objects. Here are a few ideas for other shapes: butterfly, turtle, try-on beard with strings attached, snowman, sitting dog, purse, fish, sailboat, motorcycle, car, palm tree, bag with golf clubs, birthday cake, holiday ornament, pumpkin, mittens, heart, star, teddy bear, or outline of your home state, province, or country.

MATERIALS

cardstock base	glue stick
scissors	decorative paper
craft knife	deckle scissors
tracing paper	die-cuts
pencil	fine-point black marking pen
light box (optional)	embellishments (optional)
two-sided tape	

- For all designs, make sure that the card's fold remains uncut and is either on the top or left side of the card. (You can take a decorative nick out of it, but you'll need to maintain the hinge.) For the mug, line up the handle with the fold.

- With a pencil, trace or draw the desired design onto tracing paper. Relatively flat shapes, like flip-flops, can be traced directly on the tracing paper.

- Go over the traced pencil lines with a fine-point black marking pen so that you can see the pattern through the cardstock, especially if the cardstock is a dark color.

- Using a light box or sunny window, trace the shape (mug, hat, or other) onto cardstock with a light pencil line.

- With scissors or a craft knife, use the pencil outline on the cardstock as a guide to cut out the desired shape. Depending on the cardstock's thickness, it may be easier to cut one layer at a time (first the front, then the back of the card). If you use a craft knife, be sure to protect your work table with cardboard or a cutting mat.

MUG

- Dress up the mug-shaped card with ink markers in various colors, and inside attach a packaged tea bag (or other surprise) with two-sided tape. If your friend is home on a bitter cold day, wouldn't this be a nice pick-me-up?

- To make sure the ink won't seep through to the message and vice versa, tape contrasting paper on the verso of the card face.

Silhouettes
keepsakes

Silhouettes are similar to scheren-schnitte in that you use cut paper. These silhouettes were popular in Colonial America. People and pets can be the models, seen in profile. Silhouettes are fun to shape, and they also make nice keepsakes.

You can create an earnest portrait or engage in caricature, depending on your wit, ability to whittle, and whimsy. Here we're creating more serious portraits. You can cut out simple black-on-white images or use decorative or colored papers behind them to enhance a desired theme.

MATERIALS

cardstock base	two-sided tape
black construction paper	decorative paper
sharp scissors or craft knife	deckle scissors
profile photo of subject	pencil
glue stick	

- Using a photo of your subject's profile, trace the outline on black construction paper using a pencil.

- Cut out the silhouette with scissors or a craft knife.

- If you wish, cut out decorative paper with deckle scissors to use as background for the subject.

- Adhere the decorative paper to the cardstock with two-sided tape.

- If the pencil marks show and cannot be easily erased, place the reverse side of the silhouette face up. With a glue stick, affix the silhouette to the decorative paper.

Splatter Prints
quick and easy

Splatter prints

Sponge print (far right)

A few household items can create a dashing card. Don't throw away that old toothbrush; recycle it for this project. You'll want to wear a smock or apron or clothes you don't mind getting splattered with paint.

MATERIALS

cardstock

old toothbrush

watercolor paint

artist's paintbrush

household objects

dull, flat palette knife

- Using keys, lace, doily, leaves, and other household or garden items, place them on the cardstock.

- Wet the toothbrush with water and blot dry. This will soften the bristles.

- Work up some watercolor paint with water and an artist's paintbrush.

- Put newspaper behind the card to catch any excess paint splatter.

- Place the object(s) on the cardstock.

- Put paint on the toothbrush using the artist's paintbrush.

- Hold a palette knife in one hand. Rub the toothbrush on top of the knife, away from you, aiming toward the card. Warning: if you rub the toothbrush toward you, you will get splattered with paint.

- Let the paint dry a few minutes and remove your object.

- Add a greeting or use the card as is.

Sponge Prints

SPONGE-TEXTURE PAPER
quick and easy

Making a sponge texture on paper is about as easy as it gets. I prefer a natural sea sponge found in arts and crafts stores or bath shops. Paper and acrylic or watercolor paint are all you need to work with the sponge. Use one color or many colors; the creative process is up to you.

MATERIALS

cardstock or heavy drawing paper

paint (watercolor or acrylic)

natural sea sponge

water

plastic dish

artist's paintbrush

- Use a heavy cardstock or drawing paper. Colored cardstock is fine.
- With a small artist's paintbrush, mix a little paint in a plastic dish (the kind you can throw away). Mix in a little water if needed.
- Press the sea sponge into the paint you just mixed.
- Place the sponge on the paper. Move the sponge to a new spot. Add paint as needed.

HINT: You may want to wear plastic gloves to keep paint off your hands. Clean up with soap and water.

SPONGE-PRINT CARD

average complexity

Review the technique for sponge-texture paper on p. 132. You can create wonderful textures using one or many colors. Here we've used just one color.

MATERIALS

cardstock base

colored paper

pattern

sponge-texture paper

raffia

hole punch

two-sided tape

deckle scissors

● With deckle scissors cut a center circle in the card face (cardstock base).

● Cut the sponge-print paper to size for the card.

● With two-sided tape, affix the layers of decorative paper to the inside of the card so that it appears through the circular window created in the cardstock.

● Punch two holes in the card. Thread raffia through the holes and tie it.

Squeegee Prints

quick and easy

SQUEEGEE-TEXTURE PAPER

MATERIALS

acrylic paints (in its original plastic squeeze bottle)

heavy drawing paper

squeegee

- On a sheet of heavy drawing paper, squeeze paint from the acrylic paint squeeze bottle in a small lump on top of the paper. (Or drip a few small lumps from the bottle of acrylic paint.) Put several lumps in a line. Choose another color and squeeze it in next to the previous color.

- Add as many colors as you like.

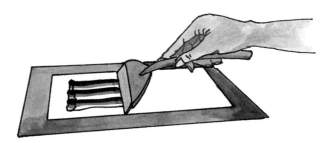

Using a squeegee to pull paint across paper.

- Position your rubber-edge squeegee at the top of the paper, above the paint lumps. With pressure on the squeegee, run it down the length of the paper. You can pull the squeegee straight down or zigzag it from side to side as you pull the paint down. The design effect will be different depending on how you spread out the paint with the squeegee.

- Just one long sweep of the squeegee will do it. If you begin to mix the paint too much or have too many colors, the final print could become muddy.

- Let the paper dry completely before using it as a card base or as decorative paper.

SQUEEGEE-PRINT CARD

Squeegee-texture paper can be as fancy or as simple as you like. You select the colors and determine whether they'll be muted or dazzling.

MATERIALS

cardstock base

squeegee-texture paper

ribbon

text

two-sided tape

deckle scissors

- Cut out with regular or deckle scissors the squeegee-texture paper, making it slightly smaller than the front of the card.

- With two-sided tape adhere the squeegee-texture paper to the card.

- Tape a length of ribbon to the card.

- Cover the tape with a greeting. Attach the greeting with two-sided tape.

Stickers
quick and easy

If you have handy stickers or a nice print that you can cut apart to create your own stickers, you can craft a last-minute card.

MATERIALS

cardstock base

assorted stickers or color print(s)

scissors (optional)

rubber cement

- Begin with colorful cardstock base.

- From a larger color print or several prints, cut out the desired figures, images, or words. Arrange them on the face of the cardstock in the desired design. Use a dab of rubber cement on the back of the homemade stickers. Attach them to the card.

- When dry, rub off excess rubber cement.

Tags

allow extra time

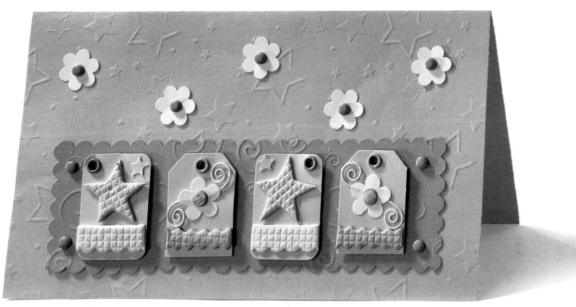

Making cards with tags can be simple or involved depending on how much time and creativity you use. One thing is for sure, you'll have fun.

NOTE: Tags are usually found in the paper crafting section of craft stores. They're also used in making scrapbooks.

MATERIALS

cardstock base

plain paper

flower die-cuts

colored or decorative paper

deckle scissors

tags

stickers (optional)

brads

two-sided tape

adhesive dots (optional)

- Cut flower shapes with a die-cut. Or if you wish, use packaged stickers from a craft or gift shop.

- With deckle scissors, cut colored paper into a rectangle. Attach the colored paper rectangle to the cardstock base with two-sided tape.

- Adhere the stickers and tags to the paper. Stickers will have adhesive. For tags, use two-sided tape.

- With brads, fasten the die-cut flowers to the cardstock and fasten the brads to the corners of the rectangle of colored paper.

- If you wish, cover your work on the reverse of the card face with colored paper cut to size and attached with two-sided tape.

- Mail the finished card in a padded envelope.

MORE TAGS

- Use a decorative card base.

- Cut out contrasting cardstock or decorative paper with deckle scissors.

- Add a decal or decorative paper to the tag, if you wish.

- Punch a hole in the card and thread raffia through the hole and tie it in a bow.

- Mail the finished card in a padded envelope.

Three-Dimensional Cards

quick and easy • fun

Who said that cards have to be flat? You can give dimension to your creation by the use of self-adhesive foam dots. They are available in craft stores and come with sticky glue on both sides. All you have to do is peel off the protective paper and press the sticky foam dots onto your card.

MATERIALS

firm cardstock base

decorative paper

heavy cardstock starfish or other appliqué

self-adhesive foam dots

deckle scissors

two-sided tape or glue stick

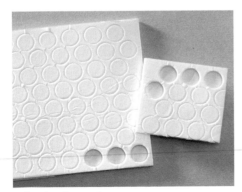

Adhesive foam dots.

- Begin with a firm cardstock base. Avoid very thin cardstock for these cards. Thicker ready-made cardstocks work better here.

- Cut a complementary decorative paper with deckle scissors as desired. Adhere the decorative paper to the cardstock with two-sided tape or a glue stick.

- The starfish shown is a heavy cardstock appliqué. Since the starfish is quite large, I used sticky dots in the middle of the body and on all points. Remove protective paper from one side of the sticky dot and adhere the sticky dot to the underside of the starfish.

- Remove the protective paper from the second side of the sticky dot and carefully place the starfish on the decorative paper. Press firmly on all sticky dots.

- Mail the finished card in a padded envelope.

Tie-dyes

fun • two-day project

Tie-dying is back in fashion on T-shirts. Did you know that you can tie-dye very easily at home with small scraps of fabric and a cup of ink or dye? It's very simple to make and you end up with wonderful results. Don't throw away those scraps of solid color or white cotton fabric from sewing projects.

MATERIALS

ink or fabric dye

plastic cup or jar (disposable)

cotton fabric

small rubber bands

cardstock base

pinking shears

iron

two-sided tape

aluminum foil

rubber gloves

large plastic spoon (disposable)

embellishments (optional)

TIE-DYED CIRCLE DESIGN

Pinch the center of the square cotton fabric scrap with your fingers and fold all the remaining fabric down, away from the area you're holding.

Pinch fabric for tie-dying.

- Using small rubber bands, wrap the first one near your center point at the tip of the fabric. Be sure to wrap this rubber band and each succeeding one as tightly as you can without breaking it

- About ½ inch (1.25 cm) from the first rubber-band wrap, wrap a second rubber band. Repeat this process until you are close to the end of the bundle.

- Pour a little ink or fabric dye into the cup, filling it about halfway.

- Wearing rubber gloves or using a large plastic spoon, submerge your bundle into the dye. Let it sit for about a half hour or the time given in the dye directions.

- With your rubber gloves or a large disposable plastic spoon, remove the bundle and place it on aluminum foil; set aside to dry. Allow a full day or more to dry.

- After the fabric is dry, carefully remove the rubber bands. If the fabric is still damp, let it air dry.

- Iron out the wrinkles. (You may want to protect your iron with another clean fabric on top of the tie-dyed fabric. Dye may leach onto the clean fabric.)

- Cut the tie-dyed fabric with pinking shears. Cut the cardstock to fit the tie-dye design. Use two-sided tape to fasten the tie-dyed fabric to the front of the card.

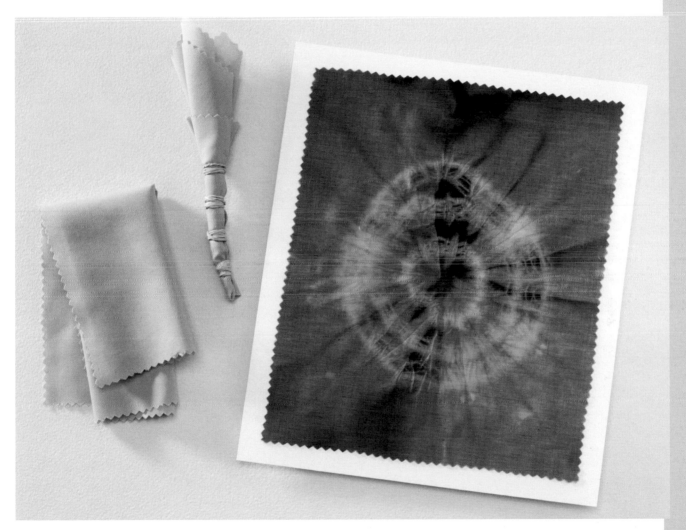

OPTION: Stitch or sew sequins or buttons to the card. To do that use a needle and thread and sew right through the front of the card. When finished, you can hide the thread on the inside of the card with decorative paper, attached with a glue stick or two-sided tape.

HINT: Save the dye in a glass or plastic jar with a tightly closed lid, and you can use it again. Waste not, want not.

TIE-DYED STRIPED DESIGN

● For a linear rather than a circular pattern, take the fabric and make accordion folds. About 1/2 to 1 inch (1.25 to 2.5 cm) folds work well.

● Using the rubber bands, wrap them around the entire bundle. Begin at one end and place the rubber bands about 1/2 inch to 1 inch (1.25 to 2.5 cm) apart.

● Follow the tie-dying procedure above for dipping, drying, and finishing.

● When you unfold the tie-dyed fabric, you'll have a striped design.

CAUTION: Ink or dye splashed on your clothes could be permanent. Wear a smock or apron to protect them. Also only use disposable tools for the tie-dying process.

Tissue Paper

quick and easy

Tissue paper is thin and creates an interesting look when you can see the paper behind it. A satin ribbon with text adds a nice touch. This creates a card with texture.

MATERIALS

decorative cardstock

tissue paper

two-sided tape

ribbon decal

- Use a decorative cardstock base.
- Carefully tear tissue paper into the shape you want. Tearing a ragged edge adds more interest to the look.
- Affix the tissue paper to the card with two-sided tape.
- Mount a ribbon decal to the top of the tissue.

Useful Cards

quick and easy • practical

Follow various card-making techniques in this book and attach or glue something useful to the card, like a business card, calendar, or paper clips.

It's fun to make a card that the recipient can actually use. The challenge is to find useful things that are around the house.

Business card

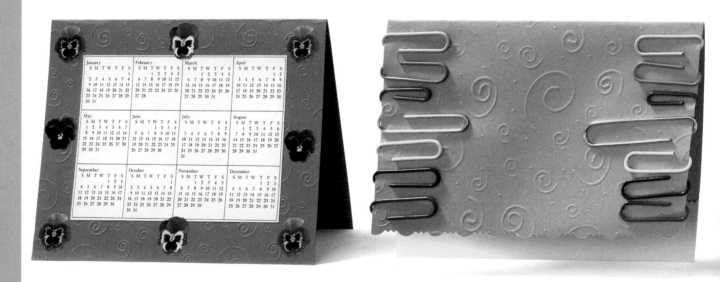

Calendar card

Paper-clip card

Vellum

QUICK VELLUM CARD
quick and easy • sophisticated

Adding a layer of vellum (a strong, cream-colored, see-through paper) to a card adds sophistication. Make a wedding invitation or another invitation to any event.

MATERIALS

white cardstock

decorative vellum

computer text

hole punch

ribbon

- Print out a greeting from your computer in a pleasing type font on white cardstock.

- Cut and fold the cardstock to the size of card you like.

- Cut and fold decorative vellum and slide it over the cardstock. You should have a front and back cover of vellum.

- Punch a hole through all four layers of vellum and card, near the edge of the fold.

- Thread a ribbon through the hole. Tie the ribbon in a bow.

VELLUM HOLIDAY CARD
quick and easy • sophisticated

We've used a pine-needle theme; you can substitute other patterns for other occasions.

MATERIALS

white cardstock base

two-sided tape

decorative paper

standard or deckle scissors

decorative printed vellum

raffia or ribbon

deckle scissors (optional)

hole punch

● Begin with a plain white cardstock base.

● Cut a strip of decorative paper to fit along one edge of the card; here I've used a pine-branch or a pine-needle print. You can cut the paper with standard or deckle scissors. Position the decorative paper on the cardstock and adhere the paper to the cardstock with two-sided tape.

● Use a pine-tree vellum print; cut and fold the vellum to fit the card.

● On the back of the card, use two-sided tape and bond the vellum to the cardstock. This will help prevent the vellum from shifting.

● Punch two holes through the cardstock, decorative paper, and vellum on the front of the card.

● Thread raffia or ribbon through the holes. Tie it in a bow on the front of the card.

Victorian Valentines & Other Fancies

BAROQUE VICTORIAN CARD
slightly challenging • feminine

The Victorians loved a highly decorated and embellished style in the various appointments of home interiors, a penchant which carried over to their elaborately detailed and ornate cards redundant with paper lace and multiple layered images.

MATERIALS
cardstock base

rhinestones

doilies

Victorian stickers

decorative paper

solid-colored paper

deckle scissors

two-sided tape

hard-bonding glue

adhesive dots

scissors

● Cover an entire cardstock base with decorative paper, such as a Victorian floral design. Use two-sided tape to adhere the paper to the card.

● Use a small round doily for the center medallion.

● With solid-colored paper and deckle-edge scissors, cut out the paper slightly larger than the doily. Trace a circle from a stencil. Or, if you're like me, you'll find a can, paper cup, or other round object to trace the circle.

● Affix a Victorian sticker (I've used a dog sitting in a teacup) to the center of the doily. Join the doily and solid paper with two-sided tape.

● Adhere the entire medallion to the card with adhesive dots. I used five on this card beneath the blue circle medallion. These "lifts" (what they were once called) give the card a very Victorian look.

● Cut a second round doily into quarters. Fasten the doily quarters to the corners of the card with two-sided tape.

● On each corner of the front of the card, fasten rhinestones on top of the doilies with hard-bonding glue.

● Mail the finished card in a padded envelope.

An alternative highly ornate Victorian card can consist of multiple stickers that create a design, like those of the dog in a tea cup or dancing cats shown on this page.

For a fussy, feminine appearance, you could also use a length of lace attached to the back of the card. Adhere the lace to the cardstock using two-sided tape. Cover the edges of the cut lace with decorative paper that's cut out with deckle scissors. (Also see lace card variations on pp. 82 to 85.)

VICTORIAN VALENTINES
quick and easy • feminine

During the Victorian age, many people created their own handmade cards with costly or artful embellishments, like hand-painted pictures, silk, lace, and other decorative items. What began in the English upper classes, perhaps with calling cards, soon spread to the middle class as card-making became increasingly popular in the 1860s for Valentine's Day and Christmastime. People spent hours making a single card.

Some wicked folks even sent vinegar valentines that anonymously delivered insults to someone rejected or disliked. Typically these cruel missives were delivered by the post office postage due, so the unwitting recipient even had to pay postage.

MATERIALS

cardstock base

stickers or decals

decorative paper

deckle scissors

two-sided tape

adhesive dots (optional)

lace

- Use ready-made cardstock to make this card quickly.

- Cut a square or rectangle with deckle scissors. Here we've made fancy corner cuts. Adhere the square or rectangle to the center of the card using two-sided tape.

- Affix a Victorian-style sticker to the square or rectangle.

- As an option, you can use adhesive dots to affix the square to the card. This will give it depth, another favorite Victorian look.

- Add lace with two-sided tape.

Weavings

WOVEN PAPER STRIPS
average complexity

You can weave strips of paper and adhere them to the front of the card. The card shown is made from music photocopied on four different colors of paper and cut into strips. We've used a sort of simple basket weave for the paper strips.

MATERIALS

cardstock base

music or another motif

photocopier

colored paper

craft knife, paper cutter, or scissors

deckle scissors

two-sided tape

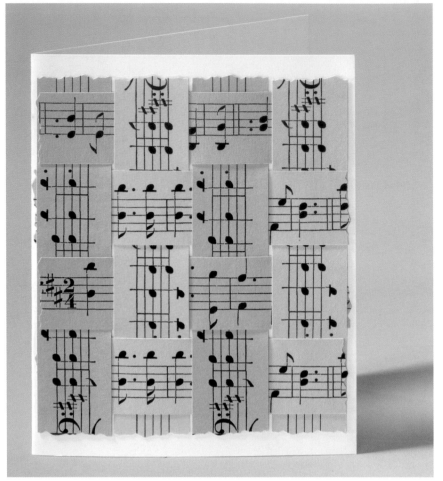

- Use ready-made cardstock as a base.
- Cut out the strips of music with a paper cutter, craft knife, or ordinary paper scissors. I've made my strips about 1 inch (2.54 cm) wide.
- Trim the ends of the strips with deckle scissors to fit the front of the card.
- Weave the strips over and under each other. Secure the strips underneath with two-sided tape to maintain the shape of the weave.
- Adhere the woven strips to the cardstock with two-sided tape.

OTHER WEAVING OPTIONS

Use colorful fabric or other ribbons, raffia, or yarn instead of paper for weavings.

If you're a knitter, you could attach a woven cloth piece (scrap) on the card face. If you're really ambitious, it could be a mini-sweater, sock, or scarf with fringe. This would be a great gift card to include with a handmade knitted present, such as a full-size sweater. Satin ribbon would also be lovely.

Windows

feminine • scented

Pretty floral cards scented with a lovely fragrance are something a greeting-card e-mail cannot deliver. Just be sure that your recipient isn't allergic to perfumes, colognes, and other scents.

MATERIALS

cardstock base

spray bottle with perfume, cologne, or natural scent

2 coordinating decorative papers

craft knife

cutting mat

metal ruler

pencil

deckle scissors

glue stick

text (optional)

embellishments (optional)

- Begin with a cardstock base.

- With deckle scissors, cut a rectangle slightly smaller than the card face. Apply the glue stick to the whole underside of the decorative paper. Center the decorative paper on the card face and be sure that it is smooth and completely adheres to the cardstock.

- Open the card and lay it on a cutting mat with card front and back "covers" face up. With a ruler and a pencil, draw a small square in the desired size in the middle of the card's front cover where you want the window.

- With a craft knife, carefully cut away the window, using your ruler to make a clean cut. If you cut along the outside of your pencil line, the line will be gone when the cutaway square for the window is removed.

- Use deckle scissors to cut another decorative paper (we've chosen one with large flowers) for the inside (right-hand page) of the card. Apply glue with a glue stick to the back of the flowered decorative paper, center it on the right-hand page, and adhere it.

- Add a greeting to the front and inside of the card if you wish.

- When finished, spray just a little perfume or cologne on the back of the card.

Wire

quick and easy • masculine

Ready-made wire in various shapes and motifs can be found in arts and crafts stores. You can also buy thin wire to shape and create your own designs. Dress up the card with a few metallic-looking brads and you'll have a unique card. You can find a wire star, heart, or another symbol or figure that suits the receiver.

MATERIALS

cardstock

small fine wire object

star or other brads

wire thread

- Use a fairly firm ready-made cardstock or make your own.

- Punch a few holes with an ice pick or thin nail in the front of the card where you plan to fasten the wire motif. Be careful not to poke your fingers.

- Thread thin wire through the holes and fasten the small wire object (we've used a wire star) by wrapping the wire thread around the object.

- To finish the wire ends, twist them around a pencil to create the loop effect.

- Fasten the brads to the front of the card in a random layout.

- To hide your work and keep your receiver from being snagged on the brads, you could cover the inside of the "front cover" of the card with sturdy decorative paper, adhered with two-sided tape.

- Mail the finished card in a padded envelope.

Wood Texture

rustic • masculine • computer-aided design (optional)

For this card, I made a photo scan of wood texture and printed it out from my computer. (See handmade wood texture on p. 111.)

However, you don't need a computer to create wood texture. If the desired wood grain is "raised," you could make a rubbing on photocopy paper of the grain using a thick, flat crayon.

MATERIALS

photocopy or other paper

two-sided tape

clip art

computer

photo scanner

computer printout or handmade wood-grain paper

- Use a ready-made cardstock as your base.

- Cut out the wood-texture paper slightly smaller than the cover of your card cover. Add a border if you wish with your graphics computer program or a drawing pen and ruler.

- Adhere the wood-texture paper to the front of the card with two-sided tape.

- Cut out a clip art design and mount the clip art on top of the wood-grain paper. If you wish, you can add a border to the clip art.

Woolly Creature

quick and easy • fun • recycled

My dog decided to take apart my new sheepskin slippers. Since I found pieces of sheepskin all over the house, I gathered up the doggone pieces to make cards. If you don't have a pooch at home to do this prep work for you, polar fleece scraps will also work well. The wild eyes for this googly-eyed creature can be found in craft stores.

MATERIALS

cardstock

colored cardstock

scissors or paper cutter

black permanent marker

hard-bonding glue

googly eyes

polar fleece or sheepskin

sewing scissors

- Cut a piece of colored cardstock slightly smaller than the cardstock base to fit the front of the card. Adhere the colored cardstock to the cardstock base.
- With sewing scissors, cut an oval shape out of sheepskin or polar fleece.
- Using hard-bonding glue, mount the fleece to the card.
- With a black permanent marker, draw legs and a head so that the fleecy oval appears lamblike.
- Affix the googly eyes to the face with a dab of hard-bonding glue.
- Mail the card in a padded envelope.

X O X O

average complexity • computer-aided

Everyone knows that X O X O means kisses and hugs. Signal your love with this card. You can use multiple X's and O's in any way that suits you.

MATERIALS

cardstock base

decorative papers

computer or typewriter

photocopier (optional)

deckle scissors

two-sided tape or glue stick

decorative die-cut decal

● Cover an entire cardstock base with X O X O decorative paper using two-sided tape. If you cannot find X O X O paper, you can make it on your computer or even with an old-fashioned typewriter. Type or print on colored paper if you wish.

● With deckle scissors, cut a square or rectangle with a heart motif and adhere it to the card with two-sided tape.

● With solid paper and deckle scissors, cut out a heart slightly larger than the die-cut decal. Adhere the heart to the card. Affix the heart-shaped or other die-cut decal to the solid heart.

● Depending on the thickness of the die-cut decal, you may need to mail this in a padded envelope.

VARIATIONS: An option would be to photocopy a strip of X O X O's and paste or tape the multiple strips to a sheet of paper, and then photocopy the finished image on colored paper.

Or cut letters out of decorative paper and adhere them to decorative paper on the face of the card.

You could also make your own X's and O's with pen and ink on colored or plain paper, using fancy calligraphy. White out any imperfections and photocopy the results on colored paper. Be sure to clean the photocopier glass.

Yarn

average complexity • recycled

With so many fancy new yarns available today, you'll have fun choosing just the right one(s) to embellish your card. Or find a snippet of leftover yarn from a knitting project. You'll need less than 10 inches (25 cm), depending on your design. The corrugated cardstock was recycled from shipping packaging.

MATERIALS

firm cardstock base

stiff solid-colored paper

decorative papers

deckle scissors

scissors

corrugated card stock or recycled shipping packing

yarn

two-sided tape

one-sided tape

hard-bonding glue

craft knife

● Use a firm cardstock base.

● With deckle scissors, cut out a rectangle or square from stiff solid-colored paper. Adhere it to the cardstock base with two-sided tape.

● With deckle scissors, cut out a star shape from decorative paper. Adhere the star to the card with two-sided tape.

● With a craft knife, cut from corrugated stock a star shape that's a little smaller than your original decorative-paper star.

● Wrap a length of yarn around the star.

● Trim the two ends of yarn and secure them to the underside of the star with one-sided tape.

● Mount the star and yarn to the card with hard-bonding glue and let dry.

● Mail the finished card in a padded envelope.

HINT: Save items, like corrugated paper, that can be recycled into cards.

Yarn Magnets

average complexity • gift

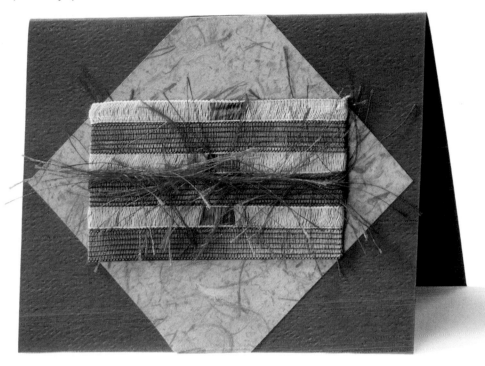

This card bears a magnet wrapped with decorative yarns. Some of the yarns we've used appear threadlike. Flexible magnets about the size of business cards are sold in packages found in office supply stores.

MATERIALS

cardstock

adhesive flexible magnet

decorative paper

yarn

scissors

deckle scissors (optional)

two-sided tape

- Begin with a firm cardstock base.
- From the decorative paper, cut a square, using deckle scissors if you wish. Adhere the square with two-sided tape in a diamond position to the cardstock base.
- Remove the protective paper from a flexible magnet.
- Cut lengths of different yarns and affix them to the sticky side of the magnet.
- Trim the excess yarn, allowing a little loose, fringy appearance if you wish.
- Position the magnet with its yarn where desired on the diamond. Fasten the magnet to the card with two-sided tape.
- Mail the finished card in a padded envelope.

Zigzags

average complexity • fun

All three examples of zigzag cards are created pretty much the same way. Photos and decorative paper can be used as part of a theme or just for fun.

MATERIALS

cardstock base

decorative paper

photo (optional)

craft knife

two-sided tape or glue stick

scissors

deckle scissors (optional)

hole punch (optional)

embellishments, such as gossamer ribbon (optional)

- Begin with the cardstock base.

- If you wish, first add a layer of decorative paper, cut with deckle scissors.

- Cut strips of decorative paper with deckle scissors, a craft knife, or ordinary scissors. They can be cut zigzag fashion or simply cut into strips and then arranged into a zigzag pattern.

- If you use a photo for your zigzag pattern, it's best to make your slices with a craft knife.

- Create a zigzag layout. Check the three finished cards shown here for ideas.

- Adhere the strips to the card using two-sided tape or a glue stick.

- Embellish as desired. We've used a gossamer ribbon threaded through a punched hole to enhance the photo zigzag card.

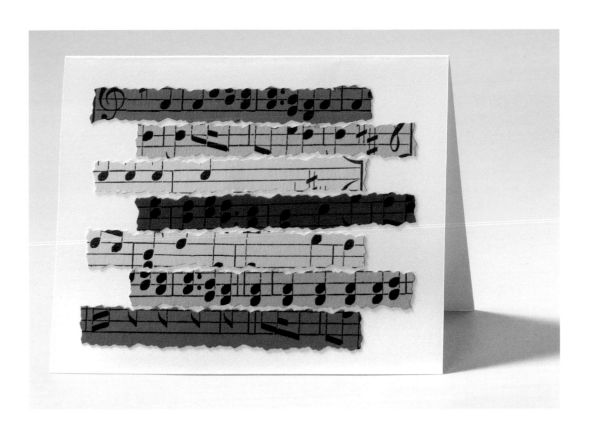

Acknowledgments

I would like to thank my editor, Jeanette Green, for her support and vision with this project. Hats off to the librarians at Cazenovia Public Library; they were key in assisting my research. I am deeply grateful to my dear husband Norman for understanding my need to meet deadlines and for forgiving dust bunnies and my time away from him. For all the pets featured in this book, I thank June for Pokie the cat, Maria for Sophia the Cavalier dog and that perfect peacock feather from her bird, and Barbara for Jazz and Tristan. Woof-woof! My special friends Sherie and Harry appear in some card photos. Avis and Luanne donated fabric scraps for a few projects. Other miscellaneous items came from local Cazenovia shops, garage sales, and friends. We've tried our best to locate the copyright owners of all materials used here.

We gratefully acknowledge the manufacturers, stores, and other companies that have provided their fine products and materials featured on various cards in this book. Note that the given company Web sites listed here were accurate at publication and are intended for product information only and not for sales or ordering products. Kindly check your local retailers for products.

Holiday cards from ©LPG Greetings, Inc., all rights reserved; Downeast Concepts, Inc., for the Beached Boat N-0302; the photo postcard of the city of Syracuse, New York, courtesy Anthony Mario of Margo Studio, Rome, New York; Paper Pizazz® and Cardmaker's™ patterned papers and foils are used with permission from Hot Off the Press, Canby, Oregon, www.paperwishes.com; Foamies™ and metal star ornament by Darice®; brads and decals from Joann™ Stores, Inc.; Paper Bliss™ tags by Westrim Crafts® and Collage Backgrounds™ papers by DMD, Inc.®; decals, stickers, and yarn from EK Success www.eksuccess.com; cards, tags, and stickers courtesy of Paper Magic Group; a special thank you to Colorbök for many donations of time and wonderful numerous supplies of paper, decals, mesh, stickers, yarn, brads, and more, www.colorbok.com; clip art from Dover Publications, Inc., www.doverpublications.com; decorative papers, quill decals, and stickers from Provo Craft, Inc., www.provocraft.com; ©C-Thru Ruler Company, Wonderful Words, www.cthruruler.com; decals from ©2004 me & my big ideas, Inc., all rights reserved under license; greeting card frames used with permission of Kristin Elliott, Inc.; embossed photo frames from Making Memories, www.makingmemories.com; photo magnets and stickers from Paper House Productions; Creative Hands® foam shapes #1621, Bug Love, www.creativehands.com; embossed photo frames from ©Masterpiece Studios, www.masterpiecestudios.com; Victorian stickers from Violette Stickers, www.violettestickers.com.; for Paper Shapers® shamrock punch by EK Success; LCI Paper Co, Inc., www.lcipaper.com; for scissors and tools by © 2005 PVA; Fiskars Brands, Inc., Fiskars.com; for die-cuts by Die Cuts with a View, 801-224-6766, www.diecutswithaview.com (wholesale information only); for lace doilies by Artifacts, Inc., www.Artifactsinc.com, 800-678-4178; and clip art from www.clipart.com.